Southern Literary Studies
Fred Hobson, Editor

Approaching
PRAYER

Approaching
PRAYER

Ritual and the Shape of Myth in
A. R. Ammons and James Dickey

ROBERT KIRSCHTEN

LOUISIANA STATE UNIVERSITY PRESS
Baton Rouge

Designer: Barbara Neely Bourgoyne
Typeface: Minion
Typesetter: Wilsted & Taylor Publishing Services
Printer and binder: Thomson-Shore, Inc.

Excerpts from poems by A. R. Ammons are reprinted with the permission of W. W. Norton &
Company. Excerpts from poems by James Dickey are reproduced with the permission of the Uni-
versity Press of New England. Chapter 2, "Ammons' Sumerian Songs: Desert Laments and Eastern
Quests," is reprinted, in somewhat different form, by permission of G. K. Hall & Co., an imprint of
Simon & Schuster Macmillan, from *Critical Essays on A. R. Ammons,* edited by Robert Kirschten.
Copyright © 1997 by G. K. Hall & Co. Chapters 3 and 4 were first published, in somewhat different
form, as "Ritual and the Shape of Myth in James Dickey's 'Approaching Prayer,'" *South Atlantic
Review,* LXI (Winter, 1996), 27–54, and "Form and Genre in James Dickey's 'Falling': The Great
Goddess Gives Birth to the Earth," *South Atlantic Review,* LVIII (May, 1993), 127–54, and are
reprinted by permission of the *South Atlantic Review.* Chapter 5, "The Momentum of Word-Magic
in Dickey's *The Eye-Beaters, Blood, Victory, Madness, Buckhead and Mercy,*" was first published in
somewhat different form in *Contemporary Literature,* XXXVI (Spring, 1995), 131–63, and is
reprinted by permission of the University of Wisconsin Press.

Library of Congress Cataloging-in-Publication Data
Kirschten, Robert, 1947–
    Approaching prayer : ritual and the shape of myth in A. R. Ammons
  and James Dickey/ Robert Kirschten.
      p.   cm. — (Southern literary studies)
    Includes bibliographical references and index.
    ISBN 0-8071-2247-5 (alk. paper)
    1. Ammons, A. R., 1926–   —Criticism and interpretation.
  2. Religious poetry, American—History and criticism.   3. Dickey,
  James—Criticism and interpretation.   4. Southern States—
  Intellectual life.   5. Prayer in literature.   6. Ritual in
  literature.   7. Myth in literature.   I. Series.
  PS3501.M6Z83   1998
  811'.54—dc21   97-51186
                                           CIP

and Jim Dickey,

for:

Archie Ammons,

Believe, too,
. . . that the flight of eagles has
For use, long muscles steeped only
In escape,
and moves through
Clouds that will open to nothing

in separating light from darkness
have we cast into death:
in attaining the luminous,
made, capable self,
have we
brought error
to perfection

But if, where the bird leaves behind
All sympathy: leaves
The man who, for twenty lines
Of a new poem, thought he would not be shut
From those wings: believed
He could be going.

Contents

Why should I pray? Why should I venerate and be ceremonious?

—WALT WHITMAN

Studied alive, myth . . . is not an explanation in satisfaction of a scientific interest, but a narrative resurrection of a primeval reality, told in satisfaction of deep religious wants, moral cravings, social submissions, asseverations, even practical requirements. Myth fulfills in primitive culture an indispensable function: it expresses, enhances, and codifies belief; it safeguards and enforces morality; it vouches for the efficiency of ritual and contains practical rules for the guidance of man. Myth is thus a vital ingredient of human civilisation; it is not an idle tale, but a hard-worked active force; it is not an intellectual explanation or an artistic imagery, but a pragmatic charter of primitive faith and moral wisdom. . . . These stories . . . are to the native a statement of a primeval, greater, and more relevant reality, by which the present life, fates and activities of mankind are determined, the knowledge of which supplies man with the motive for ritual and moral actions, as well as with indications as to how to perform them.

—BRONISLAV MALINOWSKI

O Sleepless as the river under thee,
Vaulting the sea, the prairies' dreaming sod,
Unto us lowliest sometime sweep, descend
And of the curveship lend a myth to God.

—HART CRANE, "To Brooklyn Bridge"

Abbreviations

A. R. Ammons

CP   *Collected Poems, 1951–1971* (New York, 1972)
CT   *A Coast of Trees* (New York, 1981)
LEC   *Lake Effect Country* (New York, 1983)
OM   *Ommateum: With Doxology* (Philadelphia, 1955)
S   *Sphere: The Form of a Motion* (New York, 1974)
SV   *Sumerian Vistas* (New York, 1987)

James Dickey

BB   *Babel to Byzantium* (New York, 1968)
CM   *The Central Motion: Poems, 1968–1979* (Middletown, Conn., 1983)
EB   *The Eye-Beaters, Blood, Victory, Madness, Buckhead and Mercy* (Garden City, N.Y., 1970)
EM   *The Eagle's Mile* (Hanover, N.H., 1990)
NH   *Night Hurdling: Poems, Essays, Conversations, Commencements, and Afterwords* (Columbia, S.C., 1983)
P   *Poems, 1957–1967* (Middletown, Conn., 1967)
PU   *Puella* (New York, 1982)
S   *Sorties* (Baton Rouge, 1984)
SI   *Self-Interviews* (New York, 1970)
TWS   *To the White Sea* (New York, 1993)

PREFACE

This book began as a brief presentation at a special session on James Dickey entitled "Measuring the Motion" that took place in November, 1991, at the annual meeting of the South Atlantic Modern Language Association in Atlanta. During this session, I read a paper on Dickey's long, spectacular poem "Falling," in which he depicts the fatal fall of a twenty-nine-year-old stewardess from a commercial airplane over Kansas. I had briefly discussed this poem in my book *James Dickey and the Gentle Ecstasy of Earth: A Reading of the Poems*, published by Louisiana State University Press in 1988. In my chapter on Dickey's primitivism, I attempted to explain the tragic yet ecstatic combination of the forces of life and death that attend the stewardess during her fall by using René Girard's conception of ritual sacrifice in *Violence and the Sacred*. My claim was that the stewardess attains the status of "a goddess—a sacrificial scapegoat—precisely because she is about to die and thus can 'exercise functions that are elsewhere the prerogative of the gods.'"[1] Although suggestive from a sociological point of view, Girard's terms led me to focus primarily on her death and victimage and less on the life-affirming portion of the poem, namely, "that aspect of Dickey's poetic method that changes the material act of falling from a plane into something quite different, something that accounts for our felt experience that the airline stewardess really is some sort of confluence of extraordinary powers and that her death is much more than another sensational and sympathetic item in a newspaper story."[2]

Even though my previous discussion seemed to me to be on the right track (and still does), I felt that I was missing a considerable amount of what the poem was saying, especially about Dickey's depiction of women. By focusing on the Christlike, sacrificial aspect of the dying stewardess—analogous to ritual narratives from my own cultural background—I felt that I did not spend enough time on the positive traits of her living, energized character. And although I likened her to the dying gods of vegetation from a number of primitive cultures, discussed by Sir James George Frazer in *The Golden Bough,* my previous appraisal was to some extent culture-bound.[3] As I read more extensively about goddesses in matriarchal cultures and religions, I began to see how much more complex a character she is and to understand in greater depth the religious aspect of Dickey's poetry. Thus, I thought that the poem called for a new and fuller reading. This new reading of "Falling" is also designed to address the objections of readers for whom this poem is nothing more than the celebration of the death of a woman. I have had considerable personal experience with critics who claim that "Falling" is simply another example of a masculinist ideology in which a naked woman dies while the poet's male-dominated perspective gloats over the prospect of her annihilation. From the very first time I read this poem in graduate school to the many times I listened to Dickey's extraordinary reading of "Falling" on Caedmon Records, my reaction was quite different. I was most strongly impressed not by her death but by her grace, her courage, her dazzling movement, and the overwhelming energy of her performance. Even so, one of the things that puzzled me as I reexperienced the poem was, if this poetic subject is dead or dying, how does she exercise a pervasive power that is not only continuous but expands dramatically?

This question provides a key not only to "Falling" but to Dickey's poetry in general. Rather than reiterate my argument in that chapter, I will say here that my answer centers on the mythopoeic commonplace of the transformation of life out of death—the universal cycle of killing and eating—that lies at the heart of the human and animal world. In addition to this basic cycle, a similar dialectic pervades many mythological narratives that depict the death and resurrection of divinities ranging from the biblical Christ to the Egyptian Osiris to the Greek Persephone. In many cultures, moreover, the true test of the power of a god is its ability to transcend death. This ancient topic is present not only in Dickey's invention of female gods. In "The Vegetable King," published in 1959, the same kind of metamorphosis occurs after the male speaker sleeps out overnight in his backyard, then dreams himself into the eternity of a natural cycle. This cycle occurs at a time

> when the chosen man,
>
> Hacked apart in the growing cold
> Of the year, by the whole of mindless nature is assembled
>
> From the trembling, untroubled river.
> I believe I become that man, become

As bloodless as a god, within the water,
Who yet returns to walk a woman's rooms
Where flowers on the mantel-piece are those

Bought by his death.

(*P*, 24)

In "Falling" the transformation of the stewardess into a god is less explicit, and thus even more surprising and overwhelming. Although the word *goddess* is used several times by the narrator, her transformation is effected indirectly by image groups that carry the subtextual argument of the poem. In fact, the genius of Dickey's lyric lies in his skillful fusion of the subtextual myth with a realistic fall, without lessening the realism of the fall even as the myth radically alters its nature. One major aspect of Dickey's mythic method of alteration lies in his construction of the American landscape into a sacred, empowering space in which death is not simply the termination of life. Rather, in Dickey's world, death is one of two archetypal interchanging moments within an animistic continuum, which Dickey calls "the heraldic wheel of existence" (*SI*, 68). Thus, the stewardess fall to an earth, a "Kansas," where death and life merge; for she

will drop in   SOON   now will drop

In like this   the greatest thing that ever came to Kansas   down
         from all
Heights   all levels of American breath   layered in the lungs
         from the frail
Chill of space to the loam where extinction slumbers in corn tassels
         thickly . . .

(*P*, 297)

In Dickey's animated world, "extinction" is not termination. Instead, it "slumbers in corn tassels / thickly"; that is, extinction has within it the capacity to waken from its slumber into the opposite force of life-giving corn.

Especially interesting and revealing about Dickey's metamorphic image of maize is the fact of it being found in many mythological systems. It is, for example, featured in Central American religious iconographies. Shortly after writing the chapter on "Falling," I visited an exhibition of Central American photography at the Art Institute of Chicago. One of the most striking photographs in the exhibit showed a human skull surrounded by a circle of stones. From each eye of the skull an ear of corn protruded, with remnants of the corn stalks still attached. This macabre photo contained the very image—corn emerging from a symbol of human death, within the circle of life and death—

that I had just used in my analysis of Dickey's poem. To explain the energizing nature of the stewardess' death, I had likened her to the Mesoamerican feminine god Maize Stalk Drinking Blood, who is often depicted as an ever-devouring human skull out of whose eyes grow life-giving maize. Both this photograph and the painting of Maize Stalk discussed in this book thus convey Dickey's basic premise: out of the death of the stewardess comes the life of the earth and the transcendence of her death through her participation in nature's eternal cycle.

The anthropological commonplace of cyclic metamorphosis is also central to Dickey's ritual narrative of shamanic dismemberment in "Approaching Prayer." After completing my analysis of "Falling" by reading its internal structure through the ideas of scholars and critics who work in anthropology, I thought it would be interesting to employ a similar approach with another long poem of Dickey's that had baffled readers and largely been ignored by critics. A brief glance at "Approaching Prayer" reveals its singular difficulty. Wearing spurs from his dead father's gamecocks, Dickey's speaker goes up to his father's attic, places a dead boar's head on his own, and then performs a ceremonial reslaying of the boar. Rather than the bloody mutilation of a defenseless animal, this prayer is a psychomythological passage in which a son realigns himself with the memory—now the only reality—of his dead father through the dismemberment and transformation of a boar. The boar is both the son's and the father's totem animal. Although the premise of the poem seems curious in the extreme, one may recall that animals play prominent roles in human ordeals. Whether such animals be fish (for example, in *Moby-Dick* and *The Old Man and the Sea*), boars (analogous to Dickey's, as in the myth of Adonis), or horses (in the drama *Equus*), they are externalized representatives (or totems) of the darkest, innermost parts of the human soul. Whether in literature, mythology, or our own lives, access to this dark night of the self is at times so difficult and mysterious that it necessitates the strength and guidance of a totem animal. Such is the method in Dickey's poem, where the death of the boar corresponds to the death of the father-son relation, which can only be born anew within the son. To many readers, this kind of prayer may seem preposterous, but in Algonquin Indian culture (in which the "shadow world of the dead" is accessible through the sounds of animals) or in the realm of D. H. Lawrence's "blood-consciousness," Dickey's method of worship would be far better—and somatically—understood.[4]

My chapter on Dickey's word-magic began as an investigation into the role of magical thinking in two of his most recent and demanding books of poetry: *Puella* (1980) and *The Eagle's Mile* (1990). In reading *Puella*, I was especially interested in how Dickey builds yet another powerful woman, namely, the poetic Deborah (in reality his wife, to whom the book is dedicated), who is, as poet William Harmon rightly notes, "heraldic, totemic, mythic, atavistic, primal."[5] Whatever or whoever the poetic Deborah is, her powers are conveyed by a technique of intensified hyphenates, verbals, and isolated word-groups, which to some extent resemble the "split line" that Dickey developed in the middle and late sixties. In *Puella,* the conflation of traits in such phrases as "frame-humming" (*PU,* 32) and "space-harvesting" (*PU,* 37) results in a reorganization of space and time, which are sensuously energized by means of a principle analogous to what Frazer calls "contagious magic," namely, "that things which have once been in contact with each other are always in contact."[6] So much is so closely connected with everything else in Dickey's world that the character of Deborah becomes a confluence of the magical exchanges that abound throughout the exceedingly dense topographies in each poem. Deborah's power is thus a result of how Dickey thinks through the shared traits of the objects of nature, which are so juxtaposed that a woman reconstitutes the universe and, spatially, the male poet. "A woman's live playing of the universe / As inner light, stands clear, / And is, where I last was" (*PU,* 16).

In preparation for my study of *Puella,* I began to think about how Dickey uses magic in his earlier poetry. I discovered that magical contagion is at the heart of one of Dickey's most controversial books, *The Eye-Beaters, Blood, Victory, Madness, Buckhead and Mercy.* This book was roundly criticized by many who rightly challenged several underdeveloped confessional pieces in the collection but who vastly underestimated a central core of at least seven poems that rank among Dickey's best. Not only are such poems as "Pine," "The Eye-Beaters," and "Victory" remarkable in themselves, but the magical principles in these lyrics are also direct forebears of Dickey's method of character development in *Puella* and his meditational modes of romantic reconnection in *The Eagle's Mile.* Consequently, before approaching these later works, I thought it important to understand the place of *The Eye-Beaters* within Dickey's overall conception of magical word-play, and thus to provide a rejoinder based on his own magical poetics to critics who did not consider this line of inquiry in their negative assessments. Much maligned, *The Eye-Beaters* is one of the pivotal transitional texts for Dickey in a career of continuous, often daring, experimentation. Not every poem in this book is successful, but many of them are, and they deserve serious attention.

The chapter "'This Black Rich Country': Ammons' Mythic 'Way' Begins at Sumer" itself began with my attraction to the world of Ammons' early and curiously dark poems. To me, the appeal of this darkness, like that of Eliot's "The

Wasteland," is that it is both enervating and energizing. This contradictory double darkness pervades Ammons' first book, *Ommateum* (1955); extends through his second, *Ten Poems* (1960); and continues in his poetry as late as *Sumerian Vistas* (1987). The settings in some of these poems are explicitly identified as ancient Sumer, the Near Eastern country between the Tigris and Euphrates rivers whose civilization flourished four thousand years ago. If not explicitly set in Sumer, almost all of the early poems occur in a Sumerian netherworld. These terrains oppress Ammons' speaker while he searches for even the slightest of satisfactions. Each poem, moreover, seems to be an ordeal or trial or quest of some kind, often undertaken under severe circumstances. For instance, in "Song," published in *Northfield Poems* (1966), there is a most unsonglike opening incident:

> Merging into place against a slope of trees,
> I extended my arms and
> took up the silence and spare leafage.
> I lost my head first, the cervical meat
> clumping off in rot,
> baring the spinal heart to wind and ice
>
> which work fast.

> (*CP*, 34)

When "merging" into these hostile environments, Ammons' early speaker typically responds to his circumstances by engaging in simple and arcane gestures, such as extending his arms, collecting stones, building altarcones from desert sand, or climbing plateaus and mountains.

However simple these gestures appear, they empower the speaker in various degrees by carrying with them a series of richly "religious" implications. These gestures appear to be religious partly because they are associated with traditional rituals in many religious texts; for instance, Ammons' speaker visits a mountain in "Hymn II" to behold a vision. Even if the speaker merges into nature and thus into his own death in "Song," he acquires relief from the catastrophic events that began the poem by recollecting his past pain—albeit from a resurrected consciousness beyond his dead body—in a cool, tranquil rendition. Just as Eliot's lamentational mode of voice in "The Wasteland" provides relief from a world in which "death had undone so many," so Ammons' religious gestures and vocal tone provide relief because they are stylized modes of supplication to the mysterious causes of his ordeals, causes that seem linked to some major external source of power.[7] Like the petitions in many a Sumerian lament (as recorded by such scholars as Samuel Noah Kramer and Thorkild Jacobsen), the intervention of a god in Ammons' Sumer is not forthcoming, however. The religious implications in Ammons' early poems are really enabling appeals to himself for change and strength. I have labeled the full performance—mental and physical—of these addresses the "ritualistic" component in his lyrics. Like the stewardess in Dickey's "Falling," who faces the overwhelming obstacle of death and is transfigured by defying and aligning herself with this natural opponent, Ammons' oppressed speaker ritually rearranges his relation to the things of nature and creates a new, original universe. This rearrangement is the prototypical work of the gods, namely, the creation of a new, sacred habitation. In Ammons' sacred Sumer, however, it is man who controls the spatial coordinates of a new cosmos and thus controls the beginnings of a new world, which are the beginnings of a new self.

A. R. Ammons also begins at Sumer in the sense that his desert laments lead him on a quest for satisfactions that not only complicate his poetic action but also lead to a series of sophisticated postures derived from Eastern mystical philosophies. Thus, even though my initial thesis in my second chapter on Ammons is that the poet begins at Sumer, my conclusion is that he ends up in China, India, and Japan. For instance, in "Hymn V," Ammons directly addresses a mysterious "you," who, to my mind, embodies Laotse's "Way" and Emerson's "nature" (which has its own intellectual roots in Asian thought). Whoever this "you" may be, in "Hymn IV" it (like Laotse's Tao) is "whole and undivided" (CP, 42); and in "Hymn V," the "you" has an explicit religious connotation insofar as it is called upon to satisfy the human need for continuity by means of ritual:

> Assure us you side with order: throw
> off atomicities, dots, events, endless
> successions: reveal an ancient inclination
> we can adore and ritualize
> with sapphirine cones and liturgies,
> refine through ages of
> canonical admissions and rejections; a
> consistent, emerging inclination to prefer
> the circling continuum, void receptacle,
> and eternal now . . .
>
> (CP, 42)

This passage is religious in that Ammons is consciously establishing the history and procedures of validation for his own faith. The "ancient" reality that he comes "to prefer" is less his own unique invention, however, than a cross-cultural entity that Joseph Campbell, in discussing Sumerian cosmology, calls

"the single marvelous monad of mythological inspiration." That this mythological monad is present in Ammons is conveyed by the conclusion to this
stanza, where one finds traits common to ancient celestial systems: circularity,
emptiness, and eternity.[8]

Whether in Emerson's "Circles," Plato's *Timaeus*, or Ammons' Sumerian
landscapes, not to mention Dickey's neoplatonic poems of motion and music,
the relation between the individual and the cosmos is that of a harmonious
proportion analogous to Campbell's "single marvelous monad." In the case of
both Ammons and Dickey, this proportion can be miraculous, but as I will
show, it can also be lethal. While also dwelling in an ever-threatening world of
death and decay, the Sumerians invented a proportioned cosmos in what
Campbell calls "the hieratic city state." Like Plato's magically proportioned
universe, Sumerian political and religious organizations were also predicated
on a model of celestial harmony. The harmony thus created was a "mesocosm—a mediating, middle cosmos, through which the microcosm of the individual is brought into relation to the macrocosm of the universe. And this
mesocosm is the entire context of the body social, which is a kind of living
poem, hymn, or icon, of mud and reeds, and of flesh and blood, and of dream,
fashioned into the art form of the hieratic city state." The Sumerians shared
this concept of the mesocosm with other cultures, including those of the Ori-
ent. As Campbell notes, "The Egyptian term for this order was Ma'at; in India
it is Dharma, and in China Tao."[9] If the basic model of Sumerian reality is also
shared by these Eastern cultures, it becomes easier to see how Ammon's poetic
"Way" could lead through philosophically compatible influences such as
Sumer, Laotse, and the Asian element in Emerson.

If the Sumerian landscapes in Ammons' poems are anything, they are meso-
cosms within his mind that he builds, ritually and mythically, to mediate between himself and the external world. In so doing, his religious gestures become somatic myths in which the body of Ammons and the world's body are
brought into relation. In an interview in *Diacritics*, Ammons is very clear about
the relation between these two bodies: "I use the pathetic fallacy quite a bit, but
always quite deliberately, with full knowledge of what I'm doing."[10] That the
possibility for poetic ritual and myth is grounded in Ammons' own poetic
body takes further credence from his remarks in an interview in the *Cornell
Daily Sun* in 1973. There, he noted that when he was growing up in the Depres-
sion in rural North Carolina, "It was a time of tremendous economic and spiritual privation, even loneliness. . . . I never brought a book home [from grammar school]. It was impossible. . . . But all this privation was compensated for
by a sense of the eternal freshness of the land itself. So I substituted for normal

human experience, which was unavailable to me much of the time, this sense of identity with the things around me."[11] Ammons' "identity with the things around" him is one of the fundamental issues, poetic and personal, in his early lyrics. It is also the basis for my inquiry into his artistic beginnings, rooted in the rich, complex "freshness [and terror] of the land itself"—his poetic Sumer—which have not been adequately appreciated and are as high in quality as anything he has written since.[12] Consequently, even though Dickey precedes Ammons in my remarks thus far, this study begins with Ammons and the mythopoeic land from which he initiated his poetic career.

One final word: this book is not a comparative study of the two writers. Rather, it consists of two separate lines of inquiry into how each writer employs myth and ritual. I have paired the two poets more because of my personal interest in their mythopoeic approaches than for their southernness or for the cultural and historic roots from which their work springs. These are certainly worthy topics, but they are subjects for an inquiry other than my own. Differing radically in emotion, method, and format, the poetry of A. R. Ammons and James Dickey nonetheless share ancient ceremonial strategies that require close comparison with a plurality of religious traditions to be made intelligible. It is this aspect of comparative study, in each writer taken individually, that I wish to develop.

Approaching
PRAYER

I

THIS BLACK RICH COUNTRY
Ammons' Mythic "Way" Begins at Sumer

Dispossess me of belief...
              let me walk
or fall alone...
withdraw beyond all reach of faith:

leave me this black rich country,
uncertainty, labor, fear: do not
steal the rewards of my mortality.

—A. R. AMMONS

It is his familiar everyday life that is transfigured in the experience of religious
man; he finds a cipher everywhere. Even the most habitual gesture can signify
a spiritual act. The road and walking can be transfigured into religious values,
for every road can symbolize "the road of life," and any walk a "pilgrimage," a
peregrination to the Center of the World.... [P]ilgrims and ascetics, pro-
claim by their "walking," by their constant movement, their desire to leave
the world, their refusal of any worldly situation.... Those who have chosen
the Quest, the road that leads to the Center, must abandon any kind of family
and social situation... and devote themselves wholly to "walking" toward the
supreme truth, which, in highly evolved religions, is synonymous with the
Hidden God, the *Deus absconditus*.

—MIRCEA ELIADE

In an interview in *Diacritics* in 1973, A. R. Ammons offered several observations about the relation between myth and narrative in his poetry. When asked
if, at the beginning of his career, he was "dependent on specific myths or
stories," Ammons responded affirmatively, then indicated how he uses myth
and story, especially in their relation to poetic form, or what he calls "a curvature of sentences":

A narrative provides the configuration from which many ideas may derive. In some short poems, I tell a little story. The story is quite plain; it's the first level of apprehension of the poem, but it becomes mythic in what it might suggest. . . . [T]he narrative is a body in motion . . .

[For example, a] person is walking along a dusty highroad. . . . [He] becomes aware of a presence near him and he turns and it is not something that is wandering at all. It's a mountain that is always there. It occupies a single position and . . . it retains a single prospect. So the narrative then becomes the play of these two possibilities, of being stable and of occupying a massive view about things that is unalterable; or being tiny enough to go up and down pathways to become lost. . . .

Well, that's exactly the mode I try to jump into; it's as if you were reading a newspaper—"I was walking along a dusty highroad. . . ." [I]n a normal, almost journalistic way, you go into action, things happen, then they end. Meanwhile they describe a curvature of some sort that's either narrative, or myth or structure or whatever, but it *is*, it *exists* and is no longer susceptible to analysis, to destruction by analysis or to further creation by analysis. It's *there*.[1]

Story and myth are especially prominent in Ammons' early poems, which are cast in the mode of ritual quest and take place in a Sumerian landscape of desert, dust, depravity, and darkness. In *Ommateum* ["compound eye"]: *With Doxology,* published privately in 1955, almost every poem seems Sumerian in some sense. Many contain explicit references, such as the setting in "Coming to Sumer," where a speaker named Ezra perversely plays out his role as robber of the dead:

> Coming to Sumer and the tamarisks on the river
> I Ezra with unsettling love
> rifled the mud and wattle huts
> for recent mournings
> with gold leaves
> and lapis lazuli beads
> in the neat braids loosening from the skull.
>
> (*CP,* 22)

Furthermore, almost every poem in this collection depends on some kind of progressive story to drive it forward, and each story appears to give way to larger, mysterious, mythic realities of which the story is an anecdotal fragment. At the end of "Coming to Sumer," Ammons concludes the poem's disturbing action by having Ezra abandon "the unprofitable poor." Ezra then travels on, economically, politically, and sociologically, in a higher (that is, more profitable) direction toward the "gold" and "lapis lazuli" that elude him. As the power-minded Ezra journeys hierarchically, Ammons subverts a standard mythological image of flight and ascension:

> I abandoned the unprofitable poor
> unequal even in the bone
>   to disrespect
>   and casual with certainty
> watched an eagle wing as I went
> to king and priest
>
> (*CP*, 22)

This "eagle wing" suggests Ezra's flight toward the propertied mysteries of so-cial hierarchy represented by political and religious authority, which belongs to the more affluent and thus mythic classes. The wing also closes the poem with a mythic motion of ascension—one recalls that Zeus came in the form of an eagle to carry Ganymede, the handsome Trojan prince, to Olympus to be cup-bearer to the gods—which is really a moral movement of descension. For the narrative-quest in this poem is as ethically dubious, contradictory, and self-indicting as Ezra's claim that his act of rifling "the unprofitable poor," then burning their huts, is one of "unsettling love."

By inventing a ghoulish narrator who recounts his dark deeds in a deadpan tone, Ammons not only deconstructs the generic nobility of character so often assumed by a quest myth, he also turns his poetic Sumer into a nightmare. For this is a "*black* rich country" (my italics) in which his speakers—most sympa-thetic; some not, like this Ezra—are driven by desire through oppressive ter-rains where their desire is seldom satisfied. Along their arduous routes, these speakers employ various gestures designed to turn this country from blackness to richness but which often result only in more blackness. Many of these ges-tures appear to have rich religious associations evoking the sacred. For in-stance, in "I Struck a Diminished Seventh," the speaker is "perishing for deity" during his wait for a "universal word" that will provide an "appreciation / equalling winged belief." The poem ends with the simple act of the speaker drying his feet. However unimportant this act may seem, it is really a ritual ges-ture of humility and purification, like Christ's washing of the disciples' feet at the Last Supper in John 13, which further prepares Ammons' speaker for belief and commitment. In his "black" poem, however, this gesture does not result in religious revelation. Instead, it immediately precedes the dark and threatening truth that not only will neither deity nor belief arrive for the speaker, he also will somehow be dismembered; thus the speaker concludes that the word "had almost come . . . when . . . death came over sieving me" (*CP*, 23).

Lying behind this complex of quests and gestures is Ammons' poetic and personal intention, sketched briefly in the foreword to *Ommateum*: "These poems are . . . dramatic presentations of thought and emotion, as in themes of the fear of the loss of identity . . . [and] the creation of false gods to serve real human needs." The content of these early poems bears him out. Whether his speakers fall "down in the dust" (*CP*, 2), run "dazed with grief" (*CP*, 28), or are found "diffuse, leached colorless,/ gray as an inner image with no clothes . . . [and] wasted by hills" (*CP*, 37), they are continually threatened by multifaceted deprivations ranging from a "loss of identity" to apparently meaningless searches wherein they seek for "oracles" and "belief" (*CP*, 23) yet are "without god" (*CP*, 25). Rather than dwell in a structured cosmos in which the divine plan of a supreme being offers purpose, dignity, philosophical certitude, and self-definition, Ammons' speakers forge through a land of confusion and chaos as benighted as the mythical netherworld of the Sumerian hero Gilgamesh. However "black" and "wretched" Ammons' poetic "country," its major irony is that it is also "rich" because of its theological blackness. Reasons for this existential reversal are indicated by the poet in the lines cited at the beginning of this chapter: his severance from religious belief and faith results in a human condition in which he—not God—is responsible for the events of his mortal life. By walking or falling alone, Ammons renounces all comfort in a transcendent being, divine purpose, or eternal salvation and thus faces the human "rewards" of this theological disengagement in his own "black rich" condition, namely, "uncertainty, labor, fear" (*CP*, 37).

In the interview in *Diacritics*, Ammons suggests another "rich" motivational element in his early poetics: "I [am] from a rural and defeated South . . . which, in growing up, I tended to discredit religiously and intellectually, though I could not emotionally." If Ammons has disengaged himself from the formal religion of his youth yet still feels the emotional need for religious experience—topics also central to the work of such poets as W. B. Yeats and Wallace Stevens, to name but two—it may be postulated that to a very large degree, these early poems are secular rituals in which his stories intentionally become "mythic in what [they] might suggest."[2] In other words, Ammons' quests are not merely the chaotic meanderings of a man lost and abandoned but are courses of poetic action designed to compensate for the emotional satisfaction that his former religion no longer provides yet continues to demand.[3] Consequently, these early poems may be read "blackly," as emotional reflections of the destruction of a self previously grounded in religious principle and ceremony. They may also be read "richly," as the secular reconstruction and empowerment of that self through modes of ritualized expression using mythological elements from that religious background and from those of other cultures, especially ancient Sumer. These reconstructions are especially important because they are the mythic narratives through which Ammons won his first victories in the area of poetic form. The overall direction of these narratives may be described as the internalized emotional enactment of the first two movements in a classic rite of passage: separation (from a previous self and worldview based on an externalized God) and transition (toward a new vision of self grounded in a personalized source of power). How Ammons embodies these two movements in specific poems, that is, the ways his mythic mind moves at Sumer, is the focus of my inquiry and it may best be developed by examining how ritual and myth operate in his early work.

First, however, I should clarify three central terms—*myth, ritual,* and *narrative*—that bear directly on my subject. Although the range of scholarly definitions of these topics is considerable, Jane Ellen Harrison's well-known yet strikingly simple distinction in *Themis: A Study of the Social Origins of Greek Religion* is suggestive. Harrison claims that myth is "the spoken correlative of the acted rite, the thing done."[4] In *The Cry for Myth,* psychologist Rollo May echoes and develops this distinction: "Rituals are the physical expressions of . . . myths, as in holidays and the sacraments of religion. The myth is the narration, and the ritual—such as giving presents or being baptized—expresses the myth in bodily action. . . . The myth may be prior to the ritual, as it is in the celebration of Holy Communion . . . or the ritual may come first. . . . Either way, one gives birth to the other."[5] According to these two views, myth is a narrated story, such as the recounting of the birth of Christ in Luke 2:1–20; ritual is the performance of that story, as, for example, in the display of a crèche at Christmas. If ritual is the physical performance of a narrated story, then one should be especially interested in what Ammons calls, in the remarks that opened this chapter, his "narrative," which is "a body in motion." This initiating narrative, constituting "the first level of apprehension of the poem," may be as simple as someone "walking along a dusty highroad." Bodily motion, however, is not what Ammons' narrative becomes. The somatic narrative is complicated by the speaker's perception of dialectical opposites of some kind: stasis and motion, macroscopic and microscopic views, permanence and change. Thus, the poet claims that "the narrative . . . becomes the play of these two [or more] possibilities."[6]

Simply because Ammons tells a dialectical story of topical opposites does not, of course, qualify the story as a myth. What he does to the story—how he ritually performs it—converts the narrative into something larger. I would suggest that the stylized combination of the speaker's bodily motion and his dialectical narrative becomes Ammons' mythic "curvature." The resultant combination is a *ritualized narrative* in which "the play of . . . two [or more] possibilities" is somatically enacted in ways that bring some measure of resolution to the driving needs of the speaker. To satisfy these needs, Ammons may ritually alter place and time and thus create a sacred space in which his speakers have the capacity to begin—even create themselves—anew. How Ammons performs his ritualized narratives in order to make his myths emotionally effective is the real subject of my inquiry.[7] Those moments in which Ammons converts his physical and conceptual narratives into larger mythic patterns constitute, to my mind, the major formal achievement of his early lyrics. Moreover, this mythic method initiates the entire arc of development for his poetic career. These ritual performances are elaborate rhetorics of supreme importance to his speaker, depending for their efficacy on apparently simple objects that, as I noted, transform profane spaces into sacred zones. The interactions of these objects and zones constitute major stages in Ammons' ritualizing of his narratives. Insofar as his things and spaces are magical techniques of mythic amplification, they require close attention.

STONES, SPACES, AND REALITY

To invent his ritualized space, Ammons must invent a Sumer that is not a real, historical place but an internal territory for a passage. His ritualized narratives portray his speaker's body in motion through this passage. Initially, Ammons' territory appears oppressive in the extreme. Yet it is also a space in which his speakers can master their performances to some degree. These performances depend on an enabling ground, a "Sumer," that forces the overwhelmed speaker into defensive ritual reactions by at least two major means: natural objects and bounded spaces. One group of natural objects that defines Ammons' sacred space is stones, especially those which he carries, places, or in the case of his poem "Apologia Pro Vita Sua," picks up and throws:[8]

> I started picking up the stones
> throwing them into one place
> and by sunrise I was going far away
> for the large ones
> always turning to see never lost
> the cairn's height
> lengthening my radial reach
>
> (*CP*, 38)

Although presented in a simple, minimally punctuated diction, Ammons' opening stanza reveals several complex operations. In the first two lines, the speaker performs the straightforward, apparently aimless act of picking up stones and "throwing them in one place." That this activity occurs at night is inferred, for the sun rises in line 3, where one also sees that the speaker's act has a purpose. He is building a "cairn," a monument of some kind, from which he builds mythic coordinates of time and space. The adverbs "always" and "never" amplify the cairn's status by suggesting that it is a landmark that perpetually orients the speaker and thereby exists in an eternal sacred time, not merely in the profane material sequence required to build it. The speaker's bodily gesture of "always turning" demarcates the ritualized eternal ground of the cairn, thus giving the cairn the assuring quality of being "never lost." Besides constituting a fundamental coordinate of the poem's spatial setting, the height of the cairn also enables the speaker to lengthen his "radial reach." This reach gives further form to his bodily action through the implied suggestion of a circle, which is magical in the sense that it gives him the power to build, grow, and thus extend his grasp.

If, as the title suggests, this poem is an apology or defense of the poet's life, then what can he gain from this simple if not primitive act of piling up stones? This mysterious gesture may be understood in terms of my earlier observation that a hallmark of Ammons' mythical method is its movement from a merely physical narrative to a realm in which simple actions seem filled with momentous consequences. Couched in the personified imagery of nature, these consequences grow in importance in the second stanza:

> the sun watched with deep concentration
> and the heap through the hours grew
> and became by nightfall
> distinguishable from all the miles around
> of slate and sand
>
> (*CP*, 38)

Although the speaker belittles his construction by calling it a "heap," its power nonetheless accumulates as he enters his second night of work. Even in the dark, this landmark is "distinguishable" from the surrounding "slate and sand" for "miles around." If this "heap" is taken to be his life—which the speaker is defending—then it can be seen that slowly but surely, his identity—like that of his poem—grows from the shape given to these base materials. At the end of the poem, its four-part movement from night to day to night to dawn concludes with this observation: "you can see in full dawn / the ground there lifts / a foreign thing desertless in origin" (*CP*, 38). Ending on a note of completion with the archetype of light, the poem reveals its final "ground" of transcendence in "full dawn," which suggests illumination and renewal. This light-filled final ground "lifts / a foreign thing"—*i.e.*, both the poet's invented life and his poem—which is "desertless in origin" in at least two senses. First, the speaker was, one assumes, not born in a desert; and second, the ground of the poem is not a real desert but the craft of the poet (his "cairn"), which has so altered space and time that some form of "lift" becomes possible. This lift is much more than a "heap" of stones; it is the reintroduction of the speaker to a sacred reality in which his simplest gestures now have cosmic meaning, even if the cosmos is a human one in which his body and its own space and time reconstitute each other.

If Ammons heaps mythological stones in defense—and in definition—of himself in his performative apologia, he heaps more complex mythic elements in another early poem, the title of which is identical with its opening line. The opening of this lyric reveals many of Ammons' representative ritualizing strategies from both his early and middle poetry:

> A treeful of cleavage flared branching
> through my flesh and cagey
> I sat down mid-desert
> and heaping hugged up between my knees
> an altarcone from the sand
> and addressed it with water dreams
>
> (*CP*, 24)

The poem begins with a contradictory image of life and death, a "treeful of cleavage" that is a threshold image both threatening and animating the speaker, "cleavage" indicating not only cutting but separation. To be sure, the word itself has a sexual connotation with regard to display; in this poem, however, cleavage is more like the openings and separations among the branches of a tree. Here, the image is even more aggressive; it is as if the branches were knives. This slicing force branches through the speaker's flesh, not like veins that carry life-giving blood but rather like veins that are sharpened blades. Thus, the initial condition of Ammons' speaker is presented through another of his images of dismemberment, like the one that concludes "I Struck a Diminished Seventh," where "death came over sieving me" (*CP*, 23). Ammons' cutting tree is the opposite of the cosmic tree Yggdrasil, the World Ash, which connected heaven and earth and gave man access to the gods. Ammons' bodily tree does not grow or unite but severs and flares, thus violently separating the speaker from meaningful connection. When read within the context of Ammons' early poems, this "treeful of cleavage" suggests man's absolute separation from the gods. In an oedipal sense, Ammons has committed arboreal regicide;

his initiating image has killed the divine tree-spirit, an act that initiates his internal search for a new god—or spirit—of renewal.

If Ammons' tree cleaves him from connection, it also sets his speaker and the rest of the poem into motion. The speaker is animated by this cutting tree in an archetypal manner that resembles the way the Greco-Syrian god Adonis was born through a similar threshold. Long before being slain by a boar and then resurrected by Zeus to assuage Aphrodite's grief, Adonis was born from a tree. After the maid Myrrha seduced her father and was turned into a tree for punishment, the tree gave birth to Adonis: "The tree cracked, the bark tore asunder, and gave forth its living burden, a wailing boy."[9] In Ammons' poetic "wail," the first thing his new speaker-"boy" does, being "cagey" (and caged), is to counter the tree's cutting-threat with a gesture that indicates the kind of cutting he faces. In other words, the speaker takes action against theological dispossession by building a quasi-religious monument like the cairn in "Apologia Pro Vita Sua." This time, instead of defending his life, he defends himself against the violence of disconnection by replacing the cosmic tree with another vertical monument, an altar-cone. This gesture is not exactly the biblical equivalent of constructing the golden calf. The speaker is not merely building a god—which, in Ammons' case, is a self-conscious human construction—but also a ritual environment, a complex of natural forces with which he reconnects and which in turn support him.

The fact that he sits down "mid-desert" to build this cone is crucial, for he is in the middle (mid-desert) of another middle (the desert), which doubly centers the speaker and his world. A desert setting suggests an egalitarian region in which someone in transition may obtain a special empowering status. In *The Rites of Passage,* Arnold van Gennep calls these desert regions "neutral zones," in which the traveler is "between two worlds." These zones are "ordinarily deserts, marshes, and most frequently virgin forests where everyone has full rights to travel and hunt. Because of the pivoting of sacredness, the territories on either side of the neutral zone are sacred in relation to whoever is in the zone, but the zone, in turn, is sacred for the inhabitants of the adjacent territories. Whoever passes from one to the other finds himself physically and magico-religiously in a special situation for a certain length of time: he wavers between two worlds."[10]

Ammons' speaker also dwells between two worlds: the sacred world from which he has been excluded and the profane world that he is in the process of resanctifying. His position is thus isolated yet intermediate (again, "mid-desert"); and as befits someone passing through a transitional zone, his situation is as fluid and semisubstantial as the "water dreams" with which he addresses his altarcone. Like his magico-religious self, these water dreams convey that his gesture of sanctification is to some extent unreal, that is, not as real as if the altarcone sprang from an actual, transcendent god. Consequently, a major effect of this poem is to ground (every pun intended) the speaker's ritual inclination in a reality more substantial than a dream. Thus, he clearly states this goal at the beginning of the third stanza, where he claims that he needs time (the time or duration of this poem) "to dream real these dreams."

Ammons dreams his water dreams real by using a method that he first developed in his Sumerian lyrics and that has continued to be a trademark of his poetry. However simple and straightforward this method looks in "A Treeful of Cleavage," it enables Ammons to complicate his physical and ritual narratives by enlisting natural objects in support of the speaker's quest. He makes the ritual (or questing) component of his story real by using real, natural things to carry out his religious activity, even though this activity takes place in dream space. In the world of dream space, he calls things into being—often by use of the definite article—the same way that creative Sumerian deities shaped the basic elements of their cosmos. As Samuel Noah Kramer notes, "All the creating deity had to do . . . was to lay his plans, utter the word, and pronounce the name."[11] Similarly, Ammons calls natural forces into being by declaring their presence and giving them a task to perform. "*The* wind" and "*the* sun" (my italics) are named and then portrayed as natural entities in motion that are actually in the service of the poet's cosmological motives. In the second stanza, the "wind," "chantless of rain," does not provide life-giving water or a religious chant, but it does use space and sound to spin "a sifting hum / in slow circles round [the speaker's] sphere of grief." Thus, if his grief is circumscribed by a powerful natural force, it is limited and, consequently, is more manageable.

Circular imagery continues to define and strengthen the speaker's power over his world in the second half of the second stanza, where "the sun / inched countless arms / under the periphery of my disc of sight / eager for the golden thing" (*CP*, 24). If the speaker's "disc of sight" is produced both by the "slow circles" of the wind and by the light-giving circumference of the sun, then "the golden thing" for which the sun's arms are aggressively eager is the altarcone, made "from [golden] sand." In punning on "altar," one may thus read the altarcone as a magical variation of a cosmic pillar that sets the things of nature into motions altering profane space. Shaping circular space into sacred space is a religious act shared by many cultures. It is certainly a central mechanism for the Sumerians, who organized their cities in circles, often around a palace tower (ziggurat) in a spatial scheme that was thought to reflect the circular structure of the universe.[12] If circularity constitutes a sacred space in which the powers of heaven and earth conjoin, there is another early source other than Plotinus and Emerson for Ammons' later interest in the magical properties of the circle, an interest to which his book-length poem *Sphere*, winner of the 1973–74 Bollingen Prize, convincingly testifies.

In the final third of the poem, after the sun has been "startled by the sound of time," it runs "off across the sky," and the speaker concludes with a recounting of the major themes in Ammons' Sumerian universe: the nature of belief, sacred places and sources, substitute gods, and a curious neoreligious satisfaction that he calls "bliss":

> Heaping the sand
> sharpening the cone of my god I said
> I have oracles to seek
>
> Drop leaf shade
> the wet cuticle of the leaf tipped in shade
> yielded belief
> to the fixed will and there
> where the wind like wisdom
> sweeps clean the lust prints of the sun
> lie my bones entombed
> with the dull mound of my god
> in bliss
>
>   (*CP*, 24–25)

By omitting punctuation, Ammons makes this section particularly challenging to decipher, especially the meaning and syntactic function of the opening line in the concluding stanza. For example, the specific subject of "yielded" is puzzling. Is its subject "shade," "leaf shade," or "the wet cuticle of the leaf tipped in shade"? Moreover, what part of speech is "drop"? Is it an adjective modifying "leaf shade" or a word intended to express what "leaf shade" did—that is to say, what "the wet cuticle of the leaf tipped in shade" did? If "drop" is a verbal, is it an imperative? Additionally, if Ammons intended that these questions be left open-ended, is this good or bad writing? Hence, is this first line suggestive or merely obscure?[13]

Not to impose too much on the poem, I believe that its opening is suggestive and may be clarified by placing a comma after the first and second "shade." The second line then becomes an appositional phrase modifying "leaf shade" (which I take to be a noun with "leaf" as an adjective) and specifying the precise part of the leaf shade, namely, the skin, that is the subject of the stanza's introductory clause. The poem's first line is grammatically difficult because Ammons has linked its first three terms to convey an abrupt event that aggressively reverses the setting from light to darkness. This "natural" motion, conveyed by grammatically disturbing solecism, also signals an equally abrupt change in the speaker's disturbing ritual. My understanding of this section is that the speaker sharpens (or increases) the power of his altarcone until it becomes a vertical variation of the "treeful of cleavage" that began the poem. This humanly constructed tree, which is another of Ammons' neoreligious landmarks, functions like an oracle by producing an omen, a "leaf tipped in shade," that in turn "yielded belief." What the specific content of this belief is, Ammons does not immediately say. What he does say is that the wind reappears to sweep "clean the lust prints of the sun," leaving the speaker's bones "entombed" in cool darkness with the altarcone that has now become "the dull mound" of his "god." The treeful of cleavage has thus severed the flesh from his bones. The entire poem becomes a ritual of self-burial, not merely for the speaker's "flesh" but for a death that means blissful union with his god.

In Ammons' reflexive funerary ritual, an old self is buried so that a new self may be born. This new self is distinguished from the old in that it knows that belief is not a relationship between man and divine power. Rather, belief is a function of the human will, a will that invents its own gods. This new self also knows that emotional commitment to its invented god should be cool, more like the atmosphere of "the leaf tipped in shade" than the hotter—and more transient—frenzy revealed by the sun's "countless arms . . . eager for the golden thing." Thus, if wisdom reveals anything to the speaker at the end of the poem, it is that bliss is not to be gained by "the lust prints of the sun," which are swept clean by "the wind like wisdom." The less ecstatic but more endurable truth is that the speaker's death and the death of his god are buried together in "the dull mound." This truth is endurable precisely because it is not theologically challengeable, for as Ammons notes in the lines from "This Black Rich Country," such a truth is "beyond all reach of faith" (*CP*, 37).

If Ammons' speaker is dismembering an old self and constructing a new one, then his omission of punctuation may be intended to serve yet another liminal function while simultaneously revealing a further aspect of his ritual form. In the foreword to *Ommateum*, Ammons describes his method in terms of the violence it does to a "rigid" and "unified" view of "reality." He explains that "the poems suggest a many-sided view of reality; an adoption of tentative, provisional attitudes, replacing the partial, unified, prejudicial, and rigid; a belief that forms of thought, like physical forms, are, in so far as they resist it, susceptible to change, increasingly costly and violent" (*OM,* 4). If Ammons has experienced the emotionally wrenching change from a religious world "unified" by belief in universals to an existential world of "provisional attitudes," it can be understood why his poetic forms reflect that change. They do so emotionally by presenting a semantic violence, which follows a deconstructive logic that repeatedly defers a single, centered—in Ammons' terms, "rigid"—meaning to his speaker's narratives. Instead of a single coherent line of development, his stories exhibit a "many-sided view" in which the action starts and stops in a jagged syntax that is "costly and violent" to any smooth, logical line of exposition. In the poem "Eolith" (a crude Stone Age tool), his quest for a "many-sided view of reality," which a new self sees a new way, develops through a series of fragmented narratives and thought patterns, historical periods, time zones, anachronisms, gods (for instance, Enlil, the Sumerian god of destruction), and misspellings. As one line of thought or narrative breaks, another begins; each side of each reality shows itself briefly, then splits off into a different dimension. The various sides are unified only by the poet's ritual act of carrying his primitive stone:

> I give you the wretched sympathy stone
> tears there is no end to the common matter
> dropped like suds water
>   down garbage shutes in places
>   if you wish
> Enlil has whipped your thighs with cane
> and the possibility of unloading pity is
> not greater than my giving it . . .
> I have sketched pyramids for
>   viewing splendid Hamlet
> a task waking at night in dark speed
> the pelican's over bays
>   carrying this eolith
>
>   (*CP*, 20)

Although "increasingly . . . violent" to classical forms of coherence, Ammons' early ritual forms also reveal a remarkable strength of movement. In one regard, this movement is a jagged flow whose shape—or lack of shape—recalls Kenneth Burke's idea of a "perspective by incongruity." In *Permanence and Change*, Burke calls this violent method of vision *"a shattering or fragmentation, analogous to the stage of 'rendering and tearing' (or* sparagmos*) in tragic ritual."* This process especially emphasizes *"the merging of categories once felt to be mutually exclusive,"* such as the merging—and tearing—of story lines with assertions from the middle section of "Eolith":[14]

> there have been days like
> > wasting
> > > ziggurats while
> your past spoils what is quick like river flies
> > days like
> the sweep of a steppe I have gone out
> like a northwind over the Nile
>
> > > > > (*CP,* 20)

The fourth line here clearly illustrates Ammons' process of merging and tearing. The line may be read in at least two ways. First, it merges with the initiating assertion "there have been days," if it is assumed that the line is a subordinate clause following "ziggurats." Thus, while ziggurats are "wasting," simultaneously "your past" (subject) "spoils" (verb) "what is quick" (object of "spoils"), with "quick" suggesting both the quick movement of the narrator, who two lines later says, "I have gone out / like a northwind over the Nile," and the quick of the living, which one's past spoils the way "river flies" spoil. In other words, in this world of pervasive decay and splintering change, anyone looking for sympathy or wishing to unload pity will find satisfaction for neither. There is only a universe of indifferent motion or "dark speed," in which the more delicate human emotions are driven out of existence by Enlil, the unforgiving Sumerian god of wind, who whips the quester mercilessly across the landscape. In addition to merging these ideas, the line also breaks any sense of the poem's continuity of narrative or argument in that it makes sense briefly, then has the momentum of its meaning "torn" (or interrupted) by a new unit of expression that immediately follows with a second "days like." Apart from line endings, the poem has no punctuation to signal completed thoughts, thus making any attempt at unequivocal recuperation doomed from the start. For instance, one may place a period after "steppe," thereby completing a sentence with the second, parallel appearance of "days like." Just as plausibly, "like / the sweep of a steppe" may serve as an introductory phrase modifying the "I" in "I have gone out," functioning as another geological analog to convey the velocity and scope of the perspectival movement of the speaker.

SELF AND FLOW

Like many of Ammons' early poems, "Eolith" proceeds by means of a process of merging and tearing. This process is a kind of epistemological sparagmos verging on incoherent fragmentation, if not a vertiginous mental state. This apparent chaos, however, does not reveal merely disorder or a failure of sustained method in Ammons but rather another ritual aspect of the speaker and the kind of quest he is going through. In *Myths, Dreams, and Mysteries*, Mircea Eliade notes:

> The psychopathology exhibited by the future shaman . . . closely follows the classic ritual of initiation. The sufferings of the "elect" are in every way similar to the tortures of initiation; just as the candidate was slain by the demons—"masters of the initiation"—so the future shaman sees himself being cut to pieces by the "demons of illness."
> . . . [T]hese "crises," these "trances" and this "madness" are not anarchic . . . not "profane" . . . *they are of an initiatory pattern and meaning.*
> . . . "[P]sychic chaos" . . . within the horizon of archaic spirituality, as a replica of the "pre-cosmogonic chaos," the amorphous and indescribable state . . . precedes all cosmogony. . . . *[T]he symbolic return to chaos is indispensable for any new Creation . . . it is a sign that the profane man is on the way to dissolution, and that a new personality is about to be born.*[15]

If Sumer is a nightmare world in which Ammons undergoes a major transition, I would suggest that his imagery of cutting and tearing—his ritual sparagmos—signals his initiatory "return to chaos," a primal condition of mind and body in which an old self is cut and torn, then merged with a new one. When Eliade claims that "demons . . . are shaman-ancestors and, therefore, the Masters of Initiation," it can be seen that Enlil, as befitting his role as the Sumerian god of destruction, serves this ancient function in "Eolith" by torturing the neophyte as he whips "your thighs with cane." Ammons' poem thus cuts or fragments conventional ways of seeing and being, then combines the resultant fragments into a new "chaotic" reality that is really a new cosmos. As I noted earlier, the boundaries of this cosmos are sacredly demarcated by the speaker's act of carrying the stone. That Ammons dwells to such an extent on death and destruction in his Sumerian poems is less an occasion for pathetic grief than a signal that his speaker is in one stage of a process that also promises renewal. Even these macabre lines from "Song," in which the speaker tells us that "I lost my head first, the cervical meat / clumping off in rot," suggest a mystical death or disintegration out of which rebirth is possible. For interestingly enough, the opening line of "Song" begins with a "merging": "Merging into a place against a slope of trees" (*CP*, 34). As Eliade notes, this experience of mystical death is essential for shamanic aspirants in many religious cultures. Such an experience "is related to the *contemplation of his own skeleton,* a spiritual exercise of great importance in Eskimo shamanism, but which is also found in Central Asia and in Indo-Tibetan Tantrism. The ability to see oneself as a skeleton implies, evidently, the symbolism of death and resurrection; . . . the 'reduction to a skeleton' constitutes, for the hunting peoples, a symbolico-ritual complex centered in the notion of life as perpetual renewal."[16]

Kenneth Burke calls an incongruous world of fragmented perspectives such as Ammons' "the realm of 'gargoyles.'"[17] However imagistically surrealistic and semantically violent for the reader, the poems in Ammons' early cosmos also reveal a powerful continuity, a ritual flow that has its own dynamic forward drive. Instead of being impeded by Ammons' poetic gargoyles, this momentum actually derives from the starts and stops in his early forms, and these starts and stops have a ritual dimension. Patricia A. Parker has written acutely on "the opposition between 'shape and flow'" in Ammons' early work. Using Emerson's "circle of compensation" as a paradigmatic model for Ammons' dramas of starting and stopping, Parker searches for a series of structural "centers," disclosed through the poet's metaphors, "which will keep the [poem's] 'shape' without damming up the 'flow.'"[18] To this line of inquiry, I would add the idea of a liminal ritual—that Ammons' flow is performative and that the various stops to this flow involve reflexive remanifestations of a self under reconstruction. This conception of "flow" is taken from Victor Turner's borrowing of the term in *The Anthropology of Performance:*

> Flow . . . is an interior state which can be described as the merging of action and awareness, the holistic sensation present when we act with total involvement, a state in which action follows action according to an internal logic, with no apparent need for conscious intervention on our part. Flow may be experienced . . . in play and sport, in artistic performance and religious ritual. . . . In flow, there is a loss of ego, the "self" that normally acts as a broker between ego and alter becomes irrelevant. . . . [F]low dispenses with duality and contrariety, it is nondualistic, nondialectical. . . . Reflexivity must be an arrest of the flow process, a throwing of it back against itself; framing procedures make this possible. The rejected ego is suddenly remanifested. In reflexivity, one is at once one's subject and direct object, not only in a cognitive way, but also existentially. Or, one might say, ransacking the terminology of depth-psychology, that the deepest reflexivity is to confront one's conscious with one's unconscious self. . . . A ritual performance is a flow / reflexivity dialectic. One can only "know" this in performance itself.[19]

Turner applies this conception of flow to the trancelike rituals followed by members of the contemporary Afro-Brazilian religion of Umbanda, who commune with their gods during performances called "sessions." He terms such sessions "a liminal, space-time 'pod'" in which members of the group can break from the "status-role structures" of a modern industrialized culture and bring themselves, through the flow of these rituals, into healing contact with the gods, ancestors, and traditions of their African roots. These sessions are organized by groups of the gods of mountains, forests, rivers, and other natural phenomena. By effecting a nondualistic trance with these "natural" gods, the performance of Umbanda produces a therapeutic emotional bond that reinforces cultural values preserved from the group's past, while at the same time enabling its members to deal reflexively with the problems and contradictions that beset their own lives. The healing effect of such ritual recalls Émile Durkheim's famous observation: "The believer who has communicated with his god is not merely a man who sees new truths of which the unbeliever is ignorant; he is a man who is *stronger*. He feels within more force, either to endure the trials of existence, or to conquer them."[20]

Applied to the ritualistic aspect of Ammons' early poems, Turner's conception of flow and reflexivity makes it possible to focus on these two moments as major features in the liminal process of Ammons' performed self-transformations. As his poems of quest and search develop, each feature emerges and then intertwines in a progressive alternation of enervating and energizing opposites that together constitute a new ritual flow. This final flow (or form) enables Ammons' speaker, in Durkheim's terms, to better "endure" or "conquer" the "trials of existence." First, there is the initiating flow of the poet's physical narrative, often driven forcefully forward by sentences beginning with actional participles, such as "coming" (*CP*, 36), "dropping" (*CP*, 30), "idling" (*CP*, 35), "driving" (*CP*, 33), and as I have noted, "merging" (*CP*, 34). With its focus on doing, this rush of narrative through the speaker's consciousness, performed in various settings and times, seems to me to correspond to Turner's "loss of ego." This nonreflective process of gestures and quests "dispenses with duality and contrariety" insofar as the speaker merges with landscape and cosmos in embodied performances "of voice and gesture," "action and awareness." In other words, in building an altarcone, he becomes a creator, not only of the cone but also of the space around him. This performance is not one of reflection but rather of ritual doing. "Loss of ego" is involved because the old religious self, already disposed to ceremony, merges into the new performance-self. These new gestures may be similar to those in traditional ceremonies, but the authority for their symbolic power has shifted from a divine source to the human performer. This new complex of gestures thus constitutes a separation from something old and a transition to a newly centered ontology.

The second feature of Turner's conception of ritual lies in the reflexivity that attends Ammons' poems. Turner defines reflexivity in general as "a condition" in which the "most perceptive members" of a "sociocultural group . . . acting representatively, turn, bend or reflect back upon themselves, upon the relations, actions, symbols, meanings, codes, roles, statuses . . . which make up their public selves." True reflexivity, however, occurs when an individual is both subject and object to himself, that is, when the "'self' . . . is something that one both is and that one sees and . . . acts upon as though it were another." The liminal element enters into reflexivity when the individual acts "upon the self-made other in such a way as to transform it."[21] Thus, reflexivity corresponds to the tearing apart or arresting of flow. In such a moment, one's ego—and speaking voice—is remanifested simultaneously as subject and object, seen anew. Transforming reflexive moments occur often in Ammons' work, and they are central elements in the performance of his ritual quests. Such a moment may stop the flow of the physical narrative with an epiphany, which also closes the poem. For example, in "Driving Through," Ammons concludes his "midnight rite" with a revelation of muted surprise in yet another of his hot, inhospitable deserts. The concluding reflection injects a note of hope into this hot and rainless landscape by transforming profane into human space and by transforming the narrator's physical act of driving into a threshold rite, in which the speaker prepares his house for habitation through, among other things, ceremonial purification by water. In the previous stanza, after the poet has imaginatively flooded "everything with cool / water," the poem ends optimistically:

> Driving through
> you would never suspect
> the midnight rite or seeing my lonely house
> guess it will someday hold
> laurel and a friend
>
> (CP, 34)

Even more radically and persistently, Ammons alters the flow of his physical narratives by using line endings to turn the reader back reflexively to the previous line (or narrative segment) in order to make sense of the poem. Ammons' continuous process of retrospective patterning results in a progressive form that to no small extent matches the reader's activity of recontextualizing. Thus, the overall shape of the poem becomes what Turner calls "a flow / reflexivity dialectic," and for Turner such an event constitutes a "ritual performance."[22] The flow of the physical narrative plus the pattern of reflexive stops becomes the ritually performed poem (for both poet and reader), or what I have called the "ritualized narrative." If the quest of Ammons' speaker takes its shape from the series of obstacles he needs to overcome, so too does the reader's experience become a quest of ritualized tearing and merging, of flow and reflection, in an attempt to understand the nature and value of questing in Ammons' early poems. For instance, in the opening of "Eolith," the reader encounters an obstacle while moving from the second line to the third. At the beginning of line 3, one must turn back to clarify an adequate grammatical subject for "dropped," which, in my interpretation, is "tears." One then encounters the assertion "there is no end to the common matter," which interrupts the syntactic flow between "tears" and "dropped." Additionally, at the end of the fourth line, the thought after "places" abruptly shifts into an optative "if you wish," which may be read as a concluding hypothetical following line 3 or as an introductory phrase for line 5. Whichever the case (or cases), the job of reading the poem is as semantically difficult—and delightful—as the speaker's job of carrying his "wretched sympathy stone." Or to put it another way, the ritual quest of reading "Eolith" is as challenging as the basic premise of the poem, namely that "the possibility of unloading pity is / not greater than my giving it." Thus, Ammons invites one to look again and again at these lines from a poem that one has already seen—or thought one saw:

> I give you the wretched sympathy stone
> tears there is no end to the common matter
> dropped like suds water
>> down garbage shutes in places
>>> if you wish
> Enlil has whipped your thighs with cane
>>> (*CP*, 20)

RITUAL VIOLENCE AND TRANSFORMATION

It is not only the semantic challenge that makes the reflexive element in Ammons' early forms ritualistic. It is also the aspect of ordeal, a painful physical performance that identifies his speaker's role and the kind of process the speaker undergoes. If "man is a self-performing animal," as Turner claims, then man's ritual performances are "*reflexive*" because "performing [them,] he reveals himself to himself."[23] Thus, another revelatory aspect of Ammons' ritualized flow centers on the loss (a dismembering or killing) of one ego and its reflexive remanifestation in a new mode. This deathly dimension of self-transformation—one of the most dramatic crises of liminality in Ammons—is even more "costly and violent" than his "forms of thought" because this kind of drama involves a threat to the entire body: it is the performed body that ritual so effectively defines and reveals. As Theodore Jennings has remarked, "Ritual knowledge is gained by and through the body." Such knowledge has an "'incarnate' character" in that "it is gained through 'embodiment.'"[24] More emotionally immediate and more comprehensive in effect than the ritual gesture of building an altarcone in "Apologia Pro Vita Sua," somatic violence adds to the nondualistic flow of Ammons' rites by employing a striking alteration of the whole body. This dramatic alteration necessitates a new way for the body to engage in ritual performances that is so severe the body becomes, physically and spiritually, a new self.

Within this ritual drama of drastic transformation, Ammons uses different kinds of somatic crises. For instance, in "With Ropes of Hemp," his speaker lashes himself to another vertical object—"the great oak"—with an imagery that at first suggests restraint and imprisonment (CP, 14). But the ropes also suggest a magical though painful metamorphosis. They are a kind of tortuous umbilical, which unites the speaker with an energizing tree-spirit. In his chapter "The External Soul in Plants" in The Golden Bough, Frazer notes how in the folktales of such countries as Germany, France, Denmark, and Sweden, cures for certain diseases are connected to the powers of oak trees through sympathetic magic.[25] Although Ammons' speaker watches "the ropes ravel" and his "body go raw," his life is bound up with his tree. During what he calls "my experiment"—an experiment in personal and poetic ritualization—he says "odes" and "supplications" to the tree's fiber, bark, and "root mesh / deep and reticular in the full earth" (CP, 14). In its supplicational aspect, the speaker's relation to the tree resembles that of a young man, White Youth, to the magical world tree in a hero myth of the Yakuts of Siberia. Recounted by Joseph Campbell in The Hero with a Thousand Faces, this myth is the tale of the transformation of a hero into a warrior. It tells of White Youth first coming to consciousness and wishing to learn who and where he is. When he sees a huge tree on a gigantic hill, he prays to it, expressing his need for power: "I wish to measure my strength against my kind; I want to become acquainted with men—to live according to the manner of men. Do not deny me thy blessing; I do humbly pray. I bow my head and bend my knee."[26]

Although White Youth's gesture appears submissive, the ancient, energizing employment of an achetypal tree grounds the hero to the root system of the entire earth, from which he gains strength to grow. In this process of self-sacrifice and self-renewal, Ammons' speaker recalls not only the Christian archetype involving a tree and a divinity but also Odin, the supreme Norse god of war and creation. Odin invented the cosmos, including the first human beings, Ask and Embla, who were created from two trees. The legend recounts how Odin hung for nine days on Yggdrasil as an offering to himself:

> I ween that I hung on the windy tree,
>   Hung there for nights full nine;
> With the spear I was wounded, and offered I was
>   To Odin, myself to myself,
> On that tree that none may ever know
>   What root beneath it runs.[27]

Like Christ on the cross, Odin is also pierced by a spear, not, however, to atone for man's original sin and corrupt nature but to gain a knowledge that befits Odin's station as an earthly hero and poet. "This Man of the Tree," as Campbell calls him, battles each day in his armor, then returns at night to drink magical mead given by Valkyries and to recite a poetry that celebrates the legacy of the Viking ships.[28] As Campbell notes, the power of this poetry is the power of life on earth, and to record the primordial legends of his tribe, the god-poet needs to acquire a complex wisdom of "many forms and names." In a similar way, Ammons' speaker seeks "the raucous words of the nightclouds" so that his wanderings may be recorded and, more importantly, that he too may find the words for his vocation as a poet.[29]

Like White Youth and Odin, Ammons' speaker in "With Ropes of Hemp" is bound to his tree in a relation of death and life. Within this dark night of his soul, he strives for the light of self-clarification. Once again reflecting a liminal movement from chaos to provisional cohesion, Ammons' imagery of division and combination appears in the concluding lines as splintering and "gathering":

> . . . I stand splintered to the oak
> gathering the dissentient ghosts of my spirit
> into the oakheart
> I in the night standing saying oaksongs
> entertaining my soul to me
>
> (*CP*, 14)

Campbell calls this kind of tree "a threshold image, uniting pairs-of-opposites in such a way as to facilitate a passage of the mind beyond anxiety."[30] One pair of these opposites—the imagery of splintering—clearly conveys the cutting and breaking into pieces associated with shamanic dismemberment and thus suggests that the speaker's "experiment" is initiatory. Like the bloody sacrificial boar torn apart in Dickey's magico-religious lyric "Approaching Prayer," the speaker's body going "raw" in Ammons' poem reveals a standard shamanic role that Mircea Eliade calls "the tormented and mutilated novice."[31] Effecting his ordeal in a cosmic setting of everlasting night within the realm of psychological dream space—what Ammons calls "eternity" and "nightclouds"—this novice reenacts a classic mythopoeic plot of dismemberment and reconstitution. The novice singer's reconstitution centers on an enabling process that Campbell calls above "the passage of the mind beyond anxiety."

In wishing to pass beyond lethal fragmentation, Ammons' speaker states his goal clearly when he gathers "the dissentient ghosts of my spirit / into the oak-heart"; he knows how fragile human identity can be, "how shadowy is the soul / how fleet with the wildness of wings" (*CP*, 14). To make the fragmented self whole, energized, and tangible (the opposite of "dissentient"), Ammons' "great oak" becomes what for Eliade is the speaker's "spirit guide," or what for Frazer is the "spirit of vegetation," both of which possess magical powers of renewal.[32] This oak is also Ammons' world-orienting sacred tree, that is, the world ash or world axis. Like "the primitive spindle / binding the poles of earth and air" in "I Struck a Diminished Seventh" and the cairn of stones in "Apologia Pro Vita Sua," this vertical oak-pole functions as a cosmic tree connecting heaven and earth in a timeless mythopoeic unity (*CP*, 22–23). The oak's integrating power organizes psychological space and time to such an extent that it results in the reconstitution of a poetic self, thus turning Ammons into a Whitmanesque Odin, hanging on (or, rather, tied to) his windy tree, "entertaining my soul to me."

Monstrosity and the Quietist Way

The magical connection between a supplicant human body and the strength of a "great oak" leads to another aspect of Ammons' ritual narratives. This aspect centers on a pair of dialectical opposites that establishes the dramatic conditions for one of his most striking personal peripeties, namely, the transformation between *power* and *powerlessness*. Thus far, I have focused on the first of these terms by emphasizing the active, constructive aspect of Ammons' speaker, especially his use of objects, events, and spaces to gain ritual control over desperate circumstances. The second term (which may also be referred to as *resignation*, or *disengagement*) is equally important, however—and potent, for out of this powerlessness comes another kind of power that takes its character from one of the poet's most important philosophic sources, namely, the doctrine of Tao, or "the Way." This ancient Chinese doctrine is most fully represented for Ammons in the work of the Eastern mystic Laotse. In an interview in *Diacritics*, when asked, "If you acknowledged literary fathers, who would they be?" Ammons replied: "In American literature, it's Whitman and Emerson. But Emerson led me to the same sources he discovered himself—to Indian and Chinese philosophy which, when I was younger, I read a good deal, finally coming to Laotse.... That's my philosophical source in its most complete version."[33]

Ammons' word selection bears him out. Key philosophic terms from Laotse—"the Way" ("Whose Timeless Reach" [*CP*, 33]), "inside" and "outside" ("Hymn" [*CP*, 39]), and "void receptacle" ("Hymn V" [*CP*, 43]), to name a few—provide an especially clear view of the degree to which Ammons externalizes a sophisticated religious dialectic to the things of nature. This dialectic often moves from loss to compensation or, as just suggested, from abject powerlessness to a different conception of power, which is itself compensatory and repositions the speaker's entire mode of vision. This movement occurs in various philosophic attitudes similar to Laotse's that are set within and against the scenic backdrop of Ammons' Sumerian landscapes: a pervasive stillness or spiritual darkness that seems in some sense absolute ("Turning a Moment to Say So Long"); the sense of questing for some transcendent ground beyond physical appearance and decay ("I Came in a Dark Woods Upon"); a resignation to fate that is something more than mere defeat ("Dying in a Mirthful Place"); a sense that this resignation contains mysterious knowledge of something everlasting that trivializes mordant physical motion while assimilating that motion to some larger process ("In the Wind My Rescue Is" and "Doxology"); and, finally, a ridding of the mind of earthly objects that frustrate the individual's disengagement from a world afflicted with decay and death ("Look for My White Self"). The following citation from Laotse's *Tao Te Ching* reflects many of these issues in a series of aphoristic directives:

> Push far enough toward the Void,
> Hold fast enough to Quietness,
> And of the ten thousand things none but can be worked on by you.
> I have beheld them, whither they go back.
> See, all things howsoever they flourish
> Return to the root from which they grew.
> This return to the root is called Quietness;
> Quietness is called submission to Fate;
> What has submitted to Fate has become part of the always-so.
> To know the always-so is to be illumined;
> Not to know it, means to go blindly to disaster.
>
> He who knows the always-so has room in him for everything;
> He who has room in him for everything is without prejudice.
> To be without prejudice is to be kingly;
> To be kingly is to be of heaven;

> To be of heaven is to be in Tao.
> Tao is forever and he that possesses it,
> Though his body ceases, is not destroyed.[34]

Laotse's claim—that "Though his body ceases," "he that possesses" Tao "is not destroyed"—bears most strongly on the overall direction of Ammons' early rituals. This direction characteristically begins with his speakers finding themselves in nihilistic states of darkness and self-abnegation that at first seem suicidal or as if their bodies are in some sense ceasing to exist. For example, in "Rack," the speaker notes "the great black unwasting silence" in which he is "broken" in yet another "black" country, beyond which he must quest for the "pieces of my voice":

> As I look across the fields the sun
> big in my eyes I see the hills
> the great black unwasting silence and
> know I must go out beyond the hills and seek
> for I am broken over the earth—
> so little remains
> for the silent offering of my death
>
> (*CP,* 6)

As suggested earlier, however, this "suicidal" impulse is really the second stage (often called "transition") in this poet's rites of passage, in which the killing or dismembering of an old self in a dark night of the soul is preliminary to forming a new self. And though much of the emotion that attends these rites issues from a distinctively Sumerian world of lamentational darkness (documented by Samuel Noah Kramer in *The Sumerians*), Ammons allows his speaker a distinctive kind of transcendence not found in my reading of Sumerian literature.[35] That is, in Ammons' "black rich country," there is a third stage to his liminal processes—a stage labeled "incorporation" by Arnold Van Gennep—which involves a quietistic element that issues out of monstrosity and spiritual darkness. Such incorporation helps resolve the speaker's pain by integrating it into a quietist vision of mortality that is far richer poetically and philosophically than mere suicidal paralysis or self-indulgent despair.

In many of Ammons' poems, the method of closure is profoundly religious, though not Western. Within this non-Western vision of mortality Ammons' speaker "ceases" but "is not destroyed." In Ammons' early work the speaker seems to go beyond the brokenness of his body and his universe to another realm. He appears to reach not "beyond" real, physical "hills" but beyond his current state of fragmented consciousness for an "earth" or sacred space—a "religious" or transcendent state of mind—in which he is not "broken."

Ammons dramatizes the Taoistic principle of the unbroken "always-so" in the third, closural stage of his rituals, which must be understood in conjunction with the two that precede it. His early paradigmatic ritual method may thus be seen as a three-act liminal rite, beginning with the speaker's direct engagement with a hostile world of considerable destruction (separation); next, an attempt to deal with this destruction through ritualistic gestures, such as gathering, marking, or climbing (transition); and finally, disengagement of the speaker's earthly ego from total catastrophe, whereby he enters a state of some degree of unbrokenness (incorporation). To be sure, he is not completely successful in his attempted transcendences. He often remains in a land of decay and darkness even after engaging in such power-directed gestures as circumscribing space, gathering stones, or building monuments. Yet even though Ammons' speaker concludes with a resigned awareness that many of his efforts are in vain and that he is powerless to direct his fate, he has changed—and gained something—because of his peculiar style of resignation. The central, therapeutic end of his ritual incorporation is often signaled by concluding imagery of light, elevation, higher point of view, or sign of integration.

This kind of muted resignation and integration is found at the end of "A Treeful of Cleavage Flared Branching." After the poem begins with its cleaving image of division and after the speaker heaps up sand for his "altarcone," he concludes with the observation that his bones are one with his god. His incorporation with divinity is not an ebullient unity of ecstatic transcendence but something more quiet. He is one with a "dull mound" in a condition that he calls "bliss." The announcement of this bliss, however, is delivered in an unblissful, deadpan tone, which carries with it a feeling of resignation that his invented god is less than satisfactory. Thus his "bones" lie "entombed / with the dull mound of my god / in bliss" (*CP*, 25). The movement from dismemberment to muted bliss may be found more strikingly in these lines from "Dropping Eyelids Among the Aerial Ash," where Ammons displays a powerful vision of engagement and disengagement. He begins the poem by "ascending" to the level of clouds to witness this apocalyptic, if not monstrous, sight:

> Below
> the gorged god lay on the leveled city
> and suburban bandaged
> and drowsily tolled the reckonless waste
> The clouds mushrooming rose
>   and held about his head
> like old incense of damp altars
>
> (*CP*, 30)

In the conclusion, the speaker descends "back down into the wounds and cries" of the "reckonless waste" from which he had emerged briefly. He thus circumscribes the spatial scope of the evil that confronts him while bringing some degree of light and healing to his cataclysmic universe, when in the final lines he holds "up lanterns for the white nurses / moving quickly in the dark" (*CP*, 31).

However minimal its uplifting transcendence when placed against Ammons' landscapes of overwhelming darkness, the "bliss" that concludes many of his early poems—and is found throughout his later work—is a more complex and powerful mode of closure than it first appears to be. This bliss issues from a carefully crafted combination of monstrosity and divinity, which, to my mind, has its intellectual and dramatic roots in Ammons' reading of Eastern and Mesopotamian literature. For instance, the monstrous "gorged god" in "Dropping Eyelids" recalls another pair of gods in Ammons' early work, those of cosmic strife, which appear in the second section of his long lyric "Doxology." Entitled "Paradox with Variety," this section reveals Ammons' speaker entering a temple and finding the god of creation on one side and the god of destruction on the other. Both are "tangled sensually on the floor," where "they gnawed and procreated" (*CP*, 17). Built out of the opposites of life and death, these gods constitute one of Ammons' basic principles of poetic conflict, a conflict that concludes with a curious mingling of destruction and quietness presented in yet another of his blissful images of bodily disengagement:

> Sometimes the price of my content
> consumes its purchase
> and martyrs' cries, echoing my peace,
> rise sinuously like smoke
> out of my ashen soul.
>
>   (*CP*, 18)

The martyristic or metamorphic nature of Ammons' quietist contentment becomes even clearer in light of Joseph Campbell's remarks on monstrosity and the sublime. Interestingly enough, Campbell's description of "bliss," like Ammons' poem "Dropping Eyelids," also uses "ash" to make its point:

> What we call monsters can be experienced as sublime. They represent powers too vast for the normal forms of life to contain them. . . .
>
>   By a monster I mean some horrendous presence or apparition that explodes all of your standards for harmony, order, ethical conduct. For example, Vishnu at the end of the world appears as a monster. There he is, destroying the universe, first with fire and then with a torrential flood that drowns out the fire and everything else. Nothing is left but ash. The whole universe with all its life and lives has been

utterly wiped out. That is God in the role of destroyer. . . . [T]here is a muslim saying about the Angel of Death: "When the Angel of Death approaches, he is terrible. When he reaches you, it is bliss."

In Buddhist systems . . . the meditation Buddahs appear in two aspects, one
peaceful and the other wrathful. If you are clinging fiercely to your ego and its
little temporal world of sorrows and joys, hanging on for dear life, it will be the
wrathful aspect of the deity that appears. It will seem terrifying. But the moment
your ego yields, and gives up, that same meditation Buddah is experienced as a be-
stower of bliss.[36]

Like Vishnu's universe of wrath, Ammons' Sumerian landscapes have ex-
ploded "all . . . standards for harmony, order, [and] ethical conduct." They are
settings filled with "gorged god[s]" of destruction and mythological worlds of
"ash." For Ammons' speaker, however, what begins with the compulsive monstrosity of deprivation can end with the speaker's transformative attitude,
known in Eastern thought as "sitting with blank mind" or "non-assertion, not
forcing."[37] In this state, the earthly or ashen ego yields up its earthly form and
thus the content of its earthly terror. In the moment when the Angel of Death
reaches Ammons' earthly ego, his speaker achieves the bliss of yielding or non-
assertion. This movement from worldly engagement to disengaged bliss is central to "With Ropes of Hemp," where, the speaker's raw body, though bound,
"melt[s] beyond the ruthless coil" of rope "while eternity / greater than the
ravelings of a rope / waited with me patient in my experiment" (*CP*, 14). In its
torturous transformation of a "splintered" self with its "shadowy . . . soul" into
something stronger through the process of ordeal, Ammons' ritual method
bears striking similarity in its use of paradox and contradiction to a course of
wisdom proposed in Laotse's *Tao Te Ching*:

> "To remain whole, be twisted!"
> To become straight, let yourself be bent.
> To become full, be hollow,
> Be tattered, that you may be renewed.
> Those that have little, may get more,
> Those that have much, are but perplexed.[38]

This blissful emptying or destroying of one aspect of the self "to become
full" is not otherworldly escapism presented as mere passivity. It involves, as
Campbell notes, the "centering [of] the seat of the world-shaping power in
man himself."[39] The awakening of internal strengths issues from the same dialectic of powerlessness becoming power and monstrosity becoming bliss that
informs an internalized rite of passage as a symbolic form of non-catastrophic

change.[40] Such a rite, René Girard notes, "instills" in the initiate "a respect for the power of violence" at the same time as it "promotes prudence and discourages hubris."[41] This power is also "the Way," or *Tao* in Chinese thought. Again, Campbell: "In India ... yoga enabled the ascetic to develop within himself certain 'powers' *(siddhi)* by which all kinds of magical effects could be achieved.... In China, on the other hand, it was precisely in the powers *(tê)* that interest lay. '*Tê* means a latent power, a "virtue" inherent in something,' [Arthur] Waley states. *Tao tê*, then, is 'the latent power *(tê)* of the Way, the order, of the universe *(tao)*' which the Quietist finds within, as well as without; since it is the 'Mother of all things.' "[42] Thus it is with Ezra, Ammons' "dying" neobiblical persona in "Whose Timeless Reach," who moves from a state of mortality at the beginning of the poem into a wisdom of motion (or "cool thought"), which at poem's end is "timeless." Ezra has traveled yet another of Ammons' early, ritualized roads that ultimately lead to "the Way." This is a Way of internal strength and renewal achieved through a thoroughly realistic view of death and a poetic acceptance of its overwhelming presence as an eternal law of nature. Taoistic acceptance of death yields its terror to something cooler and timeless, and this disengagement from terror becomes a Way to bliss. For A. R. Ammons, this Way begins at Sumer:

> I Ezra the dying
> portage of these deathless thoughts . . .
> taking the Way in whose timeless reach
>   cool thought unpunishable
> by bones eternally glides
>
> (*CP*, 33)

2

AMMONS' SUMERIAN SONGS
Desert Laments and Eastern Quests

This land where whirlwinds
walking at noon in tall columns of dust
take stately turns about the desert
is a very dry land

—A. R. AMMONS, "I Went Out to the Sun"

This landscape is not the portrayal of an impression, it is not the judgment of
a man on things at rest; it is nature coming into being, the world coming into
existence, unknown to man. . . . It had been necessary to see the landscape in
this way, far and strange, remote, without love, as something living a life
within itself, if it ever had to be the means and the motive of an independent
art; for it had to be far and completely unlike us—to be a redeeming likeliness
of our fate. It had to be almost hostile in its exalted indifference, if, with its
objects, it was to give new meaning to our existence.

—RAINER MARIA RILKE, on the landscape in Da Vinci's *Mona Lisa*

Suffering itself is a deception [*upadhi*]; for its core is rapture, which is the attribute [*upadhi*] of illumination.

—JOSEPH CAMPBELL

In his early lyrics, I have noted, Ammons exhibited a complex and mysterious
religious attitude, especially in those collected in *Ommateum*. This attitude is
dramatized in the form of a ritual quest that takes place in a barren, desolate
setting, often generalized, like the "dry land" cited above, in Ammons' equally
dry understatement. At times, however, this setting is identified as ancient
Sumer, in what is now modern Iraq. Written when Ammons first began publishing in the mid-fifties, poems such as "Sumerian," "Coming to Sumer,"

"Eolith," and "Gilgamesh Was Very Lascivious" make use of locales that the poet specifies as Sumerian. In addition to these specific locales, generalized Sumerian settings appear in different guises in almost all of Ammons' books. These settings range "from murky lowlands" and "the desert" in the short poem "Separations" in *Diversifications* (1975) to a Sumerian netherworld in *A Coast of Trees* (1981), where there is a "bleak land of foreverness" (*CT,* 40) in nothing less than a fast-food restaurant in "Sunday at McDonald's." In *Lake Effect Country* (1983), Ammons' speaker suffers the effects of this "very dry land" when he laments that his "lips [are] twisted with thirst / in the hot country" while observing his own "desert-precious being / swim, wily as snake-water in the sand" (*LEC,* 37). More recently, in 1987, Ammons published an entire collection of poems entitled *Sumerian Vistas.* In this collection, ironically, he does not mention Sumer. Nonetheless, he indicates its continuing importance for him in the book's title and by using his early desert landscapes (or vistas) to initiate meditations such as that in "Scaling Desire," where "a small boulder washed or / rolled down or out / of circumstance lay mid-desert" (*SV,* 65).

If Ammons' Sumerian landscapes, whether generalized or specified, initiated his career in the fifties and continue to preoccupy him, it may be asked with considerable justification why this poetic locale retains its importance for him. I addressed this question in Chapter 1 primarily with regard to beginnings. I argued that although based on historic, geographic, and cultural detail from an ancient civilization, Ammons' postmodern, mythopoeic Sumer is, among other things, a psychological space of personal passage in which he disengages himself from one mythology while building a new one. In so doing, he builds a new, existentially stronger self. The central poetic method in this undertaking is the construction of a ritualized narrative. This ritualized narrative begins realistically in a Sumerian setting and ends in a mental landscape derived in part from Asian systems of thought, which Ammons discovered through his reading of Emerson.[1] Here I will employ the same general approach but will also move in a different direction by restating the motivational ground of Ammons' ritual quests, first in human terms, then artistically. While adhering to my quasi-religious thesis that Ammons uses poetry to seek a new ground of compensatory belief, I will expand this line of inquiry by using Harold Bloom's formulation of a major psychological and poetic problem for the English High Romantic poets.

Taken from his richly suggestive article "The Internalization of the Quest-Romance," Bloom's initiating question is based on his search for a spiritual motive in the varied quests of Wordsworth, Shelley, Blake, Keats, and Coleridge:

[This is] the central problem of Romantic (and post-Romantic) poetry: what, for men without belief and even without credulity, is the spiritual form of romance? How can a poet's (or any man's) life be one of continuous allegory . . . in a reductive universe of death, a separated realm of atomized meanings, each discrete from the next? Though all men are questers, even the least, what is the relevance of quest in a gray world of continuities and homogenized enterprises? Or, in Wordsworth's own terms, which are valid for every major Romantic, what knowledge might yet be purchased except by the loss of power?

In his neo-Freudian mapping of the poetic landscapes of these writers, Bloom's answer is that the Romantics do not primarily quest for the things of nature or for unity with nature. Instead, they seek connection with "their Tharmas or id component, Tharmas being the Zoa or Giant Form in Blake's mythology who was unfallen human potential for realizing instinctual desires, and so was the regent of Innocence." According to this view, the libido moves ("falls") outward toward external objects when the inner self is compulsively overfilled. What results is an erotic quest not merely for the surrogate mother or its image but for a similar sustaining power inside oneself. Manifested by "a movement of love" of the ego toward itself, this search, for the Romantics, is actually a fusion of libido and imagination, or as Bloom says, "desire wholly taken up into the imagination." The spiritual form of the Romantics' quests is an allegorical search symbolically conducted and dramatized through nature, whereby poets seek a kind of internal consciousness, which enables them to overcome any "recalcitrance in the self" that hinders the "mature powers" of the imagination. The Romantic quest first turns inward to overcome self-defeating ego-passivity, a state in which the libido, working through the ego, endlessly repeats the "cyclic movement from appetite to repression, and then back again." In this state, what the poet must overcome is the erotic force of an ego condemned to "a self-love that never ventures out to others." Romantic transcendence occurs in a second turn of the self outward to the union of the imagination with its "ongoing creation." This ongoing creation is not redeemed nature but rather the artistic product of the poet's ongoing process of escaping excessive preoccupation with the self by making anew the externally directed poems of the imagination.[2]

Escaping excessive preoccupation with the inner-directed self is also a central topic in Eastern religious thought. In *The Mythic Image*, Joseph Campbell argues that this problem issues not only from a classic model of the Western unconscious but generally from the "field of Waking Consciousness," where "we are separate from each other . . . so long as we hold to this ego-consciousness." Based on this observation, one of Ammons' preeminent pairs of poetic terms, "the One" and "the Many," may be interpreted not only as metaphysical opposites but also as opposing states of consciousness; as Campbell notes, "what is in the mystical dimension one, is in the temporal-spatial two—and many—the very form of our 'knowledge' (in mystical terms, our 'ignorance') being multiplicity."[3] One way (or "Way") the early Ammons dramatizes the conflict between these states is, as I have shown, through the violence of an ordeal or through dismemberment, which has mythological and shamanic precedent in the concept of liminal sacrifice. I would further argue that one of Ammons' basic mythopoeic modes for reconciling "the One" and "the Many" —that is, for moving excessive and divisive ego-consciousness ("the Many," or many painful earlier selves) outward into the field of imaginative and unifying poetic action ("the One," or one new self)—is through the purification of that empirical self in the purgatory of his poetic Sumer. The purgatorial identity of land and self is explicit in these lines from the second page of Ammons' *Collected Poems*:

> The sap is gone out of the hollow straws
> and the marrow out of my bones
> > They are
> > brittle and dry
> > and painful in this land
>
> > > > (*CP*, 2)

The sacrificial method of overcoming death and division has considerable precedent in Eastern religions. For example, Ananda K. Coomaraswamy, scholar of Hindu and Buddhist philosophy, observes that "For this *ignorantia divisiva*[,] an expiation is provided in the Sacrifice, where by the sacrificer's surrender of himself and the building up again of the dismembered deity, whole and complete, the multiples selves are reduced to a single principle."[4] That Ammons' sacrificial action may very well dramatize a philosophic turn toward the East takes further credence from his observation on his methods of indention: "I usually feel that I don't have anything to say of my own until I have tripped the regular world, until I have thrown the Western mind itself somehow off."[5] Campbell notes that the stage of consciousness following such disengagement is called, variously, in Eastern thought, "rapture" or "illumination" or "bliss."

If Ammons' Sumer is some kind of purgatory, then one of his major methodological successes, to return to the Romantic vocabulary, is his marriage of heaven and hell. That is, a marriage (or what Bloom calls "an interweaving of purgatory and paradise") in which the poet externalizes the inner-directed self, with its perpetual round of desire and frustration (what Bloom calls the "Promethean libido") in its cyclic, Freudian "hell," onto a lyric model of consciousness in which the questing speaker enables the poet to discover his "mature [poetic] powers" in the ongoing "heaven" of Ammons' work.[6] Like the Romantics, Ammons' quest from purgatory to paradise has at least two major turns: inward into his own mind for the strength and confidence to write, then outward to the objects of his poetic landscape, which free him from excessive self-consciousness while paradoxically reinventing that self with an Eastern philosophic twist.[7] Insofar as Mircea Eliade claims that *"the symbolic return to chaos is indispensable for any new Creation,"* Ammons' barren, often violent, Sumerian deserts become an originating psychic ground for a poetic mythology in which he not only discovers his Blakean Tharmas—in Yeats's words, cited by Bloom, "the face I had / Before the world was made"—but also remakes that face and that world over and over again.[8] By continually reinventing this Sumerian mytho-psychic face and world, Ammons also invents a "way" to solve major artistic problems that confront any writer: namely, the plotting of a rewarding direction for his poetic action and, subsequently, the selection and arrangement of important technical elements, such as voice, motivation, and kinds of revelation, to name but three. My central claim is that this movement from Sumerian, purgatorial desire to imaginative Eastern bliss is the major ritualized narrative in Ammons' early work and, further, that this movement is so important that it plays an essential role throughout his poetry, even as late as his work of the eighties, as manifested in his title *Sumerian Vistas.*

If Ammons' songs (indeed, his career) begin as laments in Sumerian deserts, how do the routes of his lyric quests take him to Asia or, more accurately, following Emerson's description of the mystical component in Plato, "the Asia in his mind"?[9] In answering this question, I would employ the Eastern concept of illumination together with Bloom's romantic psychic mythology. Thus, I will refine my thesis from Chapter 1: Ammons' oppressive, Sumerian, mental landscapes constitute a romantic purgatory that replaces the sacred spaces of his earlier, Christian mythology and enables him to move from fallen nature (excessive self-preoccupation, due in part to the self of his earlier myth) into an internalized nature (a Sumer), which moves him outward to develop new formal and technical poetic powers, whereby he achieves an ongoing creation (the progressive body of his work) in which he continually quests for a new, "heavenly," mythological landscape, *i.e.,* "the Asia in his mind."[10]

In discussing the ritual aspect of Aristotle's conception of catharsis, Joseph Campbell notes that "tragedy transmutes suffering into rapture by altering the focus of the mind." Following Campbell, one may also say of Ammons' dark, early poems that, like Aristotle, when he refocuses his mind, his particular "mode of tragedy dissolves and [his] myth begins."[11] Even if Ammons' attempts at rapture seem to be failures—those "visions of . . . losses," as he says in "Prodigal," of a "spent / seer" (*CP*, 77)—these early lyric rituals are acts of radical refocusing that begin to dissolve his conceptual tragedies and thus commence his new myths.

My focus, however, is on the outward-turning element in Bloom's thesis, that is, the movement of Ammons' mind toward the poems that reveal his early, mature powers. Geoffrey Hartman indicates this direction in his article "Romanticism and 'Anti-Self-Consciousness,'" claiming that one of the English Romantics' central problems was to find a remedy for "the ravage of self-consciousness and the 'strong disease' of self analysis," which is also called "death-in-life." Following Hegel in his *Logic*, Hartman notes that for the Romantics, one remedy for this kind of excessive thought is found, ironically, in further thought, which transcends nature and "its own lesser forms." On this point, Hartman cites the great German idealist: "The hour that man leaves the path of mere natural being marks the difference between him, a self-conscious agent, and the natural world. The spiritual is distinguished from the natural . . . in that it does not continue a mere stream of tendency, but sunders itself to self-realization. But this position of severed life has in its turn to be overcome, and the spirit must, by its own act, achieve concord once more. . . . The principle of restoration is found in thought only: the hand that inflicts the wound is also the hand that heals it." What is most important here is Hartman's claim that "the attempt to think mythically is itself part of a crucial defense against the self-conscious intellect"—or in the case of Ammons, an intellect that self-consciously thinks itself, in Hegel's terms, from a "severed" mythology to a newer one of "concord" and "restoration." Encouraged by poetry and the imagination, this mythic mode of thought moves dialectically between the self and nature in a process of "soul-making," a route that most certainly bears on Ammons' Sumerian strategies, as does Hegel, for later poems such as "Gravelly Run" and "Bridge." I will therefore, trace the beginnings of Ammons' route of mythopoeic thought by examining central topics and devices that help to reveal the rich variety of ritualized formal strategies used by his narrator on his quests.[12]

Sumerian Laments

In *Philosophies of India*, Heinrich Zimmer recounts an incident from the legend of Mahayana Bodhisattva Avalokiteshvara, a most distinguished and beloved ambassador of Buddha to this mundane world:

When, following a series of eminently virtuous incarnations, he was about to enter into the surcease of nirvana, an uproar, like the sound of a general thunder, rose in all the worlds. The great being knew that this was a wail of lament uttered by all created things—the rocks and stones as well as the trees, insects, gods, animals, demons, and human beings of all the spheres of the universe—at the prospect of his imminent departure from the realms of birth. And so, in his compassion, he renounced for himself the boon of nirvana until all beings without exception should be prepared to enter in before him—like the good shepherd who permits his flock to pass first through the gate and then goes through himself, closing it behind him.

Every pore of the body of Avalokiteshvara contains and pours forth thousands of Buddhas, saints of all kinds, entire worlds. From his fingers flow rivers of ambrosia that cool the hells and feed the hungry ghosts.[13]

Insofar as Ammons' mythopoeic quest moves in its broadest outlines in an actional curvature from "suffering" to "illumination," his early poems may be read analogically along the lines of the legend of Avalokiteshvara. That is, Ammons' speakers dwell in a world that his voice fills with "a wail of lament," which seems to be "uttered by all natural things." This wail issues not from the prospect of Ammons' imminent departure but from his immersion in realistic, Sumerian vistas of "hells" and "hungry ghosts" that, more often than not, fail to respond to his poetic imagery of comforting "rivers" to "cool" these hells. My point here is that, like the distinguished Bodhisattva, an "uproar" precedes the attempts of Ammons' speakers at any kind of ritual disengagement. Thus, these hells constitute the inciting condition for his quests and need to be effectively dramatized as states of earthly anguish. If Ammons' myths begin when his pain dissolves (to whatever degree), then this pain must first be established as a formidable force. This initiating condition of a suffering consciousness is most strongly reflected by the lamentational voice that echoes over Ammons' vast Sumerian terrains.

The lamentational voice of the mundane earthly ego in Ammons' quester consists of at least two aspects, and these need to be distinguished from each other to see what is essentially Sumerian in this voice. The first aspect is biblical. The influence of the Bible on Ammons cannot be underestimated. Recounting how he grew up on a farm in rural North Carolina, he poignantly notes in an interview about his early education that "the only book we had in our house was the Bible."[14] Echoes of the Old Testament can be heard throughout his early work. In a line such as "Dogs ate their masters' hands / and death going wild with joy / hurried about the Sea," his view of the vicious absurdity of life and its attendant mortality has as powerful a resonance as these lines from Ecclesiastes 9:3: "The heart of the sons of men is full of evil, and madness is in their heart while they live, and after that they go to the dead." With regard to spiritual pain expressed in bodily anguish, Ammons' speaker wails in "Song" that "I lost my head first, the cervical meat / clumping off in rot, baring the spinal heart to wind and ice" (*CP,* 34). Similarly, the psalmist's cries reverberate throughout his body in Psalms 22:14: "I am poured out like water, and all my bones are out of joint: my heart is like wax; it is melted in the midst of my bowels." And while Ammons' landscapes of "ashen abnegation" (*CP,* 25) and death bear great likeness to Sumerian deserts and its underworld, they also resemble "the land of darkness" in Job 10:22: "A land of darkness, as darkness itself; and of the shadow of death, without any order, and where the light is as darkness."

To whatever degree he combines cultural voices from the ancient Near East, Ammons' speaker differs in several significant ways from those in the Bible. I would assert that these differences may be understood to some degree as "Sumerian" and that they play major roles in the development of the dramatic voice and emotional character of Ammons' early speakers. Discussing the two cultures in *The Sumerians,* C. Leonard Woolley offers a suggestive contrast that also serves as a strikingly accurate portrayal of the emotional austerity in Ammons: "Psychologically, the Sumerian was more distant and aloof than the Hebrew—more emotionally restrained, more formal and methodical. He tended to eye his fellow men with some suspicion, misgiving, and even apprehension, which inhibited to no small extent the human warmth, sympathy, and affection so vital to spiritual growth and well-being. And in spite of his high ethical attainments, the Sumerian never reached the lofty conviction that a 'pure heart' and 'clean hands' were more worthy in the eyes of his god than lengthy prayers, profuse sacrifices, and elaborate ritual."[15]

As befits this poet's austere exterior landscapes, Ammons' interior world is also "distant," "aloof," "emotionally restrained . . . formal and methodical." As I noted in Chapter 1, his poems—involving narrators such as Ezra the grave robber in "Coming to Sumer" and the speaker in "Eolith," who claims that "the possibility of unloading pity is / not greater than my giving it" (*CP,* 20)— clearly reveal an attitude of "suspicion," "misgiving," and "apprehension" toward others. In Ammons' Sumerian vistas, seldom does the speaker evince "human warmth, sympathy, and affection." Although these traits make for an unsympathetic coldness, they also balance the reader's reaction to him by providing a convincing emotional ground in a hostile cosmos for his overwhelming religious need to offer "lengthy prayers, profuse sacrifices, and elaborate ritual."

Samuel Kramer offers evidence for this last point by extending the Near Eastern cultural and poetic contrasts noted earlier. In commenting on a Sumerian poetic essay predating the Book of Job by a thousand years, Kramer notes that the Sumerian speaker resembles Job but has considerably fewer options: "The main thesis of our poet is that in cases of suffering and adversity, no matter how seemingly unjustified, the victim has but one valid and effective recourse, which is to continually glorify his god and keep wailing and lamenting before him until he turns a favorable ear to his prayers." Like Job, who finds himself in a "land of darkness" and claims that "my soul is weary of my life" (Job 10:1), the Sumerian poet in Kramer's text also cries out that "for me the day is black" and that "evil fate . . . carries off my breath of life." Yet unlike Job, the Sumerian has not even the slightest hope that he can "reason with God" (Job 13:3) or that the Lord will answer him "out of the whirlwind" (Job 38:1). Nor is there consolation for him in the special punishment reserved for the wicked (Job 24). In the cold and heartless Sumerian cosmos, the poet can only enumerate his griefs:

> "I am a man, a discerning one, yet who respects me prospers not,
> my righteous word has been turned into a lie,
> The man of deceit has covered me with the Southwind, I am
>   forced to serve him,
> Who respects me not has shamed me before you.
>
> "You have doled out to me suffering ever anew,
>
> I entered the house, heavy is the spirit,
> I, the man, went out to the streets, oppressed is the heart,
> With me, the valiant, my righteous shepherd has become angry,
>   has looked upon me inimically.
>
> "My herdsman has sought out evil forces against me who am
>   not his enemy,
> My companion says not a true word to me,
> My friend gives the lie to my righteous word,
> The man of deceit has conspired against me,
> And you, my god, do not thwart him. . . .
>
> "Suffering overwhelms me like one chosen for nothing but tears . . .
> Malignant sickness bathes my body."[16]

Ammons' speaker operates under similar situations, in which emotional pain is overwhelming and cannot be removed by appeal to divine intervention. In "A Crippled Angel," the speaker discovers a "crippled angel bent in a scythe of grief" in a temporal world so oppressive that "Grief sounded like an ocean" (*CP*, 30). In "I Came in a Dark Woods Upon," the speaker is "dazed with grief"

(*CP*, 28), and in "The Whaleboat Struck," his "body lies south / given over to vultures and flies" (*CP*, 9). Even in a poem such as "Look for My White Self," about the disengagement of the mundane ego, the speaker is "diffuse, leached colorless, / gray as an inner image with no clothes" and is "wasted by hills" (*CP*, 37).

In its emotional and spiritual darkness, the depth of longing in Ammons' speaker recalls the ancient Babylonian hero Gilgamesh. Dating approximately to 2600 B.C., *The Epic of Gilgamesh,* or "The Gilgamesh Cycle," consists of tablets containing twelve cantos or songs that describe the exploits of the Sumerian seer and hero Gilgamesh. The son of the goddess Ninsun and a human, a high priest in the city of Uruk or Erech, Gilgamesh was one-third mortal and two-thirds divine, and was known as the god of the netherworld. Fully humanized in the epic tale, he was king and protector of Erech, whose citizens he intimidated by his superior energy and formidable sexual appetite. To give peace to the citizens of Erech, the gods sent Gilgamesh a male friend, Enkidu, who was as strong as he and was meant to tame him. When Enkidu died prematurely, Gilgamesh was devastated and journeyed far and wide, even to the netherworld, to discover the secret of eternal life. His quest for such knowledge was futile, and he knew it. In John Gardner's rendering, Gilgamesh says, "I roam the wilderness in quest of a wind-puff."[17] When Gilgamesh finally discovered the plant of eternal youth, which he plucked from the ocean floor, a snake stole away with it while he was bathing, and he was left with nothing. Having lost the secret of eternal life, Gilgamesh was overwhelmed, like the Sumerian petitioner, with a fate that threatened to annihilate him. Not only did death face him constantly, it pervaded his consciousness like an existential demon:

> The one who followed behind me,
>   the rapacious one,
> sits in my bedroom, Death!
> And wherever I may turn my face,
> there he is, Death![18]

In Ammons' "Consignee," the speaker also finds death a constant companion, which restricts his alignment with natural motion:

> To death, the diffuse one
> going beside me, I said,
>   You have brought me out of day
> and he said

No longer like the fields of earth
may you go in and out.

(*CP*, 8)

After Enkidu's death, Gilgamesh searched for Utnapishtim, an ancestor whom he believed had found everlasting life and who dwelled in the farthest reaches of the earth. To gain Utnapishtim's secret, Gilgamesh traveled westward through dark mountain tunnels and immense deserts, digging wells for water and hunting wild bulls for food and clothing. Though his quest is for immortality, Gilgamesh seems to roam with little direction, moving whichever way the wind blows. In this translation from Thorkild Jacobsen's *The Treasures of Darkness: A History of Mesopotamian Religion*, he responds to the sun god, Shamash, who has urged him to abandon his hopeless quest:

Is it (so) much—after wandering and roaming
    around in the desert—
to lie down to rest in the bowels of the
    earth?
I have lain down to sleep full many a time
    all the(se) years!
(No!) let my eyes see the sun
    and let me sate myself with daylight!
Is darkness far off?
    How much daylight is there?
When may a dead man ever see the sun's splendor?[19]

"Spring Song," although more muted than Gilgamesh, is Ammons' cry for a certain kind of light, "a deep / luminosity" (*CP*, 49). By rising up from the darkened and deadening ground of elemental "dust," his speaker begins the poem, like Gilgamesh, by driving forward through a vast spiritual desert that offers no hope of fulfillment—not even the possible renewal of a "phoenix" but merely "no other choice":

I picked myself up from the dust again
and went on
phoenix not with another set of wings but with
no other choice
Oh I said to my soul may a deep
luminosity seize you
and my blanched soul smiled from its need and
dwelt on in the pale country of its bones

(*CP*, 49)

As pervasive as death, dust is an abiding presence in Ammons' deserts. Dust is not merely a geological detail in this poetic world; it is another form of death, a primal condition of uncontrollable natural force and spiritual depravity against which, yet in concert with, Ammons' speakers must act. In "When Rahman Rides," the speaker says, "There was the rush of dust and then farther on / a spiral whirlwinding," which leaves him nothing but an "ocotillo" (a spiny desert plant) "in a bloomless month" (*CP,* 13). In "The Sap Is Gone Out of the Trees," dust pervades both present and past as "the dusting / combine passed over [the wheatfields] . . . long after the dust was gone." At the end of the poem, the speaker sounds as ineffectual as dust, for he tells us that "the wind whipped at my carcass," and he could do little more than utter "Oh" and fall "down in the dust" (*CP,* 2). Even when dust is not present, Ammons' landscapes are, as Frederick Buell suggests, stifling emotional analogs of "the domain of the Queen of darkness of the Gilgamesh epic" found in Enkidu's surrealistic dream of the netherworld.[20] The word for this land in Sumerian myth is "Kur," which Kramer claims is "cosmically conceived" as "the empty space between the earth's crust and the primeval sea."[21] Kur is a place to which everyone, moral or not, goes at death. As he lay dying, Enkidu told Gilgamesh that he dreamed he saw a man with "paws of a lion" and "talons of an eagle" who overpowered and transformed him; then

> He seized me and led me down to the house of darkness . . .
> the house where one who goes in never comes out again,
> the road that, if one takes it, one never comes back,
> the house that, if one lives there, one never sees light,
> the place where they live on dust, their food is mud;
> their clothes are like bird's-clothes, a garment of wings,
> and they see no light, living in blackness:
> on the door and door-bolt, deeply settled dust.[22]

Suffocating and hopeless, dark and dusty, the Sumerian underworld reduces gods and kings to serving mud as they wait on tables. Its residents retain their worldly identities but are frail and wispy, like their birdlike garments "of wings." They are fallen deities, priests, and nobles, personages who once had access to great power or special vision, which they have now utterly lost. In short, like Ammons' "spent / seer" (*CP,* 77), they are characters who could easily dwell in the desert cosmos of his early poems.

By driving his narrator through a universe of pervasive dust and darkness, Ammons creates a trancelike state that is not merely hell or purgatory. It is a state for a peculiar kind of transition that takes place, in Eliade's words, "*be-*

yond the realm of the sensorial." To be sure, Ammons' rituals work their way through the logic of his speaker's body. At times, however, by reducing the clarity of his narrator's physical vision, Ammons provides him with an ecstatic, shamanistic view that "engages only his 'soul'" or spirit, not his entire being.[23] Throughout these early poems, the narrator's consciousness seems to be separated from his body in a nightmare world of "cleavage" (*CP*, 24) where he is losing his head (*CP*, 34) or blindly "[d]ropping [his] eyelids among the aerial ash" (*CP*, 30). As I have noted, one major aspect of Ammons' early work is his attempt to invent rituals that involve the entire body and thus rescue it from a dismembered or disunified condition. For shamans in many primitive religions, however, such dismemberment is not lethal but initiatory and anticipates the possibility of renewal. As Eliade says, "Every 'trance' is another 'death'" that "reveals the presentiment of re-birth into another mode of being."[24] Consequently, whatever anxiety is felt at death—this feeling, of course, dominates the early Ammons—is transitory and will dissipate upon the awakening to a higher consciousness. What is more important, as Eliade notes, is that this awakening is a mythological act of re-membering, an *anamnesis*, or a "recognition of the soul's true identity, that is, re-cognition of its celestial origin." In fact, only after man wakes from sleep, drunkenness, dread, or oblivion will he discover "how to act in this world."[25]

When Gilgamesh came to the island of his ancestor Utnapishtim, he was unable to stay awake for six days and nights and thus failed in his trial to achieve immortality. In contrast, through his invention of ordeals dramatized in Sumerian settings, Ammons succeeds in ecstatically awakening his narrator to a "true historiographic *anamnesis*." This kind of remembering aims to recall events that record cultural behavior not in historical but in mythical time, a world of existential, prehistoric experience that "finds [its] expression in the discovery of our solidarity with . . . vanished or peripheral peoples."[26] Hence Ammons' poem "Sumerian":

> I have grown a marsh dweller
> subject to floods and high winds,
> drinking brackish water on long hunts,
> brushing gnat smoke
> from clumps of reeds, have known
>
> the vicissitudes of silt, of
> shifting channels flush
> by dark upland rains . . .

By struggling against, then aligning himself with "natural" motions in this Sumerian landscape, Ammons' speaker gains a differentiating knowledge that enables him to gauge various spatial levels. At the somewhat cloudy end of the poem, these depths and heights demarcate a Sumerian space that extends from "underwater mud" to "blue temple tiles." With this spatial orientation comes an ability to judge the existential distance of a certain "serenity," a goal considerably "beyond approach" for this abject "marsh dweller." For he claims that after

> rising with a handful of broken shells
> from sifted underwater mud
> I have come to know how high
> the platform is, beyond approach,
> of serenity and blue temple tiles.

The depth of the speaker's need is thus measured by the geographic space he surveys, which, in turn, produces the questlike development of the poem. From the "dark upland" to "the southern salty banks," the Sumerian's "long hunts" cover considerable external ground while also conveying the equally deep (or "long") internal emptiness of "terror dawn cold across my face." The central movement of "Sumerian" is from dark, oppressive detail ("brackish water" and "gnat smoke") to the idea if not the reality of "serenity" (*CP*, 32).

By taking on the behavior of a Sumerian in a Sumerian setting, Ammons' narrator not only expresses his solidarity with a "vanished" people, but he also awakens through this solidarity from a morass of oppressive sensation to consciousness of the possibility of something higher. This something higher is a "serenity" that is sacred insofar as it is associated with the coolness of "blue temple tiles"; and further, this serenity constitutes a truth about an alternative to human suffering that has been discovered not through historical analysis or time but through the poet's recreation of a vanished culture. Such historiographic awakening has important visionary repercussions in Ammons' dark universe, especially in relation to what he discovers through his myths and rituals. In *Myth and Reality*, Eliade discusses the ancient pair of topics, forgetting and remembering, in Gnostic and Indian philosophy; in so doing, he sheds considerable light on the value of Ammons' primordial myths: "The Gnostic learns the myth in order *to dissociate himself from its results.* Once waked from his mortal sleep, the Gnostic (like the disciple of Samkhya-Yoga) understands that he bears no responsibility for the primordial catastrophe the myth narrates for him, and that hence he has no *real* relation with Life, the World, and History."[27] Ammons' entrance into a primordial past signals an incipient awareness of an ancient truth of Eastern thought: namely, that historic reality is not absolute, and insofar as this version of reality is susceptible to change, certain kinds of human suffering associated with historic time will prove mutable—even illusory—and thus subject to disappearance, just as the Sumerians and their culture have disappeared. In Gnostic and Indian thinking, the historic self mired in pain is not the true self. It may be accurate, as Denis Donoghue claims, that one of the social "limitations in [Ammons'] art" is that he "can . . . evade the responsibility of history, circumvent the claims of other people . . . [without] having to bother with the horrors of living in the slums of New York."[28] Even though Donoghue later qualifies the severity of this observation, it may be said in defense of Ammons' early work that he is all too aware of the massive destruction that history has wrought and thus has sought a personal mythico-religious view that enables him emotionally to rise above that destruction. Furthermore, this attitude involves an ancient form of remembering—a discovering and inventing a truer self than that which is determined by social catastrophe. Again, Eliade: "Waking, which is at the same time an anamnesis, finds expression in an indifference to History, especially to contemporary History. Only the primordial myth is important. Only the events that occurred in the past of fable are worth knowing; for, by learning them, one becomes conscious of one's true nature—and awakens."[29]

DIVISION, RENEWAL, AND UNDIFFERENTIATED DARKNESS

I noted earlier, following Geoffrey Hartman, that a central concern for English Romantic poets was a "fixated" self-consciousness brought on by excessive analysis that "murders to dissect," as Wordsworth says in "The Tables Turned." This imperious act of the mind to dissect and rationalize results for Wordsworth in a "false" consciousness that negates other aspects of the soul. In *Milton,* Book II, he says:

> The Negation is the Spectre, the Reasoning Power in Man;
> This is a false Body, an Incrustation over my Immortal
> Spirit, a Selfhood which must be put off & annihilated alway[30]

In the early Ammons, there is a similar fragmenting threat to a kind of holistic consciousness that he greatly values and to which he must awaken from the murderous dissection of division. Many of his later pairs of abstract philosophic terms—the One and the Many, Order and Motion, Unity and Multiplicity, Center and Periphery—seem derived from his early mythopoeic preoccupation with the dangers of division. Ammons dramatizes this danger in

"Spring Song," where, as was noted, his narrator has a dismembered "soul" that dwells "in the pale country of its bones" (*CP*, 49). In the second stanza, after a "field"—that is, a new direction or ground of thought—opens on his right, the speaker at first immerses himself in its "golden broom grass" that is "arms-high." Like a wandering Gilgamesh, he seems to drift aimlessly with the wind as he notes that he "whirled with the wind sizzling there."

In Ammons' case, however, this strategic movement alters the course of the poem by placing the speaker in the hands of nature's (his own mind's) forces. This wind grants the speaker the power to address vegetation and thus to use the things of nature as dramatic characters to complicate the poem's storyline. Ever worried about what will endure and what will not, especially in the season of growth and renewal, the speaker challenges the grass's "rising shoots" when he says, "Where, if spring will not keep you, / will you go" (*CP*, 50). When he stoops "to scold the shoots," the narrator nearly falls "in with their green en-hancing tips." That is, he nearly falls for or succumbs to a traditional image of growth in spring. In his desolate world the image seems to be a sign of separa-tion, for he exits abruptly and "nearly died / getting away from the dividing place." The poem concludes violently with a standard mythological image of darkness and blood, couched in the figures of the sun and moon. As he was at the beginning of the poem, the speaker is left utterly alone in a hostile surreal-istic setting of "sand," which is as empty and bleak as was the unknown desert beyond the gate of sunrise for Gilgamesh:

> At dusk the sun set and it was dark and having
> found no place to leave my loyalty
> I slaughtered it by the road and spilled its
> blood on sand while the red moon rose
>   (*CP*, 50)

In its response to what will last, Ammons' aggressive answer seems to be "abso-lutely nothing"; his "Spring Song" appears to be the depressing, direct opposite of a traditional seasonal poem, which would celebrate the renewing power of spring by means of fertile natural detail.

However bleak the conclusion to "Spring Song," there is more possibility for renewal than first appears. As Ammons notes in the first stanza, this possibility is not as grandiose as a "phoenix . . . with another set of wings," but it nonethe-less resides powerfully within the final lines in what Joseph Campbell calls reli-gious "play-logic" or "dream-logic."[31] The key to this dream-logic lies in the considerable natural transformation in the conclusion. The sun sets into dark-ness and dies; then, when the speaker's loyalty is slaughtered (meaning loyalty to the traditional promise of renewal in a traditional spring song, as I interpret the phrase), its blood is spilled "on sand" and the moon takes on the color of blood, then rises. In archetypal thinking, this is the movement from dawn and rebirth to night, sleep, and death, and to a new birth in the rising of the moon. Most of the speaker's movement is his passage through darkness, through a dark night of the soul in which all appears to be death and decay. In yet another netherworld of dust and darkness, even the "green enhancing tips" of "golden broom grass" do not offer solace but instead evoke fear and suspicion. Without the possibility of exit, there would be no possibility of passage for this speaker. He would be condemned to a static state of deathless nonmotion. Consequently, in this "pale country," the only possibility for significant change lies in the deathly yet cyclic motions of sky gods, namely, the sun and the moon. Encountered during the speaker's trials in his desolate landscape, only these archetypal representatives, moving in their eternal continuum from life to death and back to life, animate his world with the possibility of crossing thresholds.

The threshold-promising illumination in this parable about the dangers of division reveals much about Ammons' mythological methods of unification, for his imagery suggests that his speaker wishes to discover—or return to—an ancient kind of consciousness in which the meeting of sun and moon signals the life-giving union of other pairs of primitive opposites. These energizing opposites are found, as Campbell notes, "in the Indian Kundalini yoga of the first millennium A.D.," where "lunar and solar channels" are "two spiritual channels on either side of the central channel of the spine, up which the serpent power is supposed to be carried through a control of the mind and breath." In this religious symbolism, there is "the meeting of sun and moon . . . in significant relation to the serpent and the axial staff, tree, or spine." Such symbolism demonstrates, Campbell goes on to say, that "a fundamental idea of *all* the pagan religious disciplines . . . was that the inward turning of the mind (symbolized by the sunset) should culminate in a realization of an identity *in esse* of the individual (microcosm) and the universe (Macrocosm), which, when achieved would bring together in one order of act and realization the principles of eternity and time, sun and moon, male and female."[32] This particular "inward turning of the mind," whereby internal and external realities match (and at times dramatically mismatch), is one of the central structural principles in Ammons' poetry, whether in "Spring Song" or in his later major meditations about division and integration, such as "The Arc Inside and Out," "The Unifying Principle," and "Two Motions." In these later poems, the great circular philosophers, such as Laotse, Hegel, Plotinus, and Emerson, certainly play central roles. These later speculative reflections also find a germinating mythopoeic ground in Ammons' early poetic principle that the division between poetic microcosm and macrocosm reflects a similar inimical division in the human mind.

Whatever its positive (and considerable) analytic powers, the mental act of dividing threatens and obscures access to an ancient state of being that was especially attractive to Sumerian mythmakers. Campbell calls this state the "mystical rapture of non-duality, or mythic identification." He claims that this state of rapture is at the heart of religious imagery and experience throughout the world; it "is symbolized in . . . ancient Egypt's Secret of the Two Partners, China's Tao, India's Nirvana, and Japan's development of the Buddhist doctrine of the Flower Wreath." The loss of this state has numerous implications, including the idea of death as an absolute termination because of the introduction of differentiated linear time, which begins and ends. In ancient Sumerian myth, this loss was equivalent to Adam and Eve's expulsion from paradise. Here is Campbell's account of such loss, presented in an archetypal narrative of division and unification:

> As we know from an ancient Sumerian myth, heaven *(An)* and earth *(Ki)* were in the beginning a single undivided mountain *(Anki)*, of which the lower part, the earth, was female, and the upper, heaven, male. But the two were separated . . . by their son Enlil . . . whereupon the world of temporality appeared. . . . The ritual marriage and connubium was to be understood as a reconstruction of the primal undifferentiated state, both in meditation (psychological aspect) for the refreshment of the soul, and in act (magical aspect) for the fertilization and renovation of nature: whereby it was also to be recognized that there is a plane or mode of being where that primal state is ever present, though to the mind and eye of day all seems to be otherwise.[33]

In poem after poem, ranging from "Rack" in *Ommateum* (where "the pieces of my voice have been thrown / away" [*CP*, 5]) to "Long Sorrowing" in *Sumerian Vistas* (where Ammons' speaker listens for "the voices of / cilates & crustaceans . . . held in a dark unanswerableness / to so much loss" [*SV*, 101]), separation or differentiation seems to be the basic human condition for this poet. In its various forms, separation becomes Ammons' Sumerian version of original sin, a mythopoeic occasion of overpowering need for unity or a refreshing integrating consciousness, which so motivates his speaker that this need generates the basic action in many of his poems.

In addition to its presence in *Sumerian Vistas*, "dark unanswerableness" seems everywhere in the early Ammons. At first, this darkness appears to abrogate all hope of illumination or revelation. Indeed, darkness is often an essential ingredient of the enervating closure in these poems. At the end of "Turning a Moment to Say So Long," the speaker concludes by plunging into a well, then submerging himself in darkness with "night kissing / the last bubbles from my lips" (*CP*, 10). At the end of a poem with a similar title, "Turning," the speaker sounds like a comic Gilgamesh as he falls into another deep well of water. Instead of ascending on "wings of light," he "fumbled about" in the last two lines "in the darkness for my wings / and the grass looked all around at the evening" (*CP*, 12). Whereas darkness signals a powerful deathly alienation in this "unanswerable" universe, it also has, as Chapter 1 showed, a "rich" dimension. This dimension of Ammons' Sumerian darkness is to some extent his mystical response to the condition of division. It may be said, then, that Ammons is a contemporary Gilgamesh who seeks his own version of immortality through his continuous quest for a state of nondivision. Although in individual poems he is often frustrated in attaining this state, his entire early mythological landscape becomes an emotional and spiritual ground in which he reconstructs, as Campbell says, a refreshing and dark "primal undifferentiated state."

Paradoxical and difficult to describe, this mythological realm of undifferentiated darkness is made somewhat intelligible by using mythopoeic iconography to suggest its depth and power. One visual analogue may be taken from an ancient Sumerian (*ca.* 2500 B.C.) terra-cotta plaque of a moon-bull and a lion-bird in the University Museum in Philadelphia. This plaque depicts, according to Campbell, "the ever-dying, ever-living lunar bull, consumed through all time by the lion-headed solar eagle." This depiction is not an image merely of predatory victimage. It is a symbolic statement of an eternal, energy-transferring process whereby the bearded bull, with its serene human smile, does not exactly die but instead releases energy in fiery flashes from his legs, which are atop a "cosmic holy mountain" said to be "the goddess Earth." While the moon-bull is consumed by the sun's light, he energizes the earth in a round of fertilizing power like that of the Egyptian fertility god, Osiris, whose animal was also the bull. In this mythological realm, darkness or blackness does not signal annihilation but rather a more complex, undifferentiated state of life and death, moments in a cycle of being or eternal flow that can give rise to a "wisdom beyond death, beyond changing time." Campbell claims that this "primal state is ever present" in us, though difficult to visualize, express, or examine. If it is in myths and their provocative images of eternal mysteries that this realm is effectively displayed and experienced, it is evident why Campbell concludes that "the state of the ultimate [lunar, mythic] bull . . . is invisible: black, pitch black."[34]

Like Gilgamesh's netherworld, Ammons' Sumerian vistas also serve as thresholds to a nightmare world that is itself an "ever-dying, ever-living reality." For Ammons' mental spaces are really dream worlds or dream spaces, often surrealistic, in which familiar directional coordinates and traditional dualisms are dissolved so that the speaker can effect passage from meaningless death. In "Dying in a Mirthful Place," for instance, Ammons' speaker mocks death by narrating the poem after he has died, even while "buzzards . . . sat over me in mournful conversations / that sounded excellent to my eternal ear" (*CP*, 13). In this poem, Ammons, like Gilgamesh, searches for a kind of immortality in a barren desert "soil" (on "a hill in Arizona") in which there is "a noiseless / mirth and death" (*CP*, 13). To some extent, he finds immortality, unlike Gilgamesh; at least, he acquires an "eternal ear." What this eternity is becomes clearer in Ammons' long, three-part poem "Requiem," whose religious title is consistent with its content, namely, another of Ammons' paradigmatic acts of creation. After a middle section of surrealistic "transfigurations" in another Sumerian desert, where there are "trunks of violent trees stalking the vacant land," the opening of the final segment, entitled "Contraction," clearly indicates the poem's paradigmatic premise. "Repenting creation," God claims somewhat defensively that "I do not have to be consistent: what was lawful to my general plan / does not jibe / with my new specific will; what the old law healed / is reopened / in the new" (*CP*, 46–47). The entire middle section, with its "golden culminations and unfuneraled dead," is a welter of new reopening from old, a series of "primal rhythms" of life and death, part of which sail "into eternity" and part of which, along with "the earth . . . rolled into time" (*CP*, 46).

The opposition of time and eternity returns us to Sumer and to the ancient Mesopotamian consciousness that concludes Ammons' poem. Immediately after God claims that he has "drawn up many covenants to eternity," the poet introduces a pseudonarrative that abruptly inserts the mordant finality of the temporal world. This world is represented in Sumerian, historical detail:

> Returning silence unto silence,
> the Sumerian between the rivers lies.
> His skull crushed and moded into rock
>   does not leak or peel.
> The gold earring lies in the powder
> of his silken, perished lobe.
> The incantations, sheep trades, and night-gatherings
>   with central leaping fires,

roar and glare still in the crow's-foot
walking of his stylus on clay.

(*CP,* 47)

Like the middle section of the poem, this segment consists of two temporal
zones. First, there is an unchanging eternity of the dead, a world of "silence
unto silence" in which there is no material change. The "skull" of "the Sumerian between the rivers" (the Tigris and Euphrates, one presumes) "does not
leak or peel." On the other hand, there is the active world of "incantations" and
"leaping fires" that exist but on an artifact—an ancient clay tablet of cuneiform
script, or "crow's-feet." Like Yeats's "artifice of eternity" in "Sailing to Byzantium," the world of these events is also frozen, as is the next image of physical
decay in Ammons' poem: a "sick man" in a Sumerian temple who could not be
cured by the "anesthetic words of reciting priests." He too is long silenced, for
"dust has dried up all his tears," and he "sleeps out the old unending drug of
time" (*CP,* 47). That is, if the priests' words did not end his illness, the "unending drug of time" certainly will, albeit in the form of eternal sleep.

However static and final the deathly elements seem in this section, the poem
concludes not on a note of absolute termination but with a round or universal
rhythm that conveys an eternity quite opposite that of mordant stasis:

The rose dies, man dies, the world dies, the god
grows and fails, the born universe dies
　　　into renewal,
and all endures the change,
totally lost and totally retained.

(*CP,* 47)

By presenting this paradoxical state of death and "renewal," in which "all," including "the god," is "totally lost and totally retained," Ammons closes this
poem with a mystical rapture that assimilates the visible, dualistic world of discrete particulars to a universal realm of archetypal motion. That is, he converts
material, historical, and mythological decay—"the rose dies," "the world dies,"
"the god / grows and fails"—into a reproductive cycle that dissolves the finality
of the Sumerian's death in the previous section into something considerably
less permanent. Transformed at the close of the poem into a moment on the
eternal wheel of Ammons' transfigurations, this Sumerian portrait of pain and
suffering seems more like a momentary nightmare than a fully realistic and
disturbing termination. Such transformation is even more understandable because the poem's surrealistic atmosphere continually shifts the shapes of ob-

jects and laws of creation until its universe seems to be what is called in Indian thought "deep dreamless sleep," or in Freudian psychology, "the oceanic feeling."[35] To be sure, this is not the world of visual, waking consciousness. Instead, Ammons' mode of poetic motion takes us beyond serial time, with its discrete events and divisions, to a state of "mythic identification" often depicted as a state of darkness in which life and death dissolve into each other in an eternal round of change that does not change or, as Ammons says, "dies / into renewal."

Ammons' darkened spaces, as well as his deserts and barren terrains, constitute another way to form mythological base matter or primal chaos out of which transformation is made possible for the mind. This transformation is really an emotional recreation of the self, which presents its reinvention through a narrative of origins issuing from unformed natural material. In "Chaos Staggered Up the Hill," the speaker drolly notes that "messy chaos" gets "the daisies dirty." Itself a traditional term for unformed cosmic matter, the "chaos" in Ammons' poem engulfs then dissolves him, only to offer the possibility of renewal in the poem's final line, where it has the power "to make us green some other place" (CP, 6). As with so many of his poems, Ammons' setting contains the potential for incipient reversal and thus constitutes in various forms the very goal or ground of change that his quester seeks. Ammons' deserts are barren and dry—in a word, chaotic—because they are places for sacred beginnings. They are worlds in need of content, form, and habitation. In this sense, Ammons' Sumerian vistas are anywhere he remakes his universe. Eliade notes that through ritual—for example, the raising of the Christian cross, a variation on the sacred pole or cosmic pillar—sacred or habitable space is recreated that is the opposite of "a foreign, chaotic space, peopled by ghosts, demons, 'foreigners' (who are assimilated to demons and the souls of the dead)."[36] In Ammons' early Sumerian world, death is a constant companion in his land of "great black unwasting silence" (CP, 6); his constant challenge, in however rudimentary a form or to whatever small degree, is to recenter and resituate himself within a profane, hostile universe. In so doing, his early victories in poetic form are victories in the reforming of his own habitation—in other words, of dwelling in a Sumer that in Eliade's words is a "territory" that "can be made ours only by creating it anew, that is, by consecrating it."[37]

Working on the level of ritualized action, Ammons employs this darkness as a spatial coordinate to construct a sacred ground—albeit the ground of his own lyric performance—which results in a revelation that this ground is the result and reward of his quester's search. This quester's reward is a new, poetic Sumer so barren and empty that even the speaker's simplest gestures may be read as attempts to reorganize space and time. In reconstituting this world, Ammons' speaker thus performs what Eliade calls "the paradigmatic acts of the gods," namely, the re-creation of a time of origin that is itself the making and consecrating of a sacred reality. Ammons' world is no historic Sumer. His primitive settings and scenes are so much "fragments of a shattered universe" that his spatial movements up and down, in a poem such as "Choice," not only give direction to his "indirection" but also create direction by giving shape to "mean" or profane "space":[38]

> Idling through the mean space dozing,
> blurred by indirection, I came upon a
> stairwell and steadied a moment to
> think against the stem:
> upward turned golden steps
> and downward dark steps entered the dark:
>
> ...I
> spurned the airless heights though bright
> and sank
> sliding in a smooth rail whirl and fell
> asleep in the inundating dark
>
> (*CP*, 35)

Like the unformed darkness or primal choas at the beginning of Genesis, the darkness in Ammons' mental allegory is a kind of cosmic base matter or state of somnolence out of which gods create light—or in the case of this poem, out of which the speaker, seeking a kind of sight, emerges able to do battle with a god of limited vision, as when, in the conclusion, he "grappled with / the god that / rolls up circles of our linear / sight in crippling disciplines" (*CP*, 35).

A Wisdom Beyond Death

The lunar bull on the Sumerian terra-cotta plaque Campbell described is also a mythological variation on one of Ammons' favorite themes—the One and the Many. A version of this eternal pair (and process) can also be found in the Indian *Śatapatha Brāhmana*, which Campbell cites in *Creative Mythology:* "That One who is the Death on whom our life depends. . . . He is one as he is there, but many as he is in his children there."[39] However ineffable this "pitch black" realm, it is a prominent feature in Sumerian and Asian religions, and there are at least two kinds of wisdom to be derived from it. Both are found in Ammons' early verse, and they give these poems a substance and weight as considerable as anything he has written since. One aspect of this wisdom is its attitude toward death. Perhaps the most striking trait in Ammons' early poems is the contradictory fact that, although his world is filled with death, his speaker finds a curious solace there. By continuously moving toward a pitch-black consciousness of undifferentiation, Ammons' speaker not only quests for but also simultaneously establishes a mental landscape that philosophically and emotionally subsumes the oppressive world of decay that threatens to overwhelm him. In "Consignee," a circular blackness offers Ammons' speaker a certain consolation, a "wisdom beyond death," which is the opposite of the speaker's daylight vision. After "death, the diffuse one" brings him "out of day," the speaker tells us that he "quarreled and devised a while / but went on / having sensed a nice dominion in the air, / the black so round and deep" (*CP*, 8).

In its preoccupation with the "black so round and deep," Ammons' stance toward death seems equivalent to an inward spiritual disengagement found in Chinese mythology, a mythology that, like Ammons, conceives of life and death as evolving from one "featureless, undistinguishable mass." According to an anecdote narrated by Campbell in *Oriental Mythology,* Chuang Tzu (*ca.* 300 B.C.), a Taoist wise man, was criticized for failing to mourn properly the death of his wife. Instead of observing the appropriate rites of lamentation, he was found singing and drumming on a bowl. When reproached, he replied that when his wife died, he indeed first despaired; then, however, he began to reflect. In a style as simple and as straightforward as Ammons' poem, Chuang Tzu's reflection puts the staggering loss of his wife's death into the larger context of "nature's Sovereign Law":

> Pondering on what had happened, I told myself that in death no strange new fate befalls us. In the beginning we lack not life only, but form; not form only, but spirit. We are blent in the one great featureless, undistinguishable mass. Then a time came when the mass evolved spirit, spirit evolved form, form evolved life. And now life in its turn has evolved death. For not nature only, but man's being has its seasons, its sequence of spring and autumn, summer and winter. . . . She whom I have lost has lain down to sleep. . . . To break in upon her rest with the noise of lamentation would but show that I knew nothing of nature's Sovereign Law.[40]

In a comment on this passage, noted Orientalist and translator Arthur Waley offers a gloss that applies equally to Ammons and may very well be the central emotional focus of *Ommateum:* "This attitude toward death . . . is but part of a general attitude toward the universal laws of nature, which is one not merely of resignation nor even of acquiescence, but a lyrical, almost ecstatic acceptance. . . . That we should question nature's right to make and unmake, that we should hanker after some role that nature did not intend us to play is not merely futile, not merely damaging to that tranquility of the 'spirit' which is the essence of Taoism, but involves, in view of our utter helplessness, a sort of fatuity at once comic and disgraceful."[41]

A second aspect of Ammons' "wisdom beyond death" centers on a conception of the self in relation to the term "all," a relation noted in the conclusion to "Requiem": "and all endures the change, / totally lost and totally retained" (*CP*, 47). This paradoxical polarity has the status of an ontological assertion in this poem, but it also suggests an ancient Eastern conception of the self. Especially in its "lost" and "retained" aspects, Ammons' conception of the self forms a central element in his response to the overwhelming anguish of personal mortality that attends him in his Sumerian settings and throughout his work. These two opposing aspects of the self—dissolution and reconstitution—point to a continuous dialectical drama that his voice (or self) undergoes during his quests. One might plausibly argue that the central pilgrimage in his poetry is for the reconstitution of a constantly fragmented self. This drama is so important to him that it is found in the very first poem in *Ommateum*, when his speaker precariously identifies himself: "I am Ezra / As a word too much repeated / falls out of being" (*CP*, 1). Even in "Muse," published ten years later in the mid-sixties, Ammons continues to focus on the "anguish of becoming" when he exclaims" how many / times must I be broken and reassembled!" (*CP*, 99). In Ammons' poetry, this negative disengagement of a culturally dramatized self is positively portrayed by images of death, darkness, and termination: for example, suffocating ("Turning a Moment to Say So Long" [*CP*, 10]), splintering ("I Came in a Dark Woods Upon" [*CP*, 28]), killing ("In Strasbourg in 1349" [*CP*, 3]), wounding ("A Crippled Angel" [*CP*, 30]), and burying ("A Treeful of Cleavage Flared Branching" [*CP*, 25]). The impulse toward a disengaged self is positively portrayed by devices that turn substance into a number of disembodied items: color, or its lack ("Succumbing in the still ecstasy / sinuous through white rows of scales / I caved in upon eternity / saying this use is colorless" [*CP*, 31]); transforming fire ("all miracle hanging fire / on rafters of the sky" [*CP*, 30]); spirits ("my blue ghost" [*CP*, 38]), or assimilative motion ("cool thought unpunishable / by bones eternally glide" [*CP*, 33]).

If Ammons begins in a this-worldly state of real sensory pain, confusion, and death, he transcends these states by questing for a new self that bears close resemblance to the Eastern doctrine of the extinction or emptying of the self. That is, if Ammons seems often to begin at a realistic Sumer, he just as often finds himself on the way ("Way") to an Absolute, which is to a large degree Oriental. This radical Eastern doctrine of transcendence, so foreign to the Western mind, may be illustrated by certain branches of Buddhism. In *Buddhism: Its Essence and Development,* Edward Conze notes: "The chief purpose of Buddhism is the extinction of separate individuality, which is brought about when we cease to *identify* anything with ourself. From long habit it has become quite natural to us to think of our own experience in the terms of 'I' and 'mine.'" Conze goes on to say, however, that this habit can be abolished by thought:

> According to the doctrine of the Old Wisdom School, wisdom alone is able to chase the illusion of individuality from our thoughts where it has persisted from age-old habit. Not action, not trance, but only thought can kill the illusion which resides in thought.
>
> If all our sufferings are attributed to the fact that we identify ourselves with spurious belongings which are not really our own, we imply that we would be really much better off without those belongings. This . . . inference can also be stated in a more metaphysical way by saying that what we really are is identical with the Absolute. It is assumed . . . that there is an ultimate reality, and . . . that there is a point in ourselves at which we touch that ultimate reality. The ultimate reality, also called Dharma by the Buddhists, or Nirvana, is defined as that which stands completely outside the sensory world of illusion and ignorance, a world inextricably interwoven with craving and greed. . . . [This notion] is very much akin to the philosophical notion of the "Absolute," and not easily distinguished from the notion of God among the more mystical theologians, like Dionysius Areopagita and Eckart.[42]

The wisdom to which Ammons aspires does not result in the extinction of his speaking voice, for without that, of course, there would be no poem. Rather, in many of his major meditations, Ammons' speaker effects to some degree and in various forms the "extinction of separate individuality." That is, he severs the connection of the meditating self with the often painful, even monstrous, contents of its thought. This claim at first seems wrongheaded because Ammons' early speakers are so busy differentiating what appear to be fully realistic elements. Their minds are filled to overflowing with complex distinctions, details, and progressions, which are presented in the mode of realistic narratives. However rich and diverse the surface texture of these poems, they often close with a movement—a physical gesture or mental adjustment—that separates the speaker from his antecedent activity and from the dark emotion that attends his act. For instance, after surveying a catalogue of historical atrocity in "In Strasbourg in 1349," the speaker waits for the light of morning, then calmly exits not merely Strasbourg: "When morning came / looked down at the ashes / and rose and walked out of the world" (*CP,* 3). A more severe separation is found in a much gentler poem, "Some Months Ago," which is filled with "bright flakes from ... mist," when Ammons somewhat surprisingly concludes with

> I closed up all the natural throats of earth
> and cut my ties with every natural heart
> and saying farewell
>   stepped out into the great open
>
>   (*CP*, 5)

He does not tell us what "the great open" is. A page later in his *Collected Poems*, however, is a similar term with the same adjective—"great," which is designed to resolve conflict between the masculine sun and the feminine moon over the possession of light. At the end of "I Went Out to the Sun," the speaker calls to the sun to resolve the controversy by invoking a comprehensive reality of loss and emptiness that makes the controversy futile: "Why are you angry with the moon / since all at last must be lost / to the great vacuity" (*CP*, 7).

A Higher Way

These three poems suggest a mysterious assimilative principle or higher reality lying behind the concrete particulars of Ammons' world. Harold Bloom claims that this reality is "Emerson's 'Nature,' all that is separate from 'the Soul,'" which is identical with the "you" addressed in "Hymn," in which Ammons' speaker asserts, "You are everywhere partial and entire / You are on the inside of everything and on the outside" (*CP*, 39).[43] Although Bloom is surely on the right track, the "you" in "Hymn" also bears a strong resemblance to Laotse's conception of Tao. In *Tao Te Ching*, the paradoxical "inside and outside" are predicated of the "formless," "serene," and "empty" Tao:

> There was something formless and perfect
> before the universe was born.
> It is serene. Empty.
> Solitary. Unchanging.
> Infinite. Eternally present.
> It is the mother of the universe.
> For lack of a better name,
> I call it Tao.
>
> It flows through all things,
> inside and outside, and returns
> to the origin of all things.[44]

Like a realm of Platonic archetypes against which the things of this world pale by comparison, this "great open" or "great vacuity" or "Tao" is either inferred or stated abstractly in Ammons' poems. Although its concrete function is to offer the speaker solace in an oppressive real world when none is otherwise forthcoming, its nature appears to be as difficult to grasp as the ineffable pitch-black realm of undifferentiated consciousness discussed previously. It dwells in the world of "silence unto silence" mentioned in "Requiem," from and to which the dead Sumerian has traveled. Its presence is felt throughout Ammons' poetry, not only in his early poems but also in later lyrics, such as "The City Limits" and "A Coast of Trees." This mysterious realm is likely some analogue of what Conze calls, as noted earlier, the Buddhist "Absolute . . . which stands completely outside the sensory world of illusion and ignorance." In "Guide," the term "Absolute" is explicitly mentioned by Ammons:

> You cannot come to unity and remain material:
> in that perception is no perceiver . . .
>
> you cannot
>   turn around in
> the Absolute: there are no entrances or exits
>   no precipitations of forms
> to use like tongs against the formless:
>   no freedom to choose:
>
> to be
>   you have to stop not-being and break
> off from *is* to *flowing* and
>   this is the sin you weep and praise:
> origin is your original sin:
>   the return you long for will ease your guilt
> and you will have your longing:
>
> the wind that is my guide said this . . .
>
> (*CP,* 79)

Insofar as Ralph Waldo Emerson is everywhere in Ammons, Emerson's re-marks from "Plato; or, The Philosopher" on the Asian element in the Greek philosopher function well as a "guide" in isolating the Asian Absolute in Am-mons: "No man more fully acknowledged the Ineffable . . . that is, the Asia in his mind . . . the ocean of love and power, before form, before will, before knowledge, the Same, the Good, the One; and now, refreshed and empowered by this worship, the instinct of Europe, namely, culture, returns; and he cries,

Yet things are knowable! They are knowable, because, being from one, things correspond. There is a scale: and the correspondence of heaven to earth, of matter to mind, of the part to the whole, is our guide." In "Guide," if the perceiver "cannot come to unity and remain material," then Ammons seems to be saying that the material self somehow disappears when apprehending a wholeness amid a "diversity of sensations"—for instance, the experience of being "glad and sad at once" (*CP*, 80).[45] Moreover, he goes so far as to claim that "origin is your original sin" and "that perception is no perceiver." In other words, he is claiming that the mental act of coming to unity does not necessitate an originating sense of self accompanying the act of knowing. Even worse, such a source of self-consciousness (or "perception") places one "in the mouth of Death." It is, thus, "the Asia in [Ammons'] mind" that leads him to assert several lines later that to truly "be," one must find a motionless center in order to "come to unity," for one "cannot / turn around in / the Absolute." One must "break / off from *is* to *flowing*." An individual need not be an originating self but must engage in a process of consciousness that resembles the Buddhist method of concentration. With its emphasis on emptying, this process involves overcoming "vestiges of the object," so described by Conze: "One first sees everything as *boundless space,* then as *unlimited consciousness,* then as *emptiness,* then by giving up even the act which grasped the nothingness, one reaches a station where there is *neither perception nor non-perception.* Consciousness and self-consciousness are here at the very margin of disappearance."[46]

In "Guide," the phrase "wisdom wisdom," repeated twice for emphasis in the poem's conclusion, not only announces the object of Ammons' search for guidance but also sounds like Conze's "final salvation" in what he calls "the Old Wisdom School." This salvation "requires the complete obliteration of the individual self," such that Conze can conclude emphatically, "Wisdom alone can enter the Great Emptiness."[47] Applied to Ammons, such wisdom does not encompass a determinate personality that "is" but rather one that is a "flow." This "self" or state is not a place or origin of consciousness but a wind, which is the perfect "guide" (model) for the speaker because it contains nothing of substance but "direction." Perhaps the best way to describe this major aspect of Ammons' poetic self (or lack of self) is through religious poetry. In "The Great Forest Book," or Brihadaranyaka Upanishad, cited by Joseph Campbell in *The Flight of the Wild Gander,* there is an evocative hint as to Ammons' method of concentration, in which the "Self," as a mode of apparently constitutive motion, is really ever elusive. The "He" in the following excerpt is not a transcendental ego that retains its identity while experiencing discrete events in sequence. Beyond categories and self-contradictory, and beyond conventional coordinates of space and time as well, the "He" is identical with what is worshipped, that is, what Campbell calls the "rapture" of a consciousness that the gods of "eternal being" (*CP*, 80) are within us, not without. In the poem the subsumptive term for this assimilative mode of mythic identification is "the All":

> Him they see not; for as seen, he is incomplete.
>
>   When breathing, He is named breath, when speaking voice, when seeing the eye, when hearing the ear, when thinking mind: these are just the names of His acts. Whoever worships one or another of these, knows not; for He is incomplete in one or another of these. One should worship with the idea that He is just one's self (*ātman*), for therein all these become one.
>
>   That same thing, namely, this Self, is the footprint of this All, for just as one finds cattle by a footprint, so one finds this All by its footprint, the Self.[48]

"Guide" was first published in the *Hudson Review* as "Canto I" in 1960.[49] As late as 1981, Ammons continued to reveal a prominent interest in such words as *emptiness* and *unity*, as well as in an unnameable, ineffable reality that emerges through particulars, which are themselves transcendent signs. In the poem "Coast of Trees" from his book of the same title, Ammons' speaker conducts a quasi-religious meditation that recalls Geoffrey Hartman's observation in *The Fate of Reading* that "we moderns depend on reflective forms that have replaced religious self-consciousness":[50]

> The reality is, though susceptible
> to versions, without denomination:
> when the fences foregather
> the reality they shut in is cast out:
> if the name nearest the name
> names least or names
> only a verge before the void takes naming in,
> how are we to find holiness . . .
>   we know a unity
> approach divided, a composure past
> sight: then, with nothing, we turn
> to the cleared particular, not more
> nor less than itself, and we realize
> that whatever it is it is in the Way and
> the Way in it, as in us, emptied full.
>
>   (*CT*, 1)

Ammons' word-play with Laotse's term "the Way" is especially suggestive here. To achieve a vision of "the reality," the speaker needs to transcend the "cleared particular," which is an obstacle and thus "in the Way." As I have noted, however, transcending the particular is an essential part of the meditative process of overcoming "vestiges of the object." The particular that is "cleared" or emptied of self-consciousness is thus "in the Way" as a necessary step in the process of unifying wisdom. In addition, because inside and outside are categories that no longer apply in this undifferentiated world of mythic identification, where space and time dissolve into the One, the "Way" is also "in" the "cleared particular." That is, the Way is both inside and outside the cleared particular, which has been "cleared" of its sensory content. The particular thus becomes an avenue or Way—as do we—of achieving the "holiness" of "full" union with "the reality" (the All, the One), precisely because we are "emptied" of ourselves and of the contents of the particular.

This verbal play is not simple escapism to a reality whose existence is merely problematic. As the mundane self empties of originating thought and motion, it also divests itself of emotion, including the desperate "longing" from which Ammons' early speaker so intensely suffers. This longing is attached to a worldly ego in considerable pain, a state that can be transcended by dissolving empirical opposites, such as "elation and dejection" (Conze's words) or "sad and glad" (*CP*, 80). Such transcendence can be achieved through Buddhist concentration, which is the "means for transcending the impact of sensory stimuli and our normal reactions to it. . . . [I]n the fourth Dhyana, one ceases to be conscious of ease and dis-ease, well-fare, and ill-fare, elation and dejection, promotion or hindrance as applied to oneself. Personal preferences have become so uninteresting as to be imperceptible. What remains is a condition of limpid, translucent and alert receptiveness *in utter purity of mindfulness and even mindedness.*"[51]

This state of "purity" or "even mindedness" beyond "sensory stimuli" corresponds to the "composure past / sight" in "Coast of Trees" and to the "serenity" noted in "Sumerian." It also corresponds to a moment in "A Crippled Angel" when Ammons' speaker watches the angel "bent in a scythe of grief" emit "smoke" from its ears, which centers the angel such that surrealistically and realistically, its ears become "the axles / of slow handwheels of grief." Yet when the speaker "interposed a harp" (that is, the poem) with its "lyric strings," he watched "the agony diffuse in / shapeless loss" (*CP*, 29). The transcendence of "disease" and "dejection" through disciplined thought is an ancient commonplace in Asian thought. One form of this mediation is found in Chinese mythology in a Quietist sect (*ca.* 300–400 B.C.), the School of Ch'i. Its philosophy is *hsin shu,* or "the art of the mind." The appeal of this discipline or meditation, however, is by no means to the mind alone. Rather, it involves the whole human being in a way that explains that aspect of the human soul capable of attaining what Ammons calls "holiness" (*CT*, 1). As Arthur Waley notes of *hsin shu:* "By 'mind' is not meant the brain or the heart, but a 'mind within the mind' that bears to the economy of man the same relation as the sun bears to the sky. . . . It must remain serene and immovable like a monarch upon his throne. It is a *shen*, a divinity, that will only take up its abode where all is garnished and swept. The place that man prepares for it is called its temple *(kung)*."[52]

It must be noted immediately that more often than not, Ammons' speaker does *not* attain this divine state. For the most part, he remains mired in the particulars of this world that are not "cleared" or are cleared only to some degree. Although he aspires to a meditational "abode where all is garnished and swept," his characteristic stance is that of loss, which turns his speaker into a sympathetic if not heroic failure. Ammons' speaker is, after all his questing, "the spent / seer," who in "Prodigal" laments that

> the mind whirls, short of the unifying
> reach, short of the heat
>   to carry that forging:
>   after the visions of these losses, the spent
> seer, delivered to wastage, risen
>   into ribs, consigns knowledge to
>   approximation, order to the vehicle
> of change, and fumbles in blunt innocence
>   toward divine, terrible love.
>
>   (*CP*, 77)

By understanding what this speaker aspires to—(Ammons' mysterious Asian Absolute), the reader can better understand where his speaker stands. I believe that he stands in a poetic Sumer or in a lyric condition in which "the spent seer" yearns to disengage himself from "disease" and "dejection" by discovering a certain kind of immortality. Yet he never—or seldom—finds it. In "Written Water" from *Lake Effect Country* (1983), Ammons appears doomed to remain this-worldly:

> I hope I will go through
> the period of hunger
> for immortality and be stated—
> so that I can rise
> at least from that death into communion with things.
>
>   (*LEC*, 11)

Whatever bliss he attains is as "fragile" as the ability to "look / through" human pain. As he says in "The Bright Side,"

> Bliss is the
> trace of
> existence that
> the idea of
> nothingness—
>
> thinking
> nothingness
> is a presence
> fragile as
> the longing look
> through
>
> tragedy . . .
>   (*LEC*, 1)

Ammons' sense of loss, as I suggested earlier, can be understood in the context of Emerson's remarks on Plato, where he notes a similar opposition between "immortality" and "things" in his Greek master. After acknowledging "the Asia in [Plato's] mind," which is a mystical "ocean of love and power . . . before knowledge," Emerson turns, as he so often does, toward experience, claiming that Plato also cries, "Yet things are knowable!" They are knowable because "there is a scale . . . the correspondence of heaven to earth, of matter to mind, of the part to the whole."[53] In the final, Emersonian analysis, Ammons also knows that there is an existential scale between heaven and earth, that is, between the immortality of the heavenly "Asia in his mind" and the earthly Sumerian deserts where he begins. The reality he ends with is precisely the "scale" he has uncovered in his journey from the vast wastelands of Sumer to the "cool thought" of Eastern mysticism. This scale may be defined as the tension between the reality he aims for and the reality he must live. The reality he aims for may be expressed in this selection from the sixth chapter of the *Bhagavad Gita:*

> That supernal bliss which
>   Is to be grasped by the consciousness and is beyond the senses,
> When he knows this, and not in the least
>   Swerves from the truth, abiding fixed (in it);
>
> And which having gained, other gain
>   He counts none higher than it;

> In which established, by no misery,
>   However grievous, is he moved;
>
> This (state), let him know—from conjunction with misery
>   This disjunction,—is known as discipline;
> With determination must be practised this
>   Discipline, with heart undismayed.[54]

The reality in which Ammons lives is a middle ground between "supernal bliss" and the existential world of human "misery." This middle ground is really a disciplined refocusing of his mind, which offers a dark yet serene meditation that mediates between the extremes of hope and total loss. The knowledge that Ammons finally achieves may not be that of "immortality," but his "determination" within the craft of poetry leaves us "with heart[s] undismayed," especially insofar as his enabling myths provide moving, emotional models, like Eliot's *Quartets*, to generate the spiritual energy of belief in an age of disbelief. Ammons' lyric myths are accessible to the culture at large in the same ways that Eastern modes of meditation—practiced for centuries in religions, not to mention in the works of Emerson and Whitman—are accessible. If Ammons' use of myth is restrictively private, then it is precisely the attitudes of solitude, piety, and privacy in his vision that are so admirable, especially in our excessively loud and noisy culture. Helen Vendler is quite right to observe that in his private meditations, written in the isolation of remote Ithaca, New York, Ammons speaks movingly for our age. Ammons' motto may well be this axiom from the School of Ch'i: "Throw open the gates, put self aside, bide in silence, and the radiance of the spirit shall come in and make its home."[55] "Radiance," "swerving," and "heart"—these words play a central role in the following justly famous lines from "The City Limits." Here Ammons' radiance results in a harmony of Sumerian darkness and Eastern light, and thus produces a complex serenity in which "fear . . . calmly turns to praise":

> when you consider
> the radiance, that it will look into the guiltiest
>
> swervings of the weaving heart and bear itself upon them,
> not flinching into disguise or darkening; when you consider
> the abundance of such resource as illuminates the glow-blue
>
> bodies and gold-skeined wings of flies swarming the dumped
> guts of a natural slaughter or the coil of shit and in no
> way winces from its storms of generosity . . .

then
the heart moves roomier, the man stands and looks about, the

leaf does not increase itself above the grass, and the dark
work of the deepest cells is of a tune with May bushes
and fear lit by the breadth of such calmly turns to praise.

(*CP,* 320)

3

DICKEY'S "APPROACHING PRAYER"
Ritual and the Shape of Myth

All Shamans know that Death furnishes all with Life.

—Northern Cheyenne Medicine Chief
   HYEMEYOHSTS STORM

        If you came this way,
Taking any route, starting from anywhere,
At any time or at any season,
It would always be the same: you would have to put off
Sense and notion. You are not here to verify,
Instruct yourself, or inform curiosity
Or carry report. You are here to kneel
Where prayer has been valid.

—T. S. ELIOT

O to be delivered from the rational into the realm of pure song.

—THEODORE ROETHKE

In *Self-Interviews,* James Dickey refers to his six-page, 182-line poem, "Approaching Prayer," as "the most complicated and far-fetched poem I've written" (*SI*, 134). Even a brief look at the poem's basic narrative bears out Dickey's claim. After the poem's speaker goes into the attic of his dead "father's empty house," he puts on the father's gray sweater and the fighting spurs from one of the father's gamecocks. The speaker then kneels under a skylight and places on his head the head of a boar that he had killed on a hunt. Speaking partly in his voice and partly for the boar, he enacts a kind of prayer that recapitulates his slaying of the boar and ends with a series of capitalized, "far-fetched," and

seemingly disconnected biblical images: "PROPHECIES, FIRE IN THE SIN-
FUL TOWERS, / WASTE AND FRUITION IN THE LAND, / CORN, LO-
CUSTS AND ASHES," to name a few. When the speaker leaves his father's attic
intending never to come back, he is uncertain of the results of his prayer yet
hopes that something did occur: "That, if not heard, / It may have been somehow said" (*P*, 168). Lest these acts seem trivial, mad, or meaningless, Dickey explains his poem's reach: "When you're trying to write about miracles—and
prayer is a miracle if it's anything—it's not like having a conversation with a
stenographer; miracles *are* far-fetched. They are the most out-of-the-ordinary
things that could possibly be" (*SI*, 134).

Harold Bloom agrees with Dickey's assessment of the originality of "Approaching Prayer": "I know no poem remotely like it. If it shares a magic vitalism with Yeats and D. H. Lawrence, its curious kind of wordless, almost undirected prayer has nothing Yeatsian or Lawrentian in its vision."[1] Extremely
challenging to decipher, Dickey's narrative is so far from ordinary experience
that it has received little critical commentary.[2] One reason for the poem's
difficulty is, as Bloom suggests, that Dickey's lyric is a very unprayerlike prayer.
Although the prayer concludes with biblical imagery, it contains no pious
words nor any god, or saintly beings toward which it is directed. There seems
to be no specific petition by the speaker; indeed, he is not even certain that he
has prayed. The poem has no meditative or discursive sequence conducive to
holiness or tranquil reflection. Rather, Dickey explicitly notes that for this
prayer to be effective, his "reason" must be "slain" (*P*, 163). Instead of directing
the soul to spiritual fulfillment, the piece focuses on an animated blood-filled
hunt. During the hunt the poet imitates not the lives and visions of biblical
"desert fathers . . . who saw angels come" (*P*, 167) but the manic energy of a wild
pig. To warrant the reader's attention and Dickey's passion for its complexity,
the appropriate critical terms are required to describe its direction and evaluate
the significance of this apparently wordless and undirected prayer. In short, in
Dickey's words, what exactly, if anything, has been "heard" in this poem and
"somehow said" so that "something important" has come "to be" (*P*, 168)?

To discover what has come to be in "Approaching Prayer," one must discover
what has already been done. For what is complicated here in a classic Aristotelian sense is the course of change the speaker undergoes by virtue of three "far-
fetched" things that he performs: the speaker goes up to the attic, has a peculiar
adventure, and then returns to everyday life with a radically new if not mysterious vision. In whatever has happened to this man, he has undergone some
kind of powerful alteration—verbal and more than verbal—by means of magical communion with his dead father. Insofar as the speaker feels that he must

"slay" his reason to initiate his ritual, one can understand the sympathetic observation about prayer and putting "off / Sense and notion" from T. S. Eliot's
"Little Gidding" in the opening quotation. Moreover, to initiate this inquiry
into converse with the dead, I will turn to another correlative point shared by
both poets that bears directly on our lives and families—that the dead are with
us in many modes. This relationship Eliot indicates poignantly and paradoxically in the final section of his great poem:

> We die with the dying:
> See, they depart, and we go with them.
> We are born with the dead:
> See, they return, and bring us with them.[3]

SEPARATION

The opening section of "Approaching Prayer" may be divided into two moments: exposition and preparation. Intertwined throughout the first thirty-five
lines, these moments introduce and hint at but do not fully state the activity of
the speaker. Consisting of time, setting, and situation, the exposition itself is
minimally sketched:

> A moment tries to come in
> Through the windows, when one must go
> Beyond what there is in the room,
> But it must come straight down.
>
> (P, 163)

Two questions, both of which have no explicit answer, immediately come to
mind: What moment is this? And how does a moment try to "come in /
Through the windows"? Despite this initial ambiguity, if one assumes, as the
title suggests, that this is a poem about praying, several quasi-religious elements begin to emerge. Whatever this moment is, it involves some kind of
transcendence, a going "beyond" the material elements in the room, and it
seems to appear from above or on high because "it must come straight down."
One reason for these sketchy expository coordinates may be that Dickey's
prayer is secular, for the poem hints at celestial motivation while not explicitly
acknowledging a transcendent deity. What is transcendent, however, is the suggestion of an uplifting prayer of ascent or initiation, which occurs within a setting that contains the possibility of some kind of higher change for the protagonist. In *The Sacred and the Profane*, Eliade notes that "what is 'above,' the
'high,' continues to reveal the *transcendent* in every religious complex. . . .

[T]his celestial symbolism in turn infuses and supports a number of rites (of ascent, climbing, initiation)." Eliade locates the possibility of ascension even in minimally sketched religious dimensions that evoke a sacred world through materials that speak to more than the rational aspect of the human mind: "No world is possible without verticality, and that dimension alone is enough to evoke transcendence. Driven from religious life in the strict sense, the *celestial sacred* remains active through symbolism. A religious symbol conveys its message even if it is no longer *consciously* understood in every part. For a symbol speaks to the whole human being and not only to the intelligence."[4] Even without a specifically religious symbol in his introductory lines, Dickey has begun to create a sacred space in which some kind of prayer is possible. As I will show, this is not the discursive or meditative space of a traditional lyric in which the action is basically mental. It is rather a space in which the poet can "produce a word I can't say / Until all my reason is slain" (*P*, 163) and thus speaks, as Eliade notes, "not only to the intelligence."

At line six, this sacred space receives clearer religious definition when Dickey initiates the construction of a magical circle to prepare for the speaker's prayer. The reader witnesses this preparation when the narrator starts to "circle through my father's empty house" so that he can put on or strip himself of things (*P*, 163) in a search for apparel appropriate to his act. Joseph Campbell combines these topics—clothing, circles, and the dead—in his description of the preparations of a Lapp shaman. By extension, this description applies to key aspects of Dickey's dramatic character and method: "[The shaman is] one of these strange emissaries into the kingdoms of the dead. Since the yonder world is a place of everlasting night, the ceremonial of the shaman has to take place after dark. . . . First he summons the helping spirits; these arrive, invisible to all but himself. . . . The shaman . . . loosens his belt and shoestrings . . . and begins to twirl in a variety of circles."[5] Like the Lapp shaman, Dickey begins his ceremony under "the night sky" (*P*, 164) while his circling motion demarcates and creates the sacred space for his prayer. As Eliade observes, "A territory can be made ours only by creating it anew, that is, by consecrating it"; further, "the cosmicization of unknown territories is always a consecration; to organize a space is to repeat the paradigmatic work of the gods."[6] What Dickey begins to create is a dream-space, not the conventionally sensed space of distance separating discrete objects at intervals, but a conscious and unconscious continuum of awareness between sleep and waking that is a kind of deep-structured realm of free association. Victor Turner calls this "ritual space," or what may be called "rhetorical space," that is, the demarcation of a personal enabling territory where one can be persuaded that major therapeutic change is possible.[7] If it takes the energy of a god to effect personal separation from a powerful adult figure—as many people can testify from personal experience— then Eliade's idea that the organization of such space is to "repeat the paradigmatic work of the gods" becomes all the more relevant.

The speaker's formal preparation for prayer begins not only with his magic circle but also with a search for his peculiar vestments. Although the speaker's selection of items—his dead father's gray sweater, spurs from his father's gamecocks, and the boar's head—may seem bizarre or incongruous to practitioners of modern Western religions, it is completely appropriate to many kinds of religious acts in so-called primitive cultures.[8] In *Hero with a Thousand Faces*, Joseph Campbell remarks on the initiation of priestly figures. "The shaman of the Siberians is clothed for the adventure in a magical costume representing a bird or reindeer, the shadow principle of the shaman himself, the shape of his soul. His drum is his animal. . . . [H]e is said to fly or ride it. . . . [H]e is attended by a host of invisible familiars."[9] By wearing his father's sweater, Dickey touches his dead father's spirit (or memory) through a form of contagious magic that Frazer famously defines in *The Golden Bough* as the assumption "that things which have been in contact with each other are always in contact."[10]

Using a similar assumption of transferred power, Dickey also selects the spurs of his father's gamecocks. These manic, energized birds, signs of battle and the kill, which portend the poet's oedipal combat with the boar, are his totem animals and will enable him to fly or ride "Beyond what there is in the room" while he is attended by the invisible yet familiar spirit of his dead father. Whether or not Dickey actually believes in magical contact among such objects he does not explicitly state. He certainly believes enough in the magical power of his instruments to think them necessary for his endeavor.[11] What is important is that these things constitute triggers to memory that function like the crumb of Proust's madeleine soaked in his aunt's concoction of lime flowers, calling up whole complexes of past and present recollection that seem as if they were magically set into motion. Whereas the "spirits" summoned by contiguous association may be invisible externally and are but partially represented in the poem, such spirits of memory and emotional evocation are quite real internally to anyone who has gone through a personal ritual as simple as putting on an article of clothing from a dead parent or other loved one.

Dickey's circle and selection of ceremonial garb not only sanctify his poetic space but also alter the time in which he performs. Of this kind of sacred time, Eliade says, "Religious man lives in . . . sacred time, [which] appears under the paradoxical aspect of a circular time, reversible and recoverable, a sort of eternal mythical present that is periodically reintegrated by means of rites."[12] Dickey's circular construction of an eternal mythic present is yet another preparatory expository element that initiates the poet's search by emotionally reversing the flux of profane time. This mythical present momentarily arrests ever-changing, historical duration long enough for the narrator to begin recovery of a psychological eternity where emotional grief-work can be effected. To prepare for his unfinished personal business in an internalized past, Dickey must slow down if not annihilate the conscious world of reason and logic that splinters human response. He thus enters a world in which he can circle back to a realm of enabling recollection and possibility and to the power of work through a transition that engages him emotionally and rationally. Rather than approach this world analytically, Dickey has chosen the mode of ritual action represented in this poem. At certain stages in our lives, we all have felt completely blocked in ways that do not respond to merely rational solution, felt the need for some major breakthrough that would cleanse not only the discursive mind, but what is more important, our hearts and souls. It is access to just such a time and place of energizing change that initiates Dickey's quest.

The preliminary action in Dickey's rite not only alters profane space and time but also begins to convert his "father's empty house" and thus his own body into a specific kind of temple for prayer and transformation. Speaking of "body-house symbolism," Eliade comments that:

> The "house"—since it is at once an *imago mundi* and a replica of the human body—plays a considerable role in rituals and mythologies. In some cultures . . . funerary urns are made in the shape of a house; they have an opening above to permit the dead man's soul to enter and leave. The urnhouse . . . becomes the dead man's new "body." But it is also from a house . . . that the mythical Ancestor comes; and it is always in such a house-urn-cap that the sun hides at night to come forth again in the morning. Thus there is a structural correspondence between the different modes of *passage*—from darkness to light (sun), from a human race's preexistence to its manifestation (mythical Ancestor), from life to death and to the new existence after death (the soul).

In order to effect contact with his own "mythical Ancestor" (his dead father or, more specifically, his internalized conception of his father), Dickey kneels under the skylight that functions as his mythological "narrow gate," to use Eliade's phrase. This gate is a symbol of opening and ascension that in many cultures "makes possible passage from one mode of being to another, from one existential situation to another."[13] Campbell calls this opening the "sun door." It is "the opening at the top of the lodge—or the crown, pinnacle, or lantern of the dome—is the hub or midpoint of the sky: the sun door, through which souls pass back from time to eternity, like the savor of the offerings, burned in the fire of life, and lifted on the axis of ascending smoke from the hub of the earthly to that of the celestial wheel."[14]

To transform his dead father's empty house into his own adult "body-house" and to grieve fully the loss of his father while simultaneously initiating a ritual separation from his dead parent, the speaker chooses to "kneel down under the skylight" (P, 164) that functions as his personal sun door. This skylight/sun door is where his prayer begins and thus constitutes the threshold of his passage from within his current condition to an emotional state outside it. Encompassing both darkness and light, this threshold of opposites also suggests the "primordial image of shattering the roof," that is, the destruction of the current structure of the house which is "the dead man's new 'body,'" and thus the destruction of the poet's current unresolved relationship with his father.[15] Dickey leaves the body or foundation of his current father-son relationship for a new dynamic, a new change in emotional foundation, something other than the child-father relation they had before. By using the skylight for his sun door, Dickey creates a spiritual starting point that gives him both separation and uplift.

After he kneels down, the final preparatory step for Dickey's narrator is to put on a hollow hog's head. This head is both a helmet and another animal totem (whose mythopoeic nature I will explore more fully later). With regard to the helmet's preliminary function, I will simply note here that it is the last item Dickey employs before his adventure begins and that helmets have at least a double function for him: protection and preparation for risk-taking.[16] Risk-taking and the possibility of discovering words for prayer are also central topics in these lines from Dickey's moving war poem, "Drinking From a Helmet." After picking up the helmet of a dead soldier from the battlefield on a Pacific island in World War II, his speaker, numb from combat, drinks refreshing and life-giving water from the soldier's helmet. The narrator then magically enters a surrealistic world of unity, protection, and communion with the dead, where he recovers his "nearly dead power to pray":

IX

My nearly dead power to pray
Like an army increased and assembled,
As when, in a harvest of sparks,
The helmet leapt from the furnace
And clamped itself

On the heads of a billion men.
Some words directed to Heaven
Went through all the strings of the graveyard
Like a message that someone sneaked in,
Tapping a telegraph key
At dead of night, then running
For his life.

(*P*, 175)

By putting on the boar's head-helmet, Dickey not only closes himself off from
the world of normal vision by means of ferocious concealment "with star
points in the glass eyes / That would blind anything that looked in" (*P*, 164), he
also opens his totemic alter ego to the lethal "vulnerability" and to the unity of
life and death in the surreal hunt that follows. Precisely this dramatic combination of risk and daring generates the momentum for the rising action in the
next section of "Approaching Prayer," which may be labeled "transition."

Transition

Although, as I have noted, many of the religious elements in Dickey's drama
are sketched or merely initiated in the poem's opening lines, they come to full
ritualistic vitality in its middle segment. Circular exchanges between human
and other-than-natural voices, totemic transfers between man and beast, emotional animation between bodies of the living and of the dead, an ordeal involving death and mutilation in a cosmic night, and an incantory shamanistic
cure and resurrection—all these primitive and sacred topics constitute major
psychological transitions as he generates the beginnings of prayer. The second
act of Dickey's ritual starts at line thirty-six, when his dream-journey begins.
Ending at line 129, his journey encompasses approximately one-half of the
poem and consists of three elements: transport to a primitive world of hunting; the hunt itself, presented in a double-voiced trance, narrated alternately by
the poet and the poet-as-boar; and two effects on the poet (still kneeling) that
ensue from his trance: a terrific, internal speeding-up of what D. H. Lawrence
would call "blood-consciousness," then a near "lift" (or ascension) of some
kind.

A brief nine lines (36–44) whose function is to expedite the main action, the
first element in the transitional section—the poet's transport to the dramatic
world of hunting—occurs immediately after the speaker kneels and puts on
the boar's head. While he continues to search in his visionary blindness for
some cause "to utter words," Dickey's "night sky fills with a light / / Of hunt-

ing" and with "the sweat and panting of dogs." Inside the boar's head, he pants with what anthropologist E. B. Tylor calls the "spirit-voice" (which, in Algonquin Indian culture, allows men to converse with "the shadow world of the dead" and thus draws "the breath of life / For the dead hog" (P, 164).[17] This double vision of man and animal initiates the second element of the trance-journey at line 45—the hunt, wherein Dickey reenvisions himself with a bow and arrow, preparing to shoot the hog whose spirit he has assumed. What follows is an alternating double-voiced account of the hunt with the boar-poet (the victim) narrating the motion-filled action in italics while the human poet records his reactions, especially his "motionless" search for words, in his normal voice:

> I draw the breath of life
> For the dead hog:
> I catch it from the still air,
> Hold it in the boar's rigid mouth,
> And see
>
> > *A young man aging with a bow*
> > *And a green arrow pulled to his cheek*
> > *Standing deep in a mountain creek bed,*
> > *Stiller than trees or stones,*
> > *Waiting and staring*
>
> Beasts, angels
> I am nearly that motionless now
>
> > *There is a frantic leaping at my sides*
> > *Of dogs coming out of the water*
>
> The moon and the stars do not move
>
> > *I bare my teeth, and my mouth*
> > *Opens, a foot long, popping with tushes*
>
> A word goes through my closed lips
>
> > *I gore a dog, he falls, falls back*
> > *Still snapping, turns away and dies*
> > *While swimming.*
>
> (P, 164–65)

With dogs snapping and "leaping" all around him, the boar is shot twice with arrows—the first arrow signaled by the narrator's "yes." The scene then fills with the movement of blood as the boar dies and his *"tongue spills blood / Bound for the ocean"* (*P,* 166; italics in original). Although blood and violence abound in this hunting narrative, the poet's human voice records a series of events, cosmic and personal, that shift from a "motionless" state to one of comprehensive harmonious movement as a direct result of the hunt. Then, while "the plants attune all their orbits" (*P,* 165), a personal rhythm emerges from the cosmic harmony as the universe creaks "like boards / Thumping with heartbeats / And bonebeats." Moments later, an even more personal transformation occurs, as the narrator discovers that "my father is pale on my body"— all of which takes place in the cosmic night of "moonlight, moonlight" (*P,* 166). When the hunt ends, so does the boar's voice, but its totemic nature continues to propel the poem's harmonious energy into the third element of this section. Before these harmonizing and energizing ends are discussed, the dramatic role of the boar and the moonlit universe of blood and harmony to which he is central should be examined more closely.

In addition to representing one of the poet's self-acknowledged "best and stillest" (*P,* 163) moments from his past life, this wild boar is the poet's power animal. A power animal symbolizes, in Eliade's words, a spirit's unseen presence that is "manifested by the shaman imitating animal cries or behavior." Insofar as Dickey follows one of the basic laws of religious history by wearing the boar's head, namely, that *"one becomes what one displays"* because "there is no clear difference . . . between empirical object and symbol" to the "primitive" mind, he not only receives assistance from the "spirit" of the boar but also becomes the boar. By participating in the symbol of the boar, Dickey-as-shaman becomes what Eliade calls "the carrier of a value." This animistic mimesis is not mere child's play or superstition but an emotionally enabling method involving the transference of traits (or values) that is basic to a mythico-magical mode of power: "Imitating the gait of an animal or putting on its skin was acquiring a superhuman mode of being. There was no question of a regression into pure 'animal life': the animal with which the shaman identified himself was already charged with a mythology, it was, in fact, a mythical animal, the Ancestor or the Demiurge. By becoming this mythical animal, man became something far greater and stronger than himself." Not only does his power animal enable the shaman to become "greater and stronger than himself," it also enables him to become another self. Rather than evoke real external spirits through his power animal, the shaman enters a reflexive world of dream consciousness in which he initiates his transforming action: "This shamanistic imitation of the actions and voices of animals can pass as 'possession.' But it would perhaps be more accurate to term it a *taking possession of his helping spirits by a shaman.* It is the shaman who *turns himself* into an animal, just as he achieves a similar result by putting on an animal mask. Or, again, we might speak of a *new identity* for the shaman, who becomes an animal-spirit."[18]

When the speaker puts on the boar's head, it is already charged with a mythology because it represents a past "best" moment that is itself charged with life and death. In other words, the animal is greater and stronger than the poet because it has traversed the realm between the living and the dead and has come back to life animated by the poet's breath. This power to navigate momentous stages between existential zones not only constitutes a rite of passage but also represents exactly the kind of transitional power that Dickey needs to effect a *"new identity."* By forsaking his human condition, he "dies" and is then reborn through an animal spirit that in many cultural forms has accompanied human souls to another world or become the new shape of the deceased.[19] Dickey's description of the hunter as *"A young aging man with a bow"* (*P,* 164; italics in original) suggests someone in transition, someone dying, from the period of his youth with his living father to that of an "aging man," who no longer has a living father to draw upon (or against). In addition to Dickey's biological parent, this dead father may be partially poetic, "the composite precursor Yeats/Roethke," as Harold Bloom argues in his oedipal reading of the poem. The slain boar thus serves an even further liminal function by enabling Dickey to construct a poem distinctively different—in Bloom's word, "stronger"—from those of his incarcerating fathers. Even though he bases his lyric on their "stance and diction" (as Bloom notes), Dickey can symbolically kill off these potentially lethal influences with arrows and thus transumptively become his own strong literary precursor.[20]

Also suggesting mortal transition, Dickey's nocturnal setting of "Moonlight, moonlight" (*P,* 166) is itself conducive to the possibility of change (from the "death" of one personal state to the "life" of another); for this is a night-world that is "a symbol of death; the forest, the jungle, darkness symbolize the beyond, the 'infernal regions.'"[21] In this kind of primal darkness, life and death are intertwined in yet another sense insofar as Dickey-as-boar undergoes the first two stages in what Eliade calls the basic, "ecstatic" experience for a shaman, which is "the traditional schema of an initiation ceremony: suffering, death, resurrection."[22] By slaying the alter ego of his power animal, the poet-shaman does not engage in a sensationalized version of sadomasochism but rather gains strength from a liminal encounter that is commonplace in shamanic initiation. My point is that the intensity of violence inflicted on the boar has a direct correspondence to the intensity of internal violence necessary for the speaker's emotional separation from the father, itself a formidable psychic tearing. In this context, the poet-as-animal is "the tormented and mutilated novice" who "is believed to be tortured, cut to pieces, boiled or roasted by the demons who are the masters of the initiation, that is, by the mythical ancestors."[23] Here again, I will say that Dickey does not delight in the mutilation of an animal but instead focuses on another central component in a shaman's character. This component, a "widespread theme in shamanic training and apprenticeship[,] is *dismemberment* or shamanic sickness or the wounded healer. Shamans in training often expect to become sick or wounded as part of the initiation, or voluntarily submit to the experience of feeling oneself being dismembered, cut open, broken into small pieces, and then reconstituted, often by the animal ally or other spirit guide."[24]

As Dickey's alter ego, the boar also suffers bloody mutilation and dismemberment. Not only do *"the dogs of blood / Hang to* [its] *ears"* (*P*, 166; italics in original) but also later the boar's head is cut off. Symbolic of the poet's existential separation and death, this event is Dickey's version of the ritualistic initiatory wound that the poet shaman must overcome to become whole. The boar as animal ally thus assists the poet-shaman to reconstitute himself by means of its life-giving flow of blood, which gains considerable momentum and scope as it *"spills . . . Bound for the ocean"* (*P*, 166).[25] This flow is archetypal.[26] Like blood "derived by the Australian fathers from their subincision holes" and "used for ceremonial painting and for gluing white bird's down to the body," the flow shares animating traits with this series of analogies made by Campbell; it "symbolizes at once menstrual blood of the vagina and the semen of the males, as well as urine, water, and male milk. The flowing shows that the old men have the sources of life and nourishment within themselves; i.e., that they and the inexhaustible world fountain are the same."[27] The flow of the boar's blood also provides an occasion in which Dickey achieves an internal personal harmony, mentioned earlier, which is presented in external celestial imagery as "the planets attune all their orbits." This double-voiced narrative and vision of the hunt—a voice half animal, half human—enables different aspects of Dickey-as-wounded healer to die and live simultaneously in the practical process of ritual consciousness that generates a peculiar psychological allegory. In a world in which metamorphosis is sudden, violent, and uniquely reflexive, it is no wonder that the speaker's point of view assumes the boar's and his own: "I have seen the hog see me kill him."[28]

Dickey's double vision of exchange between man and animal has several other implications. By doubly seeing his own ritual death as the boar, the poet comes away with a fuller knowledge—emotionally and rationally, from inside and outside himself—of the transition he is undergoing. As Eliade notes, "The initiate is not only one newborn or resuscitated; he is a man who *knows,* who has learned the mysteries, who has had revelations that are metaphysical in nature."[29] Such knowledge or religious experience is intended not merely for himself but is to be passed on to the community. Just as Osiris and Dionysus were dismembered and reconstituted, so do we—whether in the vicissitudes of adolescence, career changes, divorce, death, or any form of major emotional separation—need a healing experience similar to Dickey's. Even though Dickey says at the end of the poem that "I don't know quite what has happened" (*P,* 167), he nonetheless passes on to others the poetic model of an enabling myth, a partial reversal, as Bloom suggests, of the myth of Adonis; for this time, Adonis slays the boar who is really both himself and his various fathers. Moreover, because the specific motivation for the lyric speaker in "Approaching Prayer" is sketched in the broadest possible terms, Dickey's poem can easily function as a vehicle of transference of practical wisdom for his readers so that they can effect personal rituals while they read.[30] This process is especially effective if the poem is read aloud.

Another function of Dickey's exchange with the boar is epistemological, especially in relation to the shamanic initiate's awareness of the arbitrariness of "factors" in his culture. Victor Turner notes that there is a reflective element in the transitional stage of initiation: "Much of the grotesqueness and monstrosity of liminal *sacr* [culturally essential knowledge] may be seen to be aimed not so much at terrorizing or bemusing neophytes into submission or out of their wits as at making them vividly and rapidly aware of what may be called 'factors' of their culture."[31] Working in the mode of symbolic anthropology, Mary Schmidt thinks that these factors "from one's culture are analogous to Lévi-Strauss's 'gross constituents' of myth. In the liminal state, such social categories are juxtaposed in odd ways so that the child initiate becomes aware of them as merely mental constructs."[32] Although the reader may assume that Dickey's speaker is a mature man, the child within him conducts his personal therapy by altering his previous view of reality in the "far-fetched" manner I noted earlier. In this confusing and dismaying process, the fixed entities of reality and nature are rewritten. The child learns that social categories are not eternal verities but susceptible of transformation. When the child sees an animal's head on a person's body, he witnesses an object that is a new construction made out of what were previously separate components.

Anyone who has put on an actor's costume—more so a boar's head—knows how thoroughly cultural and dramatic roles may be rewritten by altering appearance. Dickey's trance-like hunt and exchange with the boar constitute an especially dramatic reshuffling of the previously separate categories of human and animal consciousness. This topic Dickey has explored with considerable dexterity in such poems as "The Dusk of Horses" and "Reincarnation II" (in which a nondescript office worker is transformed into a majestic seabird soaring endlessly over the oceans). By undoing conventional divisions associated with "rational" (culturally given) thought, Dickey moves back and forth between and then beyond generic opposites. He moves, moreover, into an ecstatic imaginative space in which discursive conceptualizing constitutes a blockage. In this realm abstraction is, in Arthur Deikman's words, "an interference with the direct contact that yields essential knowledge through perception alone."[33] By slaying the boar of his own reason, Dickey discovers, as Schmidt notes, "that real and unreal are not differences in kind but of degree." Not only of degree, I may add, but of arrangement. In "Approaching Prayer," Dickey rewrites and rearranges culturally discrete relationships between man and animal, living and dead, and dismemberment and unification to such a degree that he not only traverses them but more importantly reverses their real relations. In the inner-directed, sacred space of his poetry, he transforms the dead into the living and then back to the dead. This animated—animistic—world for Dickey consists of an undifferentiated realm in which father, son, and sacred animal not only share identical physical traits (such as the motion of blood) but also basic ontological categories. By poetically reconstructing these categories, Dickey thereby gains the power of renewal—he can transcend or animate death, *i.e.*, emotional death—and also tears this metaphysical "insight from the spirits who have torn him, then demand[s] a passage back through glory" to the real world.[34]

To conclude the transitional section of his poem, to specify in greater detail the shamanic insight from his trance and to begin his "passage back through glory," Dickey constructs two experiences. First, while still kneeling in the dark, he sees nothing, then

> for a second
>
> Something goes through me
> Like an accident, a negligent glance,
> Like the explosion of a star
> Six billion light years off
> Whose light gives out
>
> Just as it goes straight through me.
> (*P*, 166–67)

This star imagery suggests but a partial image of illumination. The illumination is partial because the effects of Dickey's trance are just beginning to manifest themselves and are still far from verbal, much less rational, articulation. The speaker feels the effect of the past hypnotic events but cannot find the source, which, like a burnt-out star, is now long gone from his reflective consciousness. The second experience occurs immediately after this marginally conscious burst of light: the "boar's blood," still "bearing the living image / Of my most murderous stillness," sails "through rivers" then "picks up speed." Combined with "chicken-blood rust" from his father's gaffs, the "sailing" blood "freshens, as though near a death wound / Or flight" and provides the poet a near "lift / From the floor" and, more importantly, "from my father's grave," which Dickey identifies with the father's sweater "crawling over my chest" (P, 167). This physiological and emotional lift is the first sign of the poet's third stage of initiation. Such a stage is variously called by anthropologists "return," "renewal," "resurrection," "rebirth," or "regeneration." This ancient archetypal event is usually signaled by ascension of some kind, often ascension from the dark night of the soul to a world of refreshing light. Dickey's dark and bloody trance-journey thus fittingly ends with two positive moments—light and uplift—that lead to the final section of the poem, the "incorporation."

INCORPORATION

Beginning at line 130 and extending to the end of the poem (some fifty-two lines), the last major section of "Approaching Prayer" consists of three elements. The first two elements (lines 130–35) are brief and expository: Dickey removes the hog's head, the gaffs, and the sweater, then leaves his father's house, never to return. These definite physical gestures initially suggest a strong closure to the poem. But Dickey ends in a much less definite if not contradictory way. For when he reflects on what his praying has accomplished, he finds that its meaning is elusive:

> I don't know quite what has happened
> Or that anything has,
> Hoping only that
> The irrelevancies one thinks of
> When trying to pray
> Are the prayer
>
> (P, 167)

Whatever these "irrelevancies" are, they do not result from the kind of prayer practiced by "the desert fathers" in the Bible; instead, Dickey hopes that he has arrived

> . . . by my own
> Means to the hovering place
> Where I can say with any
> Other than the desert fathers—
> Those who saw angels come . . .
> To answer what questions men asked
> In Heaven's tongue,
> Using images of earth
> Almightily
>
> (*P*, 167–68)

What follows is one of the most curious sections in this already "farfetched" poem, namely, a spectacular example of the kind of biblical prayer Dickey rejects. This rejected mode, which Dickey defines as answers by angels to men's "questions," consists of a catalog of images of earth (images of elemental catastrophic forms such as "FIRE" and "LOCUSTS AND ASHES"), presented "in Heaven's tongue" (in a capitalized style marked by miraculous events, such as "PROPHECIES" and "A CHILD BORN OF UTTER LIGHT"):

> PROPHECIES, FIRE IN THE SINFUL TOWERS,
> WASTE AND FRUITION IN THE LAND,
> CORN, LOCUSTS AND ASHES,
> THE LION'S SKULL PULSING WITH HONEY,
> THE BLOOD OF THE FIRST-BORN,
> A GIRL MADE PREGNANT WITH A GLANCE
> LIKE AN EXPLODING STAR
> AND A CHILD BORN OF UTTER LIGHT—
>
> (*P*, 168)

What is contradictory and puzzling about this catalog is this: if Dickey wishes to speak—that is, to pray—in a language that is "any / Other" than that of his desert fathers, why does he use such an extensive catalog of the rejected fathers' images, and why does he feature this catalog so prominently in the poem's finale? To solve this apparent opposition and to understand how Dickey incorporates these final lines into the preceding action and into his return to the rest of his life, I propose four answers. First, one purpose of this imagery is contrast. The list consists of traditional answers (by biblical fathers) that constitute inherited responses. These responses have the credibility, as Dickey asserts, of answers written in "images of earth" by men (not by a manifestly present supreme being) who witnessed "angels" (as sources of these answers) with the dubious reality of "body glow" that reflected on standard biblical objects, such as "bushes / And sheep's wool and animal eyes." No matter how farfetched his prayer may be, Dickey has seen none of this glowing supernatural paraphernalia, nor does he offer any of it to the reader as proof of the validity of his praying. Instead of professing a thundering, spectacular burst of beatific visions exploding from the sky, Dickey is more modest. He says merely that he hopes that the "irrelevancies one thinks of / When trying to pray / Are the prayer" (P, 167), then offers in contrast a personal catalog of "irrelevancies" that consist of major moments taken from the previous events in his poem: "violent" "stillness," "blood enough," "the warmth of my father's wool grave," "love enough," and "the keen heals of feathery slaughter." These are not answers but the conditions of prayer, which the poet hopes will give him "lift enough . . . For something important to be" or "somehow said" (P, 168).

Second, the answers in this neobiblical catalog do not form a single, coherent response to a particular petition but are instead a barrage of energized and disconnected events. In this fragmented state, they constitute yet another external sign—this time, linguistic—of the internal dismemberment of the shamanic, wounded healer; that is, they constitute a "shattered language."[35] This shattering not only reflects the psychological fragmentation that Dickey has undergone in a previous stage of his initiation but also suggests the further oedipal shattering of the traditional modes of response to his biblical fathers' prayers that at one time had credence for him. As his new self emerges through his new kind of prayer, Dickey poetically appropriates the magical energy of conventional religious imagery while simultaneously shattering it and distancing himself from its paternal authority, just as he appropriates the powers of the various fathers—familial, poetic, religious—whom he buries and turns into ancestors in his mourning rite.

Third, Dickey concludes with these images because they represent examples of answers to prayer that at first appear to correspond with the creative and destructive experiences he has just undergone. Beginning with judgments from the Old Testament and ending with miraculous incarnation from the New Testament, this sequence has a three-part structure that reflects the three-part structure of the poem as a whole. Moving from promise through destruction to rebirth along an imagistic pattern from darkness to light, these biblical pictures—though theologically suspect—map out an important secularized route for the speaker-initiate that enables him to construct an effective ritual. By thinking through these images of transformation, Dickey implicitly suggests that the seeds of catastrophic spiritual change have continually been present in the ritualized myths of biblical narratives and that these ancient powers are now assimilated and reinvented in his internalized quest. Both the biblical events and Dickey's new myth depend radically on magical image-thinking to overwhelm the speaker's mind and heart in ways that abstract reasoning cannot. The images in this sequence are, as the poet noted, like "the explosion of a star / Six billion light years off / Whose light gives out // just as it goes straight through me" (*P*, 166–67). In short, they constitute a new way of using ancient archetypes to construct a neobiblical word-magic that transforms the entire soul of Dickey's speaker.

Finally, by rearranging the shattered biblical images into a new energized sequence, Dickey does what many novices do in the process of initiation; he begins to learn (or invent) what Eliade calls "a new language" or "a secret vocabulary" that is a further sign of mystical rebirth. Based on a deconstruction of conventional modes of biblical coherence coupled with signs that sum up the poem's major events in Dickey's concluding catalog ("violent" "stillness"), this "symbolism of the second birth" forms what Lévi-Strauss calls in *Structural Anthropology* a "language of symbols," which points to the heart of the psychological method in "Approaching Prayer."[36] This incipient language constitutes yet another beginning or approach by Dickey to answer his prayer, an answer that is nothing less than his entire poetic construction in which prayer and response are one. Lévi-Strauss believes that the symbols or signs in this language are the basic "elements of mythical thought" that "lie half-way between percepts and concepts" and "between images and concepts." Further, he thinks that such symbols have a peculiarly resonating referential function that empowers the mythical thinker as he "'speaks' not only *with* things . . . but also through the medium of thing."[37] When ritualized in the form of a narrative performed by certain shamans, such signs can have the curative power to shed light on emotional illnesses that "normal thought cannot fathom."[38] Lévi-Strauss goes on to say that in psychoanalysis, this process of accession is called *"abreaction"*:

> The shaman does not limit himself to reproducing or miming certain events. He actually relives them in all their vividness, originality, and violence. And since he returns to his normal state at the end of the seance, we may say, borrowing a key term from psychoanalysis, that he *abreacts*. In psychoanalysis, abreaction refers to the decisive moment in the treatment when the patient intensively relives the initial situation from which his disturbance stems, before he ultimately overcomes

it. . . . [I]ts precondition is the unprovoked intervention of the analyst, who appears in the conflicts of the patient through a double transference mechanism, as
a flesh-and-blood protagonist and in relation to whom the patient can restore and
clarify an initial situation which has remained unexpressed or unformulated.[39]

It is not enough to "reach deeply buried complexes" through the conscious
use of words alone. One cannot merely speak this abreactive process; the cure
must be physically performed or enacted through a "living myth."[40] Dickey's
poem could thus somewhat humorously be retitled "Approaching Abreaction,"
for he, like the shaman, does not psychoanalyze himself or enunciate an explicit emotional revelation. Perhaps one reason Dickey does not describe in detail the "deeply buried" complex he undergoes is that he is too busy working
through it. Although sketched briefly in relation to his father and in the allegorical terms of the hunt, this complexity of instincts, like many myths, must
remain, as Freud notes, "magnificent in [its] indefiniteness." In *The Cry for
Myth*, psychoanalyst Rollo May maintains that this "lack of definiteness" constitutes a central value of myths, "for their drama perpetually suggests surprising interpretations, new mysteries, novel possibilities."[41] Dickey is, of course,
no full-fledged shaman. He is a modern man, who resides, as do we all, in a
highly technological industrial civilization and who nonetheless is attempting
to understand the full human benefits obtainable from dwelling in mythical
time and space. Consequently, his attempt at ritual has a certain tentativeness
about it, which he explicitly acknowledges in his statement of hope and uncertainty in the poem's concluding lines. Despite this tentativeness, the emotional
issue at stake in Dickey's poem is clear and immediate enough for anyone who
has gone through a similar if not universal experience: separation from a father
and incorporation of a new father-child relation that enables the child to carry
on effectively with the remainder of his or her life.

To conclude, I will note that May's distinction between ritual and myth
sheds further light on Dickey's poem: "Rituals are the physical expressions of
the myths. . . . The myth is the narration, and the ritual—such as giving presents or being baptized—expresses the myth in bodily action."[42] What Dickey
does physically, then—kneeling, putting on the boar's head, slaying the boar—
is the ritual. His poetic telling of the tale is the myth, which encompasses considerably more than the physical ritual. Both elements, myth and ritual, performed together, empower the abreactive process by appealing to vastly more
than the rational part of the performer. As I indicated in the opening to this
chapter, Eliade observes in *The Sacred and the Profane* that "a purely rational
man is an abstraction; he is never found in real life."[43] Further, the overuse of

reason to solve problems in therapy is labeled by May as "the sin of dogmatic rationalism."[44] Insofar as the performance of ritual involves what Eliade calls "the *whole man*," it is the whole mind or psyche that uniquely benefits from a living myth such as Dickey's, and thus it is the unifying involvement of all parts of the performer—mental, emotional, and physical—that constitutes the distinctive answer to Dickey's prayer.[45] The poet, in short, prays himself whole, or at least as whole as one can be in effecting successfully the kind of transition he undergoes.[46] The poet's human role in this holistic drama may best be described by Lévi-Strauss's analogy between therapist and shaman, which centers on the incantatory power of the shaman's chant: "A prerequisite role—that of the listener for the psychologist and of orator for the shaman—establishes a direct relationship with the patient's conscious and an indirect relationship with his unconscious. This is the function of the incantation proper. But the shaman does more than utter the incantation; he is its hero, for it is he who, at the head of a supernatural battalion of spirits, penetrates the endangered organs and frees the captive soul."[47]

In James Dickey's distinguished lyric "Approaching Prayer," just such a chant has the magical power of myth to transform both poet and reader, if the reader, like the poet, is willing, in Theodore Roethke's wonderful words, "to be delivered from the rational into the realm of pure song."[48]

4

FORM AND GENRE IN DICKEY'S "FALLING"
The Great Goddess Gives Birth to the Earth

The fables of the gods are true histories of customs.

—GIAMBATTISTA VICO

I don't think that there's a deeper part of nature than a woman. The blood of women is connected with the moon, the heavens, everything. They bear the very seed of meaning and existence.

—JAMES DICKEY

Oh, golden flower opened up
                              she is our mother
whose thighs are holy
                        whose face is a dark mask
She came from Tamoanchan,
                      the first place
where all descended
                  where all was born. . . .
She is our mother,
                the goddess earth.
                                She is dressed
in plumes
          she is smeared with clay.

—Atzec poem to the Mother of the Gods

A quarter of a century ago, well before many current intellectual trends became mainstream, Dickey reaffirmed the multicultural brotherhood of his own poetic vision with Native Americans, when, in *Self-Interviews*, he lamented "the loss of a sense of intimacy with the natural process. I think you would be very hard-put . . . to find a more harmonious relationship to an environment than the American Indians had. We can't return to a primitive society . . . but there is a property of mind which, if encouraged, could have this personally animistic relationship to things. . . . It's what gives us a *personal* relationship to the sun and the moon, the flow of rivers, the growth and decay of natural forms, and the cycles of death and rebirth" (*SI*, 68–69). An exhilarating celebration of just those harmonious cycles, "Falling" is one of Dickey's best-known and most spectacular poems. The lyric runs more than six full pages in page-wide lines with minimal punctuation to interrupt its accelerating whirlwind of energy while dramatizing the fate of a stewardess who falls from an airliner over the Midwest. Although this woman starts off as the victim of a tragic accident, her fall is exhilarating because she ends up as someone significantly different.

Critics have offered clues to this transformation. Joyce Carol Oates claims that the stewardess is "a kind of mortal goddess, given as much immortality . . . as poetry is capable of giving its subjects."[1] Monroe Spears notes that she "becomes a goddess, embodiment of a myth."[2] Joyce Pair, editor of the *James Dickey Newsletter*, observes that the stewardess is "a modern incarnation of the goddess of crops and fertility."[3] Dickey himself says that the stewardess has "a goddess-like invulnerability" (*SI*, 175).[4] Even though these clues identify the stewardess as a goddess, there are few extended discussions of the poem that develop this premise.[5] My own short analysis, written in 1983 and later published in a chapter on sacrificial victims in my book on Dickey's poetry, concurs with these opinions to some degree, suggesting that "we may best read 'Falling' . . . as a ritual reenactment of the primitive practice of killing a god of vegetation to ensure both the perpetuation of crops and the continuation of the human species itself."[6] After having done more extensive reading in mythological literatures, however, I believe that my initial assessment undervalued the power and character of this woman and that a closer look is in order.

To say that the stewardess is merely a "sacrificial victim"—a description derived from Kenneth Burke and René Girard—renders her passive in a way that does not reflect her true dynamic and dramatic character. What is needed, then, is to trace more fully the process of empowerment (the plot or form of the poem) that the stewardess undergoes by looking at the kind of mythological activity (the genre) this process resembles. Through three analogies with goddesses from Native American, Asian, and Mesoamerican myths, it is possible to see "Falling" as an animistic and matriarchal creation myth—in many ways, the emotional and cultural opposite of the patriarchal narrative in Genesis—whose particular rendering in Dickey's hands reveals further insights into his conceptions of women and nature. My claim is that "Falling" is Dickey's remarkable transformation of an airline employee into an analogue of one of the great goddesses of primitive seed-planting cultures, more specifically, Mother Earth, who in the process of falling and dying gives birth to herself and the earth.

FIRST ANALOGY: BIRD WOMAN (OR LADY OF THE ANIMALS) AND THE WOMAN WHO FELL FROM THE SKY

When the stewardess falls out of the plane (line 7), she at first panics, then experiments with her fall. Dickey says, "She develops interest   she turns in her maneuverable body / To watch it" (P, 293). Not only does she begin to enjoy her fall, but she takes on the first in a series of new kinds of power, namely, the power of animals. At line 30, she changes from someone merely performing "endless gymnastics" into what I call "Bird Woman," for she now can "slant   slide / Off tumbling   into the emblem of a bird with its wings half-spread" (P, 294).[7] Whether in "Reincarnation II," where one finds "There is a wing-growing motion / Half-alive in every creature" (P, 248), or in "Eagles," where the poet says "My feathers were not / Of feather-make, but broke from a desire to drink / The rain before it falls" (EM, 3), the empowerment of human beings through magical contact with animals is a long-standing commonplace in Dickey's work. This topic recalls two of Jungian psychologist Erich Neumann's observations when he discusses animals symbolic of ancient goddesses: first, that the "birdlike character of woman points primarily to her correlation with the heavens,"[8] and second, that in Creto-Aegean culture "the Great Mother as a nature goddess . . . was mistress of the mountains and of wild animals" and that "birds . . . symbolized her presence."[9]

In "Falling," Dickey's stewardess-goddess has "time to live / In superhuman health" (P, 294) by so taking on the properties of bird flight and vision that she becomes a variation of what is called in Pali Buddhism "the great woman rich in creatures":[10]

> Arms out   she slow-rolls over   steadies out . . .
>   trembles near feathers   planes head-down
> The quick movements of bird-necks turning her head   gold eyes
>   the insight-
> eyesight of owls blazing into the hencoops   a taste for chicken
>   overwhelming
> Her   the long-range vision of hawks enlarging all human lights
>   of cars

Freight trains   looped bridges   enlarging the moon racing slowly
Through all the curves of a river   all the darks of the midwest blazing
From above. . . .

(*P*, 294)

By acquiring the "insight- / eyesight of owls" and "the long-range vision of hawks," the stewardess is not only rich in creatures but also reenacts the role of a prehistoric goddess known as "The Lady of the Animals," who often appears in the form of a bird. Citing Marija Gimbutas' *The Goddesses and Gods of Old Europe*, Carol Christ tells us that Gimbutas found a "pre-Bronze Age culture that was 'matrifocal' . . . presided over by a Goddess as Source and Giver of All. Originally the Goddess did not appear with animals but herself had animal characteristics. One of her earliest forms was as the Snake and Bird Goddess, associated with water, and represented as a snake, a water bird, a duck, goose, crane, diver bird, or owl, or as a woman with a bird head or birdlike posture. She was the Goddess Creatress, the giver of Life." Known in classical mythology as "Aphrodite with her dove, Athene with her owl, [and] Artemis with her deer," the image of the Lady of Animals, Christ notes, goes back in history beyond Homer to the Neolithic and Paleolithic eras. In the Homeric hymns (*ca.* 800–400 B.C.), "the Lady of the Animals is cosmic power; she is mother of all; the animals of Earth, sea, and air are hers; the wildest and most fearsome of animals. . . . [She] is also earth: she is the firm foundation undergirding all life."[11]

In "Falling," Dickey's Lady of the Animals possesses not only the vision of hawks and owls but also their "fearsome" power over prey and, most important, their powers and instruments of flight. With "a taste for chicken   overwhelming / Her" and "the air beast-crooning to her   warbling" (*P*, 294–95), the stewardess arranges her skirt "like a diagram of a bat" and thus "has this flying-skin / Made of garments" (*P*, 295). These diverse animal traits dramatically enable her to change both her activity and her character. Her fall becomes purposive, no longer the formless result of an unintended accident, but instead "a long stoop   a hurtling   a fall / That is controlled   that plummets as it wills" (*P*, 295). As the velocity of her fall accelerates, conveyed brilliantly by Dickey's spectacular visual imagery, so too does the stewardess' plummeting will-to-power increase. At one point, she alters the very laws of nature as she "turns gravity / Into a new condition, showing its other side like a moon   shining / New Powers" (*P*, 295; line 54). And shortly thereafter, she begins to become fully active by determining her own fate; that is, she will not "just *fall   just tumble screaming all that time.*" She will "use / *It*" (*P*, 295; line 79).

While magically connected to animals yet still in her human form, Dickey's stewardess also resembles a goddess who experiences a similar fall in an Iroquois creation myth called "The Woman Who Fell from the Sky." From J. B. N. Hewitt's "Iroquois Cosmology," one learns that in

> regions above . . . [where] Sorrow and death were unknown . . . a tree had been up-rooted . . . a hole was left . . . opened to the world below. . . . [A] woman-being . . . fell into the hole and kept on falling through its darkness, and after a while passed through its length. And when she had passed quite through onto this other world, she . . . looked in all directions and saw on all sides about her that everything was blue. . . . [S]he was now looking upon a great expanse . . . of water. . . . On the surface of the water . . . all sorts and forms of waterfowl . . . noticed her. . . . [T]hey sent up to her a flight of numerous water ducks of various kinds, which in a very compact body elevated themselves to meet her on high. And on their backs, thereupon, her body did indeed alight. So then slowly they descended, bearing on their backs her body.

Though the birds and animals in Dickey's poem do not bear the stewardess on their backs, they form an entourage of accompanying support that shapes the very contour of her fall. Her alignment with hawks, owls, and bats changes her fall from a "tumble" to a fall like those of "sky-divers on TV," which, at least hypothetically, offers her the hope that "like a diver," she may "plunge" into "water like a needle   to come out healthily dripping / And be handed a Coca-Cola" (P, 295). In addition to her birdlike motion, the Iroquois woman-being, like the stewardess, shares a similar creative relationship with the earth. When the Iroquois woman falls, there is no land below her, only water. To safeguard her from drowning, the ducks place her on the back of the Great Turtle. Beaver and Otter try to bring up mud from the bottom to fashion earth for her, but they die in the process. So does Muskrat. As he surfaces, however, mud is found in his paws, and this the animals place around the carapace of the turtle. When the woman awakes, she finds the mud, like Dickey's "enlarging" earth, transformed: "The earth whereupon she sat had become in size enlarged. . . . [S]he . . . saw that willows along the edge of the water had grown to be bushes. . . . [S]he saw . . . growing shrubs of the rose willow along the edge of the water. . . . [S]he saw take up its course a little rivulet. In that way, in their turn things came to pass. The earth rapidly was increasing in size. . . . [S]he . . . saw . . . all kinds of herbs and grasses spring up from the earth and grow . . . toward maturity."[12] Later in this legend, the woman-being gives birth to a daughter who in turn gives birth to a set of twins. The first twin, Sapling, tosses the sun and the moon into the sky and forms the race of mankind. The Woman Who Fell from the Sky is thus a kind of mother responsible for the creation of the cosmos, the earth, and humanity.

In "Falling" the stewardess gives birth to a special kind of "enlarging earth." After she determines to "use" her fall, the American landscape enlarges not only because she falls closer to ground; it becomes animated—animistic—and a tremendous source of revelation and energy for her. Dickey's earth is, in fact, created out of animated elements similar to those in Chinese and Babylonian creation myths, in which reality is said to have emerged out of original "chaos" when "all was darkness and water."[13] When the stewardess falls out of a layer of clouds, she beholds a new world likewise issuing out of chaos and darkness and water: "New darks   new progressions of headlights along dirt roads from chaos / / And night a gradual warming   a new-made, inevitable world of one's own / Country" with "its waiting waters" (*P*, 296).

These waiting waters, like those toward which the Iroquois woman falls, also come magically alive as the source of all life for Dickey's goddess. Even though, on a literal level, the stewardess stands little chance of diving safely into water, imagery of "the waters / Of life" is so pervasive that it constitutes a major element in the vast scenic receptacle of natural movement in the "new-made . . . world" that receives her. As she heads "toward   the blazing-bare lake," this world of water is "new-made" and life-giving because of its tremendous potential for burgeoning energy. Like a life-saving rope that cannot aid her, the moon is "packed and coiled in a reservoir" (*P*, 295), and in the agricultural and sexual worlds of fecundity that she will never know, "farmers sleepwalk . . . a walk like falling toward the far waters / Of life   in moonlight . . . Toward the flowering of the harvest in their hands" (*P*, 298). As nourisher and transformer, water is the vessel of life in the womb; its nutrients make it a medium for growth. And, of course, the sea is the source of life but also tragically the destroyer. Water thus unites heaven and earth in the "Great Round" of life and death.

By entering so fully into this perpetual cycle, Dickey's stewardess is the great Egyptian heaven goddess Nut, who is, Neumann reminds us, "water above and below, vault above and below, life and death, east and west, generating and killing, in one. . . . The Great Goddess is the flowing unity of subterranean and celestial primordial water, the sea of heaven on which sail the barks of the gods of light, the circular life-generating ocean above and below the earth. To her belong all waters, streams, fountains, ponds, and springs, as well as the rain. She is the ocean of life with its life- and death-bringing seasons." This realm is not the world of discursive consciousness. It is rather what Neumann calls "the primordial darkness" of "the Dark Mother," "the Nocturnal Mother," more specifically, "the matriarchal world of the beginning" of the creative uncon- scious that "the patriarchal world strives to deny."[14] And with its "moon-crazed inner eye of midwest imprisoned / Water" (*P,* 296), Dickey's night-world is far less the real Kansas than D. H. Lawrence's Etruscan universe in which "all was alive. . . . The whole thing was alive, and had a great soul, or *anima.*"[15]

Dickey's animistic conception of nature radically opposes that of the machine-world of the airliner with which the poem begins. While simulta- neously revealing even more about his main character, his animism recalls Carol Christ's statement: "To the Old Europeans the Lady of the Animals was not a power transcending earth, but rather the power that creates, sustains, and is manifest in the infinite variant of life forms on earth. Old Europe did not celebrate humanity's uniqueness and separation from nature but rather hu- manity's participation in and connection to nature's cycles of birth, death, and renewal."[16] Speaking in a similar vein about natural "connection" in *Self- Interviews,* Dickey paraphrases Lawrence's statement to the effect that "as a re- sult of our science and industrialization, we have lost the cosmos. The parts of the universe we can investigate by means of machinery and scientific empirical techniques we may understand better than our predecessors did, but we no longer know the universe emotionally" (*SI,* 67). Dickey's poetic answer to tech- nological alienation characterized by "the vast, sluggish forces of habit, mecha- nization and mental torpor" is to build a universe populated not only by what he has called elsewhere "the Energized Man" but in this poem by what may also be called the "Energized Woman." She is, among other things, a poetic adver- sary of contemporary commercialism. The Energized Woman is someone whose mind is "not used simply to sell neckties or industrial machines or to make cocktail conversation, but to serve as the vital center of a moving and changing, perceiving and evaluating world which . . . is that world of delivery from drift and inconsequence."[17] She does not dwell in an earth filled with the deadening rhetoric of advertising. Dickey even parodies advertising slogans: when opening *"the natural wings of* [her] *jacket / By Don Loper,"* the stewardess shifts in the same poetic line from the world of fashion to the primitive world of movement *"like a hunting owl toward the glitter of water"* (*P,* 295). Rather, the Energized Woman lives in a world filled with the dynamic energy of *"mana,"* which is, in Jane Harrison's description, "a world of unseen power ly- ing behind the visible universe, a world which is the sphere . . . of magical ac- tivity and the medium of mysticism."[18]

Commenting on the Iroquois myth, Joseph Campbell sheds further light on Dickey's energized Sky Woman and this magical, mystical power she possesses.

The Woman Who Fell from the Sky is, Campbell says, "a North American example of . . . a universally recognized, early planting-culture mythology, wherein by analogy with the seeded earth, the creative and motivating force (*śakti*) of the world illusion (*māyā*) was envisioned, and in fact experienced, as female (*devī*)." The Sky Woman is an "avatar from the Sky World to this earth, bearing in her womb the gift of a race of human beings, heavenly endowed to join in mutual regard the supportive animal population already present."[19] She is also a Neolithic great moon goddess or moon-messenger. Gimbutas notes that the moon goddess was "essentially a Goddess of Regeneration . . . product of a matrilinear community . . . [who] was giver of life and all that promotes fertility."[20] Lamenting that "there's no moon goddess now," Dickey once stated that from a scientific point of view, the moon is "simply a dead stone, a great ruined stone in the sky" (*SI*, 67). And so it is, at the opening of "Falling," that "the states" are "drawing moonlight out of the great / One-sided stone hung off the starboard wingtip" (*P*, 293). As the stewardess acquires momentum, however, the ancient mythological connection between the moon and water comes magically alive, for the moon is transformed into "the harvest moon," which races "slowly / Through all the curves of a river" and into "a great stone of light in waiting waters" (*P*, 294–96). This all takes place beneath and above a moon-bride who falls from "the heavenly rapture of experienced non-duality. . . . [T]he woman's fall is at once a death (to the sky) and a birth (to this earth)."[21]

Second Analogy: Mistress of All Desires and Joys, or Goddess Unchained

The role of the stewardess as Sky Woman continues throughout her fall, but at line 94, her "shining / New Powers" take on an even greater scope. Dickey provided a clue to this stage of change in *Self-Interviews* when he said that he tried "to think of the mystical possibility there might be for farmers in that vicinity" (*SI*, 175). Not only farmers, we might add, but all who feel the influence of the moon goddess are drawn, as

> . . . under her   under chenille
>   bedspreads
> The farm girls are feeling the goddess in them struggle and rise
>   brooding
> On the scratch-shining posts of the bed   dreaming of female signs
> Of the moon   male blood like iron   of what is really said by the moan
> Of airliners passing over them at dead of midwest midnight   passing

Over brush fires   burning out in silence on little hills   and will wake
To see the woman they should be   struggling on the rooftree to become
Stars

(*P,* 296)

At this passage, the stewardess acquires a pervasive sexual power that animates sexual instinct in all the women and men who fall within her range. This power accelerates in the following lines when, defiantly, "to die / Beyond explanation," the stewardess rids herself of the restrictive trappings of her airline uniform, "the girdle required by regulations," and "the long windsocks of her stockings" (*P,* 297). She is now Goddess unchained, and her flight is superhuman because her mystical, sexual power is even more comprehensive. She is

desired by every sleeper in his dream:
Boys finding for the first time their loins filled with heart's blood
Widowed farmers whose hands float under light covers to find
   themselves
Arisen at sunrise   the splendid position of blood unearthly drawn
Toward clouds   all feel something   pass over them as she passes
Her palms over *her* long legs   *her* small breasts   and deeply between
Her thighs

(*P,* 297)

From lines 94 to 141 (just before she enters the ground and becomes the earth's creative force), the stewardess' procreative powers lead to a stage of empowerment at which one may call her the "Mistress of All Desires and Joys" or the "Great Maya." Speaking of the Buddhist "mother-goddess or earth-mother" who "signifies the triumph of the feminine principle over the masculine," Heinrich Zimmer says, "The goddess, who 'consists of all the beings and worlds' is herself the pregnant salt womb of the life sea, holding all forms of life in her embrace and nourishing them; she herself casts them adrift in the sea and gives them over to decay, and in all innocence rebuilds them into forms forever new." She is the agreeable side of the hideous Indian goddess Kali, who after she drinks blood, changes faces and becomes the world mother; she bestows "existence upon new living forms in a process of unceasing procreation." In "Hinduism," Zimmer says, "the male looks upon all womanhood . . . as the self-revelation of the goddess in the world of appearances." And "in the secret orgiastic ritual of the Tantras, reserved to the initiate, the erotic sacrament of the sexes stands above the enjoyment of meat and drink as the supreme intoxicant by which men can attain redemption in their lifetime." She has a "magic power, which fulfills and hallows, is embodied in everything feminine. . . . [A]ll [women] have a shimmer of superhuman dignity, as vessel and symbol of the supreme natural force (*śakti*) of the mother-goddess, to whom all things owe their existence."[22]

Phrases such as "the supreme intoxicant" and "orgiastic ritual" lead to further considerations about the erotic aspect of Dickey's poetic method. This method centers on an intoxicating dream like ecstasy signaled early in the poem as the stewardess falls "with the delaying, dumfounding ease / Of a dream of being drawn   like endless moonlight to the harvest soil / Of a central state of one's country" (*P*, 293). Both nightmare and adrenalin rush these dream-states run throughout "Falling," suggesting Nietzsche's Dionysian and Apollonian forces upon which art depends, "as procreation is dependent on the duality of the sexes, involving perpetual conflicts with only periodically intervening reconciliations."[23] Insofar as Monroe Spears notes in *Dionysus and the City* that Dickey's poetry is at its best when "basic Dionysian preoccupations . . . operate in proper balance with the Apollonian elements," it is worthwhile to look at how these two Nietzschean opposites   in balance and perpetual conflict—operate in "Falling."[24]

The Apollonian or dream component of the poem can be found in the fantastic stream of explosive celestial images that flow about the stewardess as she falls and in the Olympian point of view from which she has a godlike scope of vision. Nietzsche claims that such dream-states conduce to extraordinary modes of holistic consciousness, a philosophic topic that runs throughout Dickey's poetry and is incorporated in two oxymorons at the end of the elegiac "The Eagle's Mile," where one finds Justice William O. Douglas' "death drawing life / From growth / from flow," so that in the poem's last line he may "splinter uncontrollably whole" (*EM*, 27). Of this kind of ecstatic dream vision, Nietzsche says: "In dreams, according to the conception of Lucretius, the glorious divine figures first appeared to the souls of men, in dreams the great shaper beheld the charming corporeal structure of superhuman beings. . . . [F]or Apollo, as the god of all shaping energies, is also the soothsaying god. . . . The higher truth, the perfection of [the inner world of fantasies] . . . in contrast to the only partially intelligible everyday world, ay, the deep consciousness of nature, healing and helping in sleep and dream, is at the same time the symbolical analogue of the faculty of soothsaying and, in general, of the arts, through which life is made possible and worth living."[25]

In Dickey's poem, what is prophetic (and healing) about the stewardess' visioning powers is not that she attains a truth that can be put in the form of an oracle or conceptual proposition but rather that the panoramic faculty of her eye and its streaming "openness"—that of Apollo, Nietzsche's "sculptor-god"—result in her accessibility to the Dionysian powers of the "more than human," to "metamorphosis and transfiguration."[26] That is, though she faces certain death, the energy from her Apollonian rush of consciousness and its Dionysian content "prophesizes" (meaning foretells and foreshadows) an ecstatic, life-affirming reversal of her fate; for not only are "her eyes opened wide by wind" so that she sees the earth approaching, but she also is "lying in one after another of all the positions for love / Making dancing" (P, 294) in a vibrant Dionysian ecstasy.

The result of yet another of Dickey's monstrous combinations of poetic "good / And evil" (P, 294), the stewardess's drama explodes in power by representing her Nietzschean opposites in a "perpetual conflict" that produces a stunning kind of frenzy (or ecstasy). The dramatic method involved here is, as Nietzsche says, "the Apollonian embodiment of Dionysian perceptions and influences," which produces "enchantment" as a kind of reverse irony. Instead of the audience distancing itself from the central action by knowing more than the performing character, the end of this ironic frenzy is "to see one's self transformed before one's self and then to act as if one had really entered into another body, into another character. . . . [H]ere we actually have a surrender of the individual by his entering into another nature. . . . In this enchantment the Dionysian reveller sees himself as a satyr, *and as satyr he in turn beholds the god.* . . . [In] his transformation he sees a new vision outside him as the Apollonian consummation of his state. With this new vision the drama is complete." The stewardess becomes a goddess—as does the reader, participating emotionally with her—precisely through this Dionysian state of intoxicating new vision, itself a delirious peripety. Her frenzy is a "rapturous transport," a "narcotic potion," which, like certain varieties of mysticism, erases "all sense of individuality in self-forgetfulness" or, one might add, like a mystical transport that produces movement transfiguring the vulnerable self into a greater power, when, for example, one feels the sensation of being intoxicated by speed:

> She is watching her country lose its evoked master shape   watching
>   it lose
> And gain   get back its houses and peoples   watching it bring up
> Its local lights   single homes   lamps on barn roofs   if she fell
> Into water she might live   like a diver   cleaving   perfect   plunge
>
> Into another   heavy silver   unbreathable   slowing   saving
> Element
>
>   (P, 295)

Produced by Dickey's technical virtuosity in "Falling"—the long, Whitmanesque lines punctuated by caesura, his terraces of spectacularly ascending rhythm, his striking image groups conveying the sensation of a free fall—his Dionysian goddess of motion, like Nietzsche's, gives the sensation that she is "on the point of taking a dancing flight into the air. His gestures bespeak enchantment. . . . [S]omething supernatural sounds forth from him: he feels himself a god." Of such frenzy, Nietzsche says, "The essential thing in all intoxication is the feeling of heightened power and fullness. With this feeling one . . . compels [things] to receive what one has to give. . . . One enriches everything out of one's own fullness: whatever one sees, whatever one wills, is seen swelled, taut, strong, overloaded with strength. The individual in this state transforms things until they mirror his power—until they are reflections of his perfection."[27]

The frenzy in "Falling" is not simple escapism; it is entrance into an archetypal mode of motion that features the cycle of desire and death (Eros and Thanatos) but transcends death by participating fully in this eternal cycle. Whereas Dickey's stewardess-goddess fills boys' "loins with heart's blood," she will also soon become part of "the loam where extinction slumbers in corn tassels thickly" (P, 297). This concept of life-in-death fits Nietzsche's conception of the "orgiastic," which underscores the fabulous life-affirming impulse of the stewardess even in the face of her own death: "The orgiastic [is] an overflowing feeling of life and strength where even pain has the effect of stimulus. . . . Tragedy is . . . [the] repudiation and counter-instance [of pessimism]. Saying Yes to life, even in its strangest and hardest problems, the will to life rejoicing over its own inexhaustibility even in the very sacrifice of its highest types—that is what I called Dionysian. . . . [Tragic feeling is] [n]ot to be liberated from terror and pity, not in order to purge oneself of a dangerous affect by its vehement discharge—Aristotle understood it that way—but in order to be *oneself* the eternal joy of becoming . . . even joy in destroying . . . [say] I, the teacher of eternal recurrence."[28] In "Falling," this yea-saying Dionysian power features a matriarchal component that is reflected in Nietzsche's own metaphor; he claims that this is a world in which "nature speaks to us with its true undissembled voice: 'Be as I am! Amidst the ceaseless change of phenomena the eternally creative primordial mother, eternally impelling to existence, self-satisfying eternally with this change of phenomena!'"[29]

This orgiastic power is not the power of domination or control. Rather, it is what Herbert Marcuse calls an erotic stance, which reconciles Eros and Thanatos in "a world that is not to be mastered and controlled but to be liberated." In such a realm, the "opposition between man and nature, subject and object, is overcome. Being is experienced as gratification." The stewardess' shedding of her clothes is thus an enabling ritual or dance, designed to affirm a social order without repression and to amplify her basic bodily powers, as Dickey says, in a "last superhuman act" (*P,* 297) that defies the death of the body and expresses what Marcuse calls "a non-repressive erotic attitude toward reality." Instead of the functionary of a commercial airline, the stewardess is, in Marcusian terms, "no longer used as a full-time instrument of labor"; her body is "resexualized" such that "Eros, freed from surplus-repression, would be strengthened" and "death would cease to be an instinctual goal." This transforming dance and ecstatic vision of sexuality are not limited to gender.[30] Dionysian rapture as a sexual mode of holistic motion transcending death also attracted Theodore Roethke, who reveals this account in his notebooks:

> I got into this real strange state. I got in the woods and started a circular kind of dance. . . . I kept going around and just shedding clothes. Sounds Freudian as hell, but in the end, I had a sort of circle—as if, I think, I understood intuitively what the frenzy is. That is, you go way beyond yourself, and . . . this is not sheer exhaustion but this strange sort of a . . . not illumination . . . but a sense of being again a part of the whole universe. I mean, anything but quiet. I mean, in a sense everything is symbolical. . . . [I]t was one of the deepest and [most] profound experiences I ever had. And accompanying it was a real sexual excitement also . . . and this tremendous feeling of actual power. . . .
>
> The *real* point is that this business of the dance accompanies exaltation of the highest, the human thing, and it also goes into the Dionysian frenzy, which in modern life hardly anyone even speaks of anymore. . . . [W]hen Vaughan says, "When felt through all my fleshy dress, / Ripe shoots of ever lastingness," well, *that's* the feeling. You feel . . . that you are eternal, or immortal. . . . [F]urthermore, death becomes . . . an absurdity, of no consequence.[31]

That Dickey should feature this kind of movement in "Falling" comes as no surprise, for the "Delphic trance" and world of "perpetual genesis" (*BB,* 148) are aspects of Roethke's poetic vision that Dickey has long admired.

THIRD ANALOGY: MAIZE STALK DRINKING BLOOD

It is precisely these Nietzschean opposites in orgiastic combination—joy and destruction, tragedy and inexhaustibility, power and pain—in "Falling" that lead to the third analogy. The stewardess' flight ends abruptly when she strikes the ground with a tremendous impact, which Dickey does not show but represents symbolically with pronouns—"This is it   THIS" (*P,* 298; line 143), an effect that is all the more powerful and tragic for its indirect symbolization. At first glance, this moment exhibits a cataclysmic reversal of the life-force of her flight, for immediately after she lands, she is terrifyingly:

>   impressed
> In the soft loam   gone down   driven well into the image of her body
> The furrows for miles flowing in upon her where she lies very deep
> In her mortal outline   in the earth as it is in cloud
>
> (*P,* 298)

She continues to live for a time after the impact; at the end of the poem, some thirty lines later, her last words are given in capitals: "AH, GOD—." Though she dies, this final poetic space, composing approximately one-sixth of the entire lyric, exhibits her full goddesslike nature and power in a way more compelling even than her fall. It bears repeating that Dickey does not dwell here on a mutilated woman. It is not her death that is his focus but a circle (or cycle) much wider in scope. In addition to a natural feeling of compassion for her death, one's response to her issues from a deeper recognition of the universal in Dickey's dramatization of the intermingling forces of life and death. For those who find her, the poet says,

>   can tell nothing
> But that she is there   inexplicable   unquestionable   and remember
> That something broke in them as well   and began to live and die more
> When they walked for no reason into their fields to where the whole
>   earth
> Caught her
>
> (*P,* 298)

At this point, this contemporary airline stewardess bears comparison to the great Mesoamerican mother of the gods, Maize Stalk Drinking Blood. In a painting from Codex Borgia, Mexico (*ca.* A.D. 1500), entitled "The Tree of the Middle Place," these striking images occur: "Rising from the body of an earth goddess recumbent on the spines of the . . . alligator . . . of the abyss, the Tree, encircled by the World Sea, is surmounted by a quetzal bird of bright plumage. Two streams of blood pour into the goddess, and from her body rise two ears of maize, a yellow and a red. . . . Personifying the fertile earth, this goddess of life out of death is . . . known as the Maize Stalk Drinking Blood . . . [whose] skeletal remains were . . . regarded as the seat of the essential life force and the metaphorical seed from which the individual, whether human, animal, or plant, is reborn."[32]

This voracious image of death points to a different aspect of the stewardess and of Great Goddesses in many cultures, that is, their terrible power of destruction. As Erich Neumann explains it, "The Great Mother as Terrible Goddess of the earth and of death is herself the earth, in which things rot. The Earth Goddess is 'the devourer of the dead bodies of mankind' and the 'mistress and lady of the tomb.' Like Gaea, the Greek Earth Mother, she is mistress of the vessel and at the same time the great underworld vessel itself, into which dead souls enter, and out of which they fly up again."[33] The power of this goddess, also called the "Terrible Mother," is double-edged, suggesting not only death and destruction but also new life, for out of the body of Maize Stalk grow two ears of corn, signs of regeneration and rebirth. Discussing the story of Demeter and Persephone in the Greek festival Thesmophoria, Joseph Campbell emphasizes this redemptive power in the Great Goddess when he notes that in certain primitive Indonesian cycles "goddesses [are] identified with the local food plants . . . the underworld, and the moon, whose rites insure both a growth of the plants and a passage of the soul to the land of the dead. In both the marriage of the maiden goddess . . . is equivalent to her death, which is imaged as a descent into the earth and is followed, after a time, by her metamorphosis into food."[34]

These redemptive and sexual powers constitute one phase of the cycle of life and death through which humankind passes. Dickey's goddess is Mother Earth giving birth and death to herself, for the goddess of sex is the goddess of death. Campbell notes that "the death god, Ghede, of the Haitian Voodoo tradition, is also the sex god. The Egyptian god Osiris was the judge and lord of the dead, and the lord of the regeneration of life."[35] And commenting on the primitive-village mythology of certain New Guinea tribes that include the death-feast of a divine maiden who died by sinking "into the earth among the roots of a tree" to rise later in the sky as the moon, he notes this dialectical pairing of sex and death: "The plants on which man lives derive from this death. The world lives on death. . . . Reproduction without death would be a calamity, as would death without reproduction. . . . [T]he interdependence of death and sex, their import as the complementary aspects of a single state of being, and the necessity of killing and eating [—] this deeply moving, emotionally disturbing glimpse of death as the life of the living is the fundamental motivation supporting the rites around which the social structure of the early planting villages was composed."[36]

A considerably less violent figure than the goddess in "The Tree of the Middle Place" or the New Guinean moon-maiden, Dickey's stewardess nonetheless enters the earth in a way suggesting that she gives birth to a similar cycle of generation and decay and that her death is not merely the termination of a single, discontinuous individual:

> All the known air above her is not giving up quite one
> Breath   it is all gone   and yet not dead   not anywhere else
> Quite   lying still in the field on her back   sensing the smells
> Of incessant growth try to lift her
>
> > (*P*, 298)

By accretions of these cyclic moments of death-in-life, Dickey often builds his poems out of magical circles, poetic *mandalas* (Sanskrit for "circle"); "Falling" also suggests the transference (and continuance) of the stewardess' fertile powers in the comic totems of her clothes, which, magically, are "beginning / To come down all over Kansas": "her blouse on a lightning rod" and "her girdle coming down fantastically / On a clothesline, where it belongs" (*P*, 298). Further proof that her all-sustaining, all-nourishing sexual power continues is that it is felt sympathetically in the lives and in the fields of local farmers who perpetuate and participate in her extraordinary energy when the erotic dream sequence impels them to

> sleepwalk without
> Their women from houses   a walk like falling toward the far waters
> Of life   in moonlight   toward the dreamed eternal meaning of
> their farms
> Toward the flowering of the harvest in their hands
>
> > (*P*, 298)

When "Falling" is read aloud, the poem's cumulative energy is so overwhelming by the end of the performance that although the death of the stewardess is a necessary, realistic outcome of her accident, her death has in it the feeling of a beginning. This beginning resembles the tremendous burgeoning that Kenneth Burke sees as the "frantic urgency of growth"[37] in Theodore Roethke's "greenhouse poems," where "nothing would give up life: / Even the dirt kept breathing a small breath."[38] What truly animates Dickey's earth is the stewardess' cyclone of energy that is magically transferred to the ground she enters. Rather than a death, her impregnation of the land is the beginning of a new cycle of growth and decay. At poem's end, this cycle has been put in full motion by the poet. The reader's or listener's poetic experience of the stewardess' death is not a sense of cessation but of transformation. Just as the form of the poem is the reversal of the journalistic narrative that begins the action by announcing the airplane accident, the stewardess is never more alive than when she dies into her new life. Yet one more variation on Dickey's favorite topic of poetic motion, the stewardess' death is a "fresh enactment, here and now" of a "god's

own sacrifice . . . through which . . . she . . . became incarnate in the world process"; she is a constant reminder to us that "sudden, monstrous death" is a
"revelation of the . . . inhumanity of the order of the universe," yet one is also
reminded that "to see the twofold, embracing and devouring, nature of the
goddess, to see repose in catastrophe, security in decay, is to know her and be
saved."[39]

SOCIAL AND POLITICAL ENDS OF "FALLING"

Because it involves an erotic component and the death of a woman, "Falling"
has received a considerable amount of negative commentary. By way of completing an inquiry into the form, genre, and value of this poem, the preceding
analysis may be used to address various statements about this poem and Dickey
himself. Some of these statements assess not only "Falling" negatively but also
Dickey's work in general.

First, there are the charges of sexual perversion and insensitivity to women.
In *Thinking about Women,* Mary Ellmann states that Dickey's depiction of
women is "unnerving":

> James Dickey's poem "Falling" expresses an extraordinary concern with the un-
> derwear of a woman who has fallen out of an airplane. While this woman, a stew-
> ardess, was in the airplane, her girdle obscured, to the observation of even the
> most alert passenger, her mesial groove. The effect was, as the poem recalls,
> "monobuttocked." As the woman falls, however, she undresses and "passes her
> palms" over her legs, her breasts, and "deeply between her thighs." Beneath her,
> "widowed farmers" are soon to wake with futile (and irrelevant?) erections. She
> lands on her back in a field, naked, and dies. The sensation of the poem is necro-
> philic: it mourns a vagina rather than a person crashing to the ground.[40]

Ellmann's charge that Dickey is victimizing women requires some time to sort
out. With regard to her claim that Dickey shows an "extraordinary concern
with the underwear of a woman," there is little concern about underwear that
is extraordinary at all in "Falling." The stewardess' underwear, mentioned only
twice in a poem of more than 175 lines and even then quite briefly, with no de-
tailed description of the garments or lingering preoccupation whatsoever, emphasizes the transformation of a rigidly and commercially clothed woman who
is nonetheless a goddess. In the first instance where the underwear appears, it is
mentioned briefly in four lines and is part of the stream of clothes shed by the
stewardess, not to titillate men but to animate the earth sexually as part of her

ritual defiance of mortality so that she may "die / Beyond explanation." When the underwear is mentioned, it is treated comically: "absurd / Brassiere" and "the girdle required by regulations." The poem's second reference to underwear appears in one line only and, once again, in a comic context, with the steward- ess' girdle described as "coming down fantastically / On a clothesline, where it belongs" (*P*, 298).

Second, Ellmann's claim that the stewardess is "monobuttocked" misses the point. The passenger's view of her condition is never mentioned in the poem. One scarcely sees the stewardess in the plane; she falls out at line 7, and not un- til line 118 does one read that the girdle is "squirming / Off her." Rather than stressing the girdle's "obscur[ing], to the observation of even the most alert passenger, her mesial groove," the poem emphasizes the stewardess' act of re- moving it and revealing herself as a goddess. The poem says that the stewardess is "*no longer* monobuttocked" (my italics). The poem does not "recall" the view that Ellmann derides; instead, it describes the stewardess' liberation from the unnaturally confining condition.

Third, Ellmann offers a brief comment on the stewardess' running her hands over her naked body, then dying in a field when she lands. In the last line of the excerpt, Ellmann claims that "the sensation of the poem is necrophilic; it mourns a vagina rather than a person crashing to the ground." Ellmann's sum- mary does not, however, conform to Dickey's poem. Her rewriting of Dickey turns "Falling" into a narrative of punitive reparation for the stewardess' sexu- ality, independence, and strength, a narrative whose tendency runs totally op- posite to the poem's true course; her paraphrase does not admit of the tremen- dous energy of the poem or the fabulous series of powers that the stewardess acquires. The key point Ellmann misses, as noted earlier, is that Dickey's poem reverses the tragic journalistic narrative (which begins the poem) by convert- ing a mortal stewardess into an earth goddess who lives and dies in the perpet- ual natural alternation of generation and decay. Ellmann's omission of the poem's subtext that reverses the text is a severe misreading that turns a goddess into an inanimate corpse.[41]

Rather than mourn a dynamic woman unfairly reduced to a body part, one does better to question the social and political values of Dickey's poem and to address these issues with the ideas of four strong and intelligent women. Does "Falling" challenge traditional conceptions of divinity as masculine, inherited from a Judeo-Christian religious history? What implications does the meta- morphosis of a woman into an earth goddess from so-called "primitive" cul- tures have for a contemporary Western audience? What does the poem, as an enabling matriarchal creation myth with a distinctive conception of nature, say politically to both women and men? And, finally, does Dickey's mythological conception of woman impose any limit on feminine power?

First, with regard to conceptions of divinity as masculine, Carol Christ thinks that the idea of goddesses is revolutionary. Goddesses "are about female power. . . . This power is so threatening to the status quo that the word *Goddess* still remains unspeakable even to many of the most radical Christian and Jewish theologians."[42] Joseph Campbell agrees with this traditional image of female power: "There can be no doubt that in the very earliest ages of human history the magical force and wonder of the female was no less a marvel than the universe itself; and this gave to woman a prodigious power, which it has been one of the chief concerns of the masculine part of the population to break, control, and employ to its own ends."[43] The claim that Dickey's matriarchal creation myth in "Falling" is literally a revolution—a reversal or turning around—of the Western biblical tradition of Genesis and its concept of woman may be buttressed by Campbell's interpretation of the Iroquois tale of the Woman Who Fell from the Sky:

> [T]he flight of ducks ascending to ease the woman's fall; the earth divers in willing sacrifice of their lives preparing hastily a place upon which to receive her; Great Turtle becoming also willingly, the supporting ground of a new earth, upon which . . . a new arrival from the sphere of Air, would rest . . . while the new earth took form around her—[all this] represents a point of view with respect to the relationship of man to nature, and of the creatures of nature . . . that is in striking contrast to that defined in Genesis 3:14–19, where man is cursed, woman is cursed, the serpent is cursed, and the earth is cursed to "bring forth thorns and thistles" . . . [T]he basic and sustaining sense of the relationship to mankind of the natural world and its creatures in this Native American origin myth, is of compassion, harmony, and cooperation.[44]

Borrowing from Christine Froula's article "When Eve Reads Milton," one may say that Dickey's goddess is the opposite of Adam's God, "who is a *perfected* image of Adam: an all-powerful *male* creator who soothes Adam's fears of female power by Himself claiming credit for the original creation of the world."[45]

The second question centers on current implications of the stewardess' divinity. Summarizing Rita Gross's article "Hindu Female Deities as a Resource for the Contemporary Rediscovery of the Goddess," Christ indicates five lessons that the goddess symbol of ancient myth can teach modern Westerners. Analogues to these points can be found in this analysis of "Falling":

First, the Goddess's obvious strength, capability, and transcendence validate the power of women as women that has been denied in Western religion and culture. Second, Goddess symbolism involves the coincidence of opposites—of death and life, destruction and creativity—that reminds humans of the finitude of life and points to its transcendent ground. Third, Goddess religion values motherhood as symbolic of divine creativity, but without limiting female power to biological destiny. Fourth, Goddess symbolism also associates women with a wide range of culturally valued phenomena, including wealth, prosperity, culture, artful living, and spiritual teaching. Fifth, the Goddess requires the explicit reintroduction of sexuality as a religious metaphor in a symbol system where God is imaged as both male and female.

Also addressing the meaning of a primitive goddess for a Western audience, Christ lists four reasons "why women need the goddess" (one of her chapters is also so titled) that may serve as a description of the social ends effected by the enabling mythic drama in "Falling":

First, the Goddess is symbol of the legitimacy and beneficence of female power in contrast to the image of female power as anomalous or evil in biblical religion. Second, the Goddess validates women's bodily experiences, including menstruation, birth, lactation, and menopause, and validates the human connection to finitude, which has been denigrated in Western religions. Third, the Goddess symbol in the context of feminist goddess worship values the female will, which has been viewed as the origin of evil in biblical mythology. Fourth, the goddess points to the valuing of woman-to-woman bonds[,] . . . which is celebrated in the story of Demeter and Persephone. . . . The symbol of Goddess . . . legitimates and undergirds the moods and motivations inspired by feminism just as the symbol of God has legitimated patriarchal attitudes for several thousand years.[46]

Third, speaking of "the ritual poem in feminist spiritual circles," Alicia Ostriker offers a conception of ritual that articulates the kind of potential political effects one senses in Dickey's ritualized form: "For poet and reader-participant alike, ritual poetry implies the possibility of healing alternatives to dominance-submission scenarios. It suggests nonoppressive models of the conjunction between religion and politics, usually by re-imaging the sacred as immanent rather than transcendent, by defining its audience as members of a potentially strong community rather than as helplessly lonely individual victims, and by turning to nature (seen as sacred and female) as a source of power rather than passivity."[47]

Finally, to those who argue that Dickey's treatment of the Great Goddess confines female power to maternity, one may counterargue by defining the stewardess in terms of the active powers she employs. Ranging from emotional to athletic to perceptual, these capacities far exceed nourishing or bearing only. Her dramatic character may be expressed in gerunds that disclose the plot of her transformation from victim to Energized Woman: falling out of the plane; blacking out; screaming; despairing; developing interest in her fall; dreaming; slanting; tumbling; diving; flying, seeing, and tasting like a bird; controlling her fall; arranging her skirt like a bat and thus changing the shape of her fall; energizing and watching the earth magically grow below; being born out of "chaos"; planing superhumanly; using her fall; feeling the goddess in her and other women emerge; affirming her fate; shedding her clothes "to die / Beyond explanation"; sexually animating herself and those below; landing; living into her dying; breathing "at last fully . . . AH, GOD—"; and, finally, dying into a new round of living.

In "Falling" Dickey's Energized Woman, like his Energized Man, acquires, in this writer's own words about the power of poetry, "an enormous increase in perceptiveness, an increased ability to understand and interpret the order of one's experience . . . bringing only the best of oneself: one's sharpest perceptions, one's best mind, one's most hilarious and delighted and tragic senses."[48] Exchanging electrifying traits of goddesses from a plurality of cultures and religious traditions, "Falling" is James Dickey's exhilarating mythopoeic celebration of tragedy transformed into delight and ecstasy, with a woman at the center of creation.

5

THE MOMENTUM OF WORD-MAGIC IN DICKEY'S
The Eye-Beaters, Blood, Victory, Madness, Buckhead and Mercy

Magic, then, is not a method, but a language; it is part and parcel of that greater phenomenon, *ritual,* which is the language of religion. Ritual is a symbolic transformation of experiences that no other medium can adequately express. Because it springs from a primary human need, it is a spontaneous activity—that is to say, it arises without intention, without adaption to a conscious purpose; its growth is undesigned, its pattern purely natural, however intricate it may be. . . .

[I]f ritual is the cradle of language, metaphor is the law of its life. It is the force that makes it essentially *relational,* intellectual, forever showing up new, abstractable *forms* in reality . . . in an increasing treasure of general words.

—SUSANNE K. LANGER

In the late sixties, when he collected his first five books of poetry into one volume, James Dickey had reached a considerable level of literary success. Louis Untermeyer stated that *Poems, 1957–1967* "is the poetry book of the year, and I have little doubt that it will prove to be the outstanding collection of one man's poems to appear in this decade."[1] Peter Davison and James Tulip ranked Dickey and Robert Lowell as the two major poets in the country, but John Simon was even more enthusiastic, declaring, "I place Dickey squarely above Lowell."[2] In 1968, however, with the appearance of Dickey's very next book, *The Eye-Beaters, Blood, Victory, Madness, Buckhead and Mercy,* critics seemed annoyed, even dismayed, at the new direction of his highly experimental collection of verse. Herbert Leibowitz noted that the "balance of pure abandon and meticulous observation breaks apart in Dickey's latest volume," and further, that a "stagy, unpleasant hysteria enters the poems."[3] Benjamin DeMott charged that the "poet runs on unrestrainedly," giving "no shapely object to delight in, little refinement of feeling or subtlety of judgment, no intellectual distinction, no hint of wisdom."[4] Even as staunch an early supporter as Richard Howard lamented that "the look of these poems on the page is disconcerting: forms are sundered, wrenched apart rather than wrought together." Howard then concludes with a statement of considerable strength: "The cost to [Dickey's] poetry is tremendous, for it has cost him poems themselves—there are not poems here . . . only—only!—poetry."[5]

Despite the severity of these appraisals, *The Eye-Beaters* contains at least seven of Dickey's major poems and constitutes one of the central transitional texts in his poetic canon.[6] During this period, his experiments in two basic areas—form and diction—opened a number of technical poetic doors that enabled him to produce his remarkable and controversial book-length poem *The Zodiac* in 1976 and, in the 1980s, *Puella* and *The Eagle's Mile,* two of his best volumes of verse. In *The Eye-Beaters,* Dickey still kept his eye at times on a classical sense of narrative—the story-based poem on which he built such a wide following of readers; however, he also began to highlight word-groups that radically altered his techniques of telling and gained him especially dramatic entrance to the world of darkness and terror that strongly unsettled Leibowitz, DeMott, and Howard. These word-groups reveal fundamental methods in Dickey's word-magic and the subsequent momentum of his poetic thought, which, to my mind, has been misrepresented by many of his critics—those who look for intellectual or discursive thinking in a poet who is not understandable only to the rational mind, and as a result, they find Dickey's poems lacking in elements that are completely irrelevant to his poetic program.[7] Dickey's best poems in this book are not hysterical, unrestrained, unshaped, unsubtle, or wrenched apart but are intricately constructed forms generated by a mode of thinking that is rooted in anthropological and mythopoeic criticism, namely, contagious magic.

Presupposing an ancient universal law of contact between animate and inanimate objects, even those that are geographically distant, such as the moon and stars, contagious magic seems at first primitive, simple, or scientifically mistaken. When developed through the complex combinations within his extraordinary diction, however, Dickey's version of this practical causal principle allows him to reinvent a world in which magic not only seems plausible but natural and even necessary. For out of his animated series of natural connections, Dickey constructs a diverse range of rituals, ranging from sacrificial rites to linguistic acts of creation, which, reflexively, depend on his magical ontology for their effectiveness. When constructed properly, these rites reveal special therapeutic powers designed to bring some measure of human control to the catastrophic, real worlds of "blood" and "madness." The plausibility of Dickey's word-magic takes its authority from its appeal to deeper reaches of the human mind that are closed to more discursive modes of lyric action. Not "deep image poetry" exactly, his poetry operates through archetypal images within a deeply appealing and personal mode that also engages and alters the social self, especially the self traumatized by war.[8] Although his verbal and formal magic has distinguished precedents in the work of Hart Crane, Dylan Thomas, Theodore Roethke, and even Samuel Taylor Coleridge, critics often fail to judge Dickey by the principles that have been used to canonize these writers. To establish critical criteria—especially those in a mythopoeic mode—more accurately attuned to Dickey's true poetic vision in *The Eye-Beaters*, one must focus on the issues that preoccupied the poet at this point in his career: the construction of poetic form in relation to word-magic, the subsequent shift of formal momentum in his poetry from action to image, and the shaping elements in at least one of the historic genres in which he was writing.

To initiate his keynote speech to the South Atlantic Modern Language Association in November, 1982, Dickey borrowed a distinction from the *Notebooks* of poet Winfield Townley Scott.[9] Centering on two kinds of poetry, or rather two kinds of poetic diction, this distinction is simple enough yet reveals much about Dickey's poetic practice. The first type of poetry is, according to Scott, literalistic and is marked by its capacity for moving, external reference. It is "a commentary on human life so concentrated as to give off considerable pressure." Two of its central practitioners are Wordsworth and Hardy, and it "is represented by [Edwin Arlington] Robinson's [line]: 'And he was all alone there when he died.'" The second and opposite type, less literal and more evocative in character, "is a magic gesture of language" (*NH,* 125), among whose proponents are Poe and Rimbaud; this second type is illustrated by lines from Hart Crane's poem "Voyages":

> O minstrel galleons of Carib fire,
> Bequeath us to no earthly shore until
> Is answered in the vortex of our grave
> The seal's wide spindrift gaze toward paradise.

For Dickey, the key word in these lines is "spindrift," whose peculiar qualities place Crane among what Dickey calls, following Scott, the "Magic-Language exemplars" of poetry. Instead of a literal or essential component of the seal's manner of seeing, "spindrift" belongs less to the "reality world" of animal vision than to the "word world" of verbal association (or what Crane calls, in his well-known phrase, the "logic of metaphor").[10] Dickey explains that "'Spindrift' is sea-foam, wave-foam, usually wind-blown along beaches, and, though the seal's eyes may be wide, and his gaze toward Paradise, 'spindrift' is really not, cannot be part of his vision: the word is word only, associational and in its way beautiful, but word" (*NH*, 126).[11]

Instead of inventing poems characterized by statements that have an empirical or external referential direction, the poets of word-magic work from inside a reverberating, self-generating world of linguistic interplay. According to Dickey, these writers are less interested in realistic narratives or personal anecdotes that convey maxims about the world of human action and ideas than in the evocative powers and suggestions of words themselves. This word-play may be further understood by considering its opposite: the kind of diction that belongs to poets whom Dickey calls "the literalists." Unlike the "magic-language practitioners," "literal-minded poets" believe "in words as agents which illuminate events and situations that are part of an already given continuum" (*NH*, 131). For example, "The Robinson line . . . is simply factual. There are only plain words in it: a statement. Plain words in ordinary order; nothing unusual, much less exotic. The line puts the reader into contemplation of something that happened to someone, and the condition of the happening; it is the clear pane of glass that does not call attention to itself, but gives clearly and cleanly on a circumstance" (*NH*, 126). On the other hand, word-magicians do not give primacy to plot or to the discursive revelations of character but to a dream-mode or some kind of surrealistic space in which the powers of reason have little importance. Although Dickey's remarks were made with *Puella* (1982) in mind (the book with his fullest use of word-magic and to which this chapter is a preliminary study), these observations reveal much about his magical approach throughout his poetry. This approach is evident as far back in Dickey's work as the opening poem, the magical chant "Sleeping Out at Easter," in his first collection of poems, *Into the Stone* (1960). Of word-magicians, Dickey said in 1982: "For the Magicians, language itself must be paramount: language and the connotative aura it gives off. . . . The words are seen as illuminations mainly of one another; their light of meaning plays back and forth between them, and, though it must by nature refer beyond, outside itself, shimmers back off the external world in a way whereby the world—or objective reality, or just Reality— serves as a kind of secondary necessity, a non-verbal backdrop to highlight the dance of words and their bemused interplay" (*NH*, 126–27).

However magical Dickey's interests became at this point, he never fully divorced himself from his commitment to literal-mindedness or his belief in the necessity of basic storytelling; in the same essay, he criticizes purely magical poetry for its considerable limitations. In magical poetry divorced from public concerns, Dickey says that "the *world* is lacking" and that "the buzz of language and the hit-or-miss metaphor-generation is everything; the poem itself is nothing; or only a collection of fragments" (*NH*, 138). Although he admits to being profoundly interested in "the absolute freedom" that the magical making of metaphors offers the poet, Dickey also wants lyrics "bound into one poetic situation, one scene, one event after the other" (*NH*, 139). A further problem with the magical method, especially in the surrealistic school, is that it invents without discovering, as Wallace Stevens noted. It does not reveal the contents of the unconscious but mere phantasms. Also, it has no *"drama,"* for it "cannot *build."* Of poems in this style, Dickey observes that they have no narrative, no logic, no idea-development, no transformation, no "publically available" themes (*NH*, 137).

If one wonders in which camp Dickey places his own poetic language, he provides what appears to be a decisive response earlier in his essay. Although he greatly admires the best of them, he claims, "I am not of the party of the magic-language practitioners" (*NH*, 129). At first glance, this self-classification seems true. Because so much of Dickey's early poetry depends on anecdotal narrative and extrinsic reference to topics and events from his own life (world war, family, animals, even a southern Baptist preacher), he seems justified in placing himself among those poets whom he calls "literal-minded" (*NH*, 129), for example, Robert Frost, Edgar Lee Masters, and Randall Jarrell. From a stylistic or linguistic point of view, however, Dickey's poetry also suggests an extremely strong magical orientation. In the mid- and late sixties in particular, Dickey began to experiment with word-groups bunched together by means of techniques such as the "block format" (*CM*, v) and the "split line" (*SI*, 184–85). At this time, words and their "connotative aura" (*NH*, 127) became singularly featured on the pages of his lyrics. In "May Day Sermon," "Falling," "The Shark's Parlor," "The Fiend," and to some extent in "The Firebombing," he built "wall[s] of words" (*NH*, 116) out of distinctive visual and semantic combinations that were not only striking to behold but, more important, approximated, as Dickey says, "the real way of the mind as it associates verbally . . . in bursts of words, in jumps" (*SI*, 184).

One major effect of the method (or "real way") of these mental "word-bursts" and "jumps" is the construction of an emotionally immediate if not obsessive universe in which the magical contiguity of natural forms of life and death is conveyed by Dickey's imagistic contiguities. He calls the semantic aspect of this magical contact "apparently unjustifiable juxtapositions" and "shifts of meaning or consciousness" (*SI*, 185). These juxtapositions may be rationally "unjustifiable," but from a poetic and emotional point of view, they enable the objects inside his visually bracketed word groups to exchange or share properties in an especially dramatic and vivid manner. These stylistically fused traits build scenes so rich in texture that they constitute the animating ground of the poem's action and thus possibility for Dickey's characters. "May Day Sermon" provides an especially vivid example of how the poet's word-magic "jumps" across the page with a stunning momentum that energizes the woman preacher who delivers the lines. This momentum also animates the objects of nature in Dickey's universe and reveals how he thinks magically through them:

> Sisters, understand about men and
>   sheaths:
> About nakedness: understand how butterflies, amazed, pass out
> Of their natal silks   how the tight snake takes a great breath   bursts
> Through himself and leaves himself behind   how a man casts finally
> Off everything that shields him from another   beholds his loins
> Shine with his children forever   burn with the very juice
> Of resurrection . . .
>
>   (*P*, 7)

In this section, Dickey's word-magic builds the poem's (and nature's) momentum by means of his striking grammatical strategies of predication, strategies that, as I will show, are also central to his magical method in "Pine." In the arrangement of word blocks in "May Day Sermon," nouns such as "Butterflies," "the tight snake," "man," and "his children" share the ejaculatory, universal motion of sheaths and nakedness that "pass out," breathe, burst, "shield," behold, "[s]hine," and "burn . . . with resurrection." This sharing is effected by an elaborate series of delayed predicates in parallel constructions in which the poet omits punctuation and connectives in favor of breath spaces. By keeping mechanical interrupters and conjunctions to a minimum, Dickey creates an oratorical and ontological momentum marked by "fluidity and flux," which is his specification of William James's famous stream of consciousness.[12] Dickey's poetic flow—more like a tidal wave in this poem—makes objects exchange attributes by making the mind "jump" between nouns and predicates such that a verb (and its textural traits) in one clause may be plausibly predicated of two or more preceding subjects. In the lines cited above, the subject of "burn" is "loins" but may as well be "children," for both "loins" and "children"—albeit in different modes—"burn" with "with the very juice / Of resurrection."

Dickey does not only use this technique for single terms. Because he begins his word blocks with dynamic verbs, gerunds, and present participles, he drives these blocks forward in a stream of sexual, natural, and grammatical motion while simultaneously allowing the eye to linger upon visually separated word groups so that entire groups of words appear to serve as nouns for several series of subsequent verbals. Several lines later in "May Day Sermon," a trout flows and slides upstream, but Dickey's spatial arrangement of his word-groups makes it appear that the trout's "cold Mountain of his birth" does the same, for the trout "heads upstream, breathing mist like water, for the cold / Mountain of his birth   flowing   sliding in and through the ego- / maniacal sleep of gamecocks" (*P,* 7). The metaphysical mechanism behind these shared predicates is a mode of connection that Frazer calls "contagious magic," in *The Golden Bough,* namely, "that things which have once been in contact with each other are always in contact."[13] In Dickey's poetic universe, these grammatical and ontological connections produce a magical animism in which, as Joseph Campbell expresses it, "there is no such thing as absolute death, only a passing of individuals back and forth, as it were, through a veil or screen of visibility, until—for one reason or another—they dissolve into an undifferentiated ground that is not of death, but of potential life, out of which new individuals appear."[14]

Not only objects and groups of objects are animated by mental word-magic in Dickey's world. Dickey's word-magic also drives the emotionally animating end of "May Day Sermon," which is nothing less than the resurrection in springtime of nature, sexual instinct, and the vocalized anima (or soul) of the victimized daughter, all under the aegis of the oratorical triad of energized women: preacher, audience, and subject of the sermon (the daughter). The daughter of the abusive, backwoods, bible-reading father is able to return from the dead each year precisely because in Dickey's lyric universe, "there is," in Campbell's words, "no such thing as absolute death." Dickey's world is one in which life and death cyclically and magically dissolve into and out of each other and in which the animating power of the woman preacher's eternal logos—like "men" and "nakedness"—also "bursts," "shine[s], and "burn[s] with the very juice / Of resurrection." The daughter does not die for her sexual freedom but dies as a fertility goddess who transcends death each spring, like the earth, by riding the eternal continuum of decay, regeneration, and rebirth. She is empowered, in Dickey's worldview, by the words of women and the poet's magical modes of "resurrection." The very possibility for the daughter's archetypal transcendence is thus rooted in a magically empowered and conceived setting that eternally energizes her.

If the ritualized methods and the ground of action in Dickey's lyrics took on a special primitive power in the mid-sixties, the effects of his word-magic and its reverberating linguistic momentum become even more pronounced in the late sixties and the early seventies. His magical diction is primarily effected through catalogs of tactile, concrete metaphors, hyphenated word combinations, and explosive, staggered groups of action-packed gerundives. When working in a distinctively surrealistic or hallucinatory dream mode, Dickey distances himself even further from his earlier formal strategies, realistic anecdotes, and the relatively sober revelations of romantic perception in favor of an exuberant emphasis on magical imagery. For instance, in "The Eye-Beaters," the narrator does not go inside the minds of blind children for internal revelation when he visits a home for the children in Indiana but instead externalizes his imagined vision of what they see as he addresses himself:

> Smudge-eyed, wide-eyed, gouged, horned, caved-
> in, they are silent: it is for you to guess what they hold back inside
> The brown and hazel   inside the failed green   the vacant
>   blue-
> eyed floating of the soul.
>
> (*EB*, 50)

At first, there appears to be little here of what could be traditionally called a complicated plot that changes the fortunes of its characters. Neither the children nor the narrator can change. Try as he may, the speaker cannot alter the condition of the blind children, who beat their eyes in frustration. In a sense, then, the animating end of this poem is the realistic failure of poet's magical and elaborate techniques of animation. This failure, however, is only half the equation. After acknowledging the therapeutic limits of his poetry, the speaker frantically continues to build his fictional wall of mythic images for his own sake and for that of the real vision of the children. He argues rationally that in spite of their blindness, these children are still important and that "what they see must be crucial / To the human race." Despite his claim to reason, Dickey's magic produces nothing more than a semi-hysterical nightmare of his own darkness and rage as the poet tries to see what is "under their pummeled lids" (*EB*, 54).

His word-magic is thus closer to word-madness than magic. Yet this madness has a peculiar visioning power. In "May Day Sermon," while partially maddened by her belief system, by abuse to the farmer's daughter, and by Dickey's enflamed rhetoric, the woman preacher nonetheless effects an optimistic mythopoeic reincarnation of the victimized girl. In *The Eye-Beaters*, Dickey's word-madness seeks a magic that at first appears ineffective. This magic is built out of nothing but the "sheer / Despair of invention" (*EB,* 55) in the real world, where the narrator's poetic powers cannot heal. What comes most alive, however, in this world—even more than plot and character—is the poet's mental cave of magical images, that is, the cave of "perversity" and "madness" constituted by Dickey's wall of words. It is as if he wants to take readers inside Plato's cave of illusions or inside one of the Paleolithic caves at Montesquieu-Avantes in the Pyrenees and then leave them in the dark. In such a world, "half-broken light flickers" briefly and shows us partial images of "ibex   quagga . . . cave bear aurochs   [and] mammoth" (*EB,* 54, 51). But this is a mental world that is even darker and more claustrophobic, where the poet's reason has "gone / Like eyes" (*EB,* 55), and only his primal images offer him solace from despair. One thus comes closer to experiencing the dark world of these children than one ever would have without Dickey's disturbing and dazzling poem, at the heart of which is yet another of his extraordinary primitivistic exchanges. This exchange transforms speaker and reader by linking sighted readers to blind children, even though the mode of shared vision is only—or to use Richard Howard's exclamation noted above, "only!"—poetic.

In tracing the evolution of Dickey's use of magical language, what is important to note in "The Eye-Beaters"—as well as in "Mercy," "Victory," and "Pine" in the same volume—is that Dickey's walls of words are so powerful that their contagious magical energy appears to displace plot, character, and revelation as emotionally central parts of his poetic action. These traditional shaping elements are, of course, still prominent in his work of this period. But one may well be able to claim—using Dickey's description of poetic word magicians—that in these boldly experimental poems, he has gone farther than ever toward giving primacy to "language and the connotative aura it gives off." This new primacy of parts enables him to invent a new poetic "reality [which] . . . serves as . . . backdrop to highlight the dance of words and its bemused interplay" (*NH,* 127). To put it another way, Dickey's radically magical walls of reality establish settings that not so much displace thought and character as they take on the functions of character, revelation, and the solution (or opposition) to the protagonist's driving needs. In "May Day Sermon," magical word-groups not only create the physical setting but also the animating ground of change and motivation for the woman preacher. Yet they also constitute a formal revolution, what in contemporary criticism would be called a "deconstruction," in which Dickey's word-magic achieves a parity of power with the classic Aristotelian elements of thought and action, and even becomes the central pattern of thought and action. By focusing on "the action of words upon each other, for whatever meaning or sensation they may throw off, evoke" (*NH*, 131), Dickey uses these networks of meaning or sensation not to remain mired in sensation but to invent what is for him a new kind of poetic form. Insofar as his new diction produces a connotative aura that radically alters his speaker's fundamental mode of perception while also shaping and guiding the reader's point of view, Dickey's mythical language becomes both his poetic action *and* his basic method of representation. This collapse—or fusion—of analytic distinctions is true for all poetry insofar as poetry's shaping causes are synthesized within its verbal materials. But for Dickey, his distinctive change in emphasis yields especially vivid insights into a new way of thinking through words, which themselves revolutionize his poetry.

If in this middle period of his career Dickey begins to think in a radically mytho-magical mode while quite consciously moving away from anecdote and narrative, one sees yet another reason why his poetry upsets the Aristotelian causal hierarchy that privileges plot the way did Dickey in his early work. The very nature of thought manifested in Dickey's word-magic demands this formal shift. As Ernst Cassirer notes, "Mythical consciousness . . . knows nothing of certain distinctions. . . . [I]t lacks any fixed dividing line between mere 'representation' and 'real' perception, between wish and fulfillment, between image and thing." Further, by using a mode of thought that burkes classical logical axioms and assumes instead magical principles—such as "the part not only *stands for* the whole but positively *is* the whole"—Dickey confounded many critics in the late 1960s and early 1970s by inventing an "aura" that baffled them when they applied discursive or meditative criteria.[15] When Dickey's linguistic aura became a dominant force, it produced a dream world like that of the undifferentiated reality of primitive consciousness; thus many readers dismissed the poems in "The Eye-Beaters" as formless or poorly constructed. On the contrary, these poems are intricately constructed, and further, they are designed to convey an atmosphere of nightmares or dream consciousness, which by nature is cloudy or phantasmic.

One magical mode—the conversion of properties or attributes of objects into bodies—appears in the scenic imagery of "Mercy," a nightmare poem about the narrator's lover, Fay, a nurse at a hospital in "slum Atlanta," whom he picks up at the nurses' dormitory, "Mercy Manor." By mixing hypostatized, imagistic traits of love, mortality, blood, and banal pop culture in a dazzling scene of surrealistic transformation, Dickey converts Fay into a contemporary

Persephone, macabre yet heroic. While "perfume and disinfectant battle / in her armpits" (*EB*, 15), she straddles the worlds of life and death, goddess-like, when, in the poem's conclusion, the speaker imagines himself "collapsed on the street," having a kind of heart (or love) attack: "I nearly am dead / In love." Herself a stark contrast in the colors of healing and of death, Fay leans over him as he calls for her kiss to silence the cry of mortality from his lips and to bear him safely from the world of darkness into the "mercy" of St. Joseph's Hospital:

> She would bend
> Over me like this   sink down
> With me in her white dress
> Changing to black   we sink
> Down flickering
> Like television   like Arthur Godfrey's face
> Coming on   huge   happy
> About us   happy
> About everything   O bring up
> My lips   hold them down don't let them cry
> With the cry   close   closer   eyeball to eyeball
> In my arms, O queen of death
> Alive, and with me at the end.
>
> (*EB*, 16)

If Fay, like Persephone, possesses a goddesslike power of healing and re-newal, she does so because the poet rescues her from a convincing technical, pop-cultural hell that enervates yet simultaneously animates her. As he does in "The Eye-Beaters," Dickey builds another dynamic wall of words—this time, down the middle of the page—that makes the night world of hospitals come alive in a sensuously dark dream scene. This scene is not static. As the drama develops, the setting not only gains emotional power by means of the affective accumulation of Dickey's detail; it propels the action forward by providing an overwhelming opponent of night and mortality against which the speaker bat-tles for care and love. In the night world of this hospital, love, if not life, has never felt more vulnerable. One cause of this vulnerability is the massive sense of indifference that the setting—indeed, the world—evinces toward the speaker. This anomie is reflected in Dickey's magical, imagistic hypostatization of Arthur Godfrey's smiling television face, whose mind-numbing, happy countenance benignly smiles over the night world of pain and death with the comic indifference of a plastic Halloween mask. In magical thought, Cassirer says, "The 'image' does not represent the 'thing'; it *is* the thing; it does not merely stand for the object, but has the same actuality, so that it replaces the thing's immediate presence." The reader does not confuse Arthur Godfrey with his image. Rather, Dickey so animates the banality of the image that its preposterous happiness becomes an oppressive body that is real, actual. In this animated and surrealistic space, the poet turns a complex of cultural and technological relations into "a pre-existing material substance" in which, Cassirer says, "all mere properties or attributes . . . become bodies."[16] By magically making banality a substance, Dickey provides one element in the poisoned substratum of a contemporary urban scene against which the energized passion of a goddess-woman offers temporary redemption from the speaker's hysterical wail and the dark cold world of mortality and indifference.

In this stage of Dickey's poetic career—which may be labeled a magical period in which he makes a radical move from action to image—voice, points of view (reader's and speaker's), and plot seem less like specific separable literary devices than undifferentiated aspects of the dreamy aura of his word selection. These strategically constructed word-groups reveal the movement of his mind from linguistic block to block in modes of nondiscursive, nonanalytical thought that Ernst Cassirer discusses in his chapter on word-magic in *Language and Myth:*

> Mythic ideation and primitive verbal conception [involve] a process of almost violent separation and individuation. Only when this intense individuation has been consummated, when the immediate intuition has been focused and . . . reduced to a single point, does the mythic or linguistic form emerge, and the word or the momentary god is created. . . . [T]he process of apprehension aims not at an expansion, extension, universalizing of the content, but rather at its highest intensification. . . . The conscious experience is not merely wedded to the word, but is consumed by it. Whatever has been fixed by a name, henceforth is not only real, but is Reality.[17]

In the momentum of Dickey's thought in the best poems from *The Eye-Beaters,* objects and events are individuated through narratives that antagonize and separate agents. Things and acts are also individuated through strategic spatial separations (different from the split line but an offshoot of it) and through the arrangement of his words on the page. His word blocks isolate images in focused impressions that, when grouped in his distinctive series of sequences, give the sense that a name and its referent are magically connected; indeed, that reality is built out of momentary bursts of tangible, tactile names. These names not only share the properties of what they signify but feel as if they are some essential part (or the whole) of their referents while simultaneously amplifying the emotional impact of those parts. At times, Dickey's focused images give us an animal's surrealistic enlarged perspective of heads and eyes in word-groups that themselves enlarge the objects represented. For example, in "Madness," a family hound is bitten by a rabid female fox, and the experience of sound and pain is conveyed and enlarged in a poetic form marked by the isolation of intensified moments from the story:

she bit down

Hard on a great yell

To the house being eaten alive

By April's leaves. Bawled; they came and found.

The children cried

Helping tote to the full moon

Of the kitchen   "I carried the head"   O full of eyes

Heads kept coming across, and friends and family

Hurt   hurt

The spirit of the household, on the kitchen

Table being thick-sewed . . .

(*EB*, 48)

To no small degree, the basic representational device in this poem progressively becomes the form of the poem. That is, the strategic isolation of the names of fragments of events results in a magic pointillism that fixes as its primary patterned reality the surrealistic aspects of the core event that pattern depicts. Summarized under the title "Madness," the basic narrative is simple: a family dog is bitten, becomes rabid, is hunted down, then beheaded. The stylized, magical story is considerably more complex, however, primarily because of the way it is told: the conversion of a family hound into an energized manic god of the hunt and kill who, through a narrative of hallucinatory frenzy marked by the contagious and explosive escalation of sexuality and violence, dies a divine death as a nonretaliatory scapegoat; the humans in the poem project their mimetic desire for violence upon this sacrificial monster, who is expelled from the circle of domestic safety then closes the poem's process of overflowing violence with his own execution. Dickey's verbal methods of separation, individuation, and amplification are essential to the monster-making process because they amplify the dog's bizarre and dangerous traits into monstrous proportions; his sacrificial death, dramatically mandated, purges the stable world that he has infected and threatened. One instance of this amplification process occurs after the dog is bitten. It is carried into the family kitchen, and the phrase "O full of eyes" floods the moment with what Dickey construes to be the animal's vision yet also isolates that moment with an image in which eyes seem disembodied and bizarre, as would befit a being that is in the process of transgressing normal social boundaries. That the poem is so effectively disturbing and dark reveals that Dickey's vibrant word-magic makes fully tangible the traits of surrealistic monstrosity that the poem requires for its sacred drama.[18]

Although there is none of the archetypal pairing of the intensely dramatic mythopoeic opposites of sex and violence in the three-page lyric "Pine," this poem reveals several other aspects of Dickey's remarkable—and difficult— mode of magical meditation.[19] Cast in a sequence of "successive apprehensions" (or "four ways / Of being") with a fifth concluding single-word section ("Glory"), "Pine" examines a pine tree by means of four senses: hearing, smell, taste, and touch. At first glance, the poem's process of thought appears to be built out of compounds—or in Dickey's words, "a dark / Flood"—of traits that the speaker is "opening one by one." Each section features, though not exclusively, one of the senses, which Dickey examines by means of a series of percepts, analogies, intuitions, and visceral experiences of the body. This flood of synaesthetic experience combines to form a whole of some kind when at the end Dickey claims:

> A final form
> And color at last comes out
> Of you alone putting it all
> Together like nothing
> Here like almighty
> V.
> Glory.
>
> (EB, 46)

To some extent, Dickey's mode of perception resembles the kind of accumulation that, according to Denis Donoghue, constitutes the self in Whitman's lengthy catalogs: "He begins by saying, Let x equal the self. The x equals A plus B plus C plus D plus E . . . where each letter stands for a new experience contained and possessed, and the self is the sum of its possessions. This is the law of Whitman's lists. If you say that the self—x—is the sum of its possessions . . . then the more you add to the righthand side of the equation, the more you enrich the left, and you do this without bothering about the 'nature' of the x. You assume, as most Romantic poets did, that the self is not at any moment fixed, complete, or predetermined, and then you are free to develop or enlarge it at any time by adding to its experience."[20] The Romantic aspect of Dickey's poetic identity certainly coincides with the latter part of Donoghue's observation about flow and indeterminacy. Dickey's mental method of accumulation— and, consequently, his conception of his poetic self—does not, however, depend on a mere unity that is the "sum of its possessions." Dickey does not build his perceptual objects out of discrete properties only but instead conceives a different kind of whole constituted by an empathic mode of consubstantiality. One best sees the method in his word-magic in the Melanesian concept of *mana,* the general, undifferentiated power that appears in different forms and objects in a sacred, rather than profane, world. In such a realm, not every animate thing possesses *mana,* only certain objects that evoke a sense of wonder and delight. Sacred wonder and delight in the world of physical sensation and magical things (especially animals and natural objects in motion) are constants in Dickey's lyric universe, whose various elements are bound together by a principle of shared power that Ernst Cassirer calls the "law of concrescence or coincidence": "Mythical thinking . . . knows such a unity neither of combination nor of separation. Even when it seems to divide an action into a number of stages, it considers the action in an entirely substantial form. It explains any attribute of the action by a specific material quality which passes from one thing in which it is inherent to other things. Even what in empirical and scientific thought appears to be a mere dependent attribute or momentary property here obtains a character of complete substantiality and hence of transferability."[21]

Even though the major parts of "Pine" are divided by individual sense, Dickey builds the poem's progression out of a fluid merging of properties, which is effected by collections of hyphenated compounds and jammed fragments of thoughts and feelings.[22] These compounds—especially Dickey's phrase "sift-softening"—and his fragmented syntactic shorthand recall the opening lines from the fourth stanza of Gerard Manley Hopkins' "The Wreck of the Deutschland":

> I am soft sift
> In an hourglass—at the wall
> Fast, but mined with a motion, a drift,
> And it crowds and it combs to the fall

Hopkins' "soft sift / In an hourglass" serves to remind him that his body decays with time and that he can achieve redemption only by Christ's gift of eternal salvation, "proffer[ed]" in the gospel.[23] In "Pine," Dickey's "sift-softening" does not stand for the motion and drift of a heightened sense of personal mortality. Rather, "sift-softening" is one stage in his poetic process of rendering both sensible and transferable the motion of the wind through pine needles. If yet another mark of magical thinking is that substance and force are not distinguished sharply, then Dickey's fusion of force and thing demonstrates even more fully his mythopoeic mode of transforming relations among objects into tactile living presences that he offers to perception. For instance, here is Dickey's flow of compounded properties that he unifies—or, as he says, "assign[s]"—as he makes the force of the sound of pine sensuous and therefore substantial:

> Low-cloudly it whistles, changing heads
> On you. How hard to hold and shape head-round.
> So any hard hold
> Now loses; form breathes near. Close to forest-form
> By ear . . .
> Overhead assign the bright and dark
> Heels distance-running from all   overdrawing the only sound
> Of this sound   sound of a life-mass
> Drawn in long lines in the air   unbroken   brother-saving
> Sound merely soft
> And loudly soft just in time   then nothing and then
> Soft   soft and a little caring-for   sift-softening
> And soared-to.
>
> (*EB*, 44)

Because the form of the sound of pine is difficult to grasp—as Dickey says, "any hard hold / Now loses"—he hypostatizes the pine's "sound of a life-mass" by inventing a sequence of modes of motion, each of which is assigned a distinctive trait such as sifting, soaring, and whistling. By giving even the softest sound a tangibility, Dickey makes his poetic process of perception—and thus his poetic form—substantial. What was "hard to hold" now has elements that can be held, and in a discernable sequence or form. Further, by making sound a mode of motion shared among the fragments of his "apprehension," Dickey also makes these substantial traits transferable from one part of the apprehension to another and thus to the whole percept. The form of the stanza is the flow of the traits of felt motion commingling and building toward a whole. This process of substantiation and consubstantiation begins to culminate in the phrase "O ankle-wings lightening and fleeing," which represents the magical fusion of the substantiated properties of the "sound" of pine; these properties include speed, lightness, evanescence, alternation, and texture. A few lines later in its conclusion, the stanza reveals one whole unified aspect of pine in terms of hearing. Pine's basic properties merge in the figure of "footless flight," which the reader understands can both be heard yet is difficult to hear—like the sound of pine—for it is "coming and fleeing / From ear-you and pine, and all pine" (*EB*, 44).

Another way to examine the poem's formal momentum is to think of Dickey's cataloging and combining of properties as a mythopoeic mode of predication, that is, as a preliminary process of naming—and thus dividing—an undifferentiated subject into specific predicates from which he builds a differentiated reality. As an analog of this preliminary linguistic stage of cognition, Dickey's poem makes pine feel like *mana* in that it emerges through his word-groups with what feels like its own mysterious energy and power. Like the Sioux conception of Wakanda (meaning "Great Spirit" or world creator or mystery or grandeur or sacred—the term is nearly untranslatable in English), the spirit-force of pine grows magically through animated substances and, in Dickey's case, toward an ultimate, imaginatively conceived unity that differentiates it from its ground of perception. In his primitive predication of properties and in his conception of an animated whole, Dickey's poetic method is radically perspectival. As Cassirer notes: "For mythical thinking[,] the attribute is not one defining the aspect of the thing; rather, it expresses and contains within it the whole of the thing, seen from a different *angle*."[24] Not only is each perceptual sense in each major part of the poem "a different angle," each tangible attribute of each sense is also a different angle. Further, as I have noted, each angle reveals and incorporates the whole by means of Dickey's complex movement of concrete imagery. These new angles are themselves new views, new names of aspects of pine rendered plausible, determinate, and separable from the preconscious welter of sensation out of which pine reveals itself to consciousness.

In his verbal act of distinguishing perspectives, Dickey calls pine into being through the magical power of naming. With regard to this constitutive, predicative dimension, Dickey's perspectival form is a linguistic act of Creation. Like the narrative thrust in many primitive creation myths, the direction of Dickey's mythic speech moves a differentiating human preconsciousness away from the chaotic condition of heaven and earth before things had names and thus could be verbally distinguished. What is magical and sacred about this naming is that in Dickey's poem, names do not merely signify but convey the potential powers of the things named and thus symbolically created. In "Pine," Dickey's series of imagistic potencies—for example, "Your skull like clover   lung-swimming in rosin" (*EB*, 45)—literally become the poetic essence of the identity of pine as the speaker's whole being, not just the rational component of the human mind, and engage the world of nature and its emerging objects through his nascent language. No better description of the epistemological implications of Dickey's unity-effecting word-magic can be found than in an analogy between the primitive process of object formation and its relation to language, taken from the biblical narrative of creation. Cassirer recalls that after the word of God separated darkness from light to produce heaven and earth, the distinctively human element then entered the linguistic process of genesis: "The names of earthly creatures are no longer given by the Creator, but have to wait their assignment by man. . . . In this act of appellation, man takes possession of the world both physically and intellectually—subjects it to his knowledge and his rule. . . . This unity, however, cannot be discovered except as it reveals itself in outward form by virtue of the concrete structures of language and myth, in which it is embodied, and from which it is afterward regained by the process of logical reflection."[25] Dickey's one-word conclusion to "Pine" thus signals his sacred finale to the linguistic process of inventing a momentary god. In this kind of holy and mythico-religious atmosphere, the unity-effecting name and the god's nature (or power) are thus felt, however evanescently, to be one: "Glory."

Another formal achievement derived from the momentum of word-magic and magical thinking in *The Eye-Beaters* is the most dramatic aspect of Dickey's neoromanticism: his reinvention of the ode of terror. To be sure, Dickey has explored the world of nightmares and dream consciousness from the very beginning of his work, in such poems as "The Vegetable King" (1960) and "The Firebombing" (1964). In "Mercy" and "Madness," however, his word-magic in this volume signals his fullest and most frightening contribution to a genre of poetry that was extremely popular in the late eighteenth and early nineteenth centuries. Represented on Coleridge's dark side by "The Rime of the Ancient Mariner" and "Dejection: An Ode," this genre took its criteria for excellence from Longinus' classic treatise *On the Sublime,* especially the aspect of the sublime that focuses on "the most striking and vehement circumstances of passion."[26] In Edmund Burke's opinion, because the sublime produces "the strongest emotion which the mind is capable of feeling" and because terror was felt to be an emotional corollary of the feeling of religious dread occasioned by nothing less in importance than "the supreme evil," the ode of terror was held by many to be the highest form of lyric.[27] Although there is no explicit theological component in "Victory," this historic genre—"so wildly awful, so gloomily terrific," as the eighteenth-century critic Nathan Drake enthusiastically put it—combined a number of traits that bear directly on Dickey: "To excel in this species of Ode demands a felicity and strength of genius that has seldom been attained; all the higher beauties of poetry, vastness of conception, brilliancy of colouring, grandeur of sentiment, the terrible and the appalling, must combine, and with mysterious energy alarm and elevate the imagination. A lightning of phrase should pervade the more empassioned parts, and an awful and even dreadful obscurity, from prophetic, or superhuman agency, diffuse its influence over the whole."[28]

Terrible and appalling, with a mysterious energy that appears to issue from a "superhuman agency," "Victory" is Dickey's striking nightmare poem about one of the most "supreme evils" of human experience: world war. The poem recounts the story of a GI in the Pacific Theater who anticipates the surrender of the Japanese on V-J Day (September 2, 1945) two years before the event. "[T]wo birthdays / back, in the jungle, before [he] sailed high on the rainbow / Waters of victory," the soldier drinks whiskey sent by his mother as a present, then explains to her—apparently, in a letter—how he later found himself drunk in a tattoo parlor in Yokahama, with "four / Men ... bent over me." They tattoo his entire torso with a brightly colored snake that follows the contours of his body:

> ... it was at my throat
> Beginning with its tail ...
> moving under
> My armpit like a sailor's, scale
> By scale. ...
> I retched but choked
> It back, for he had crossed my breast. ...
> Oh yes and now he lay low
>
> On my belly, and gathered together the rainbow
> Ships of Buckner Bay. I slumbered deep and he crossed the small
> Of my back   increased
> His patchwork hold on my hip   passed through the V between
> My legs, and came
> Around once more   all but the head   then I was turning   the snake
> Coiled round my right thigh and crossed
> Me with light hands ...
>
> (*EB*, 40–41)

The soldier's experience with this all-devouring, demonic snake warrants immediate comparison with two turbulent moments from Coleridge's odes of terror. Dickey's snake-filled nightmare world in "Victory"—especially "the dark side / Of the mind" (*EB,* 40)—recalls Coleridge's "viper thoughts, that coil around my mind, / Reality's dark dream!" from "Dejection: An Ode." When Coleridge turns from these viperous thoughts to "listen to the wind," he hears, with greater terror, the "groans . . . of trampled men, with smarting wounds— / At once they groan with pain, and shudder with the cold!" Similarly, Dickey's world of war is filled with the pain of men, that of his living "buddies," ready, as he is, "to sail . . . toward life / After death," along with the memories of "others long buried / At sea" (*EB,* 38). Even more important, the retching and choking of Dickey's soldier in a time of war suggest the sixth stanza from "Ode to the Departing Year," which records Coleridge's rage and shock at human slaughter carried out in the name of liberty during the French Revolution and in the massacre of Ismail in 1770. After experiencing a nightmare vision "on no earthly shore" of the departing year, whose past events and "robe [is] inscribed with gore," this Romantic poet awakes to find that his predatory dream continues to flood traumatically through his soul to the same degree that World War II traumatically pervades Dickey's poetry and fiction (even half a century later in Dickey's best and most recent novel, *To the White Sea*).[29] One has only to place sections side by side from "Victory" and "Ode to the Departing Year" to note the emotional frenzy and pain shared by the two poets.[30] After two hundred years, Coleridge's words are still striking:

> Yet still I gasp'd and reel'd with dread.
> And ever, when the dream of night
> Renews the phantom to my sight,
> Cold sweat-drops gather on my limbs;
>   My ears throb hot; my eye-balls start;
> My brain with horrid tumult swims;
>   Wild is the tempest of my heart;
> And my thick and struggling breath
> Imitates the toil of death!
> No stranger agony confounds
>   The Soldier on the war-field spread,
> When all foredone with toil and wounds,
> Death-like he dozes among the heaps of dead![31]

Whereas terror signals the presence of an emotionally animating form in both poems and indicates the genre to which each belongs, the method of closure in each differs considerably. This difference sheds further light on the momentum of Dickey's word-magic. To be sure, both poems close with a suffocating terror that demands release. Each poet has worked his way through considerable psychological pain; to remain in a state of such dread, however, is emotional, moral, and political paralysis. In short, the pervasive terror in the body of each ode demands the poet's return to action in his conclusion, lest the momentum in each piece remain mired in pathetic tragedy.[32] This two-step process—stasis and renewal—occurs in Coleridge's ending, when he warns England that it has been protected from the political terrors of the Departing Year primarily because of the military value of its geographic isolation. Threatened even as he closes, Coleridge hears "the Birds of warning sing," then personally resolves to be "unpartaking of the evil thing" and to remain alert, "Cleans'd from the vaporous passions that bedim / God's Image."[33]

Dickey, also acutely aware of catastrophic evil in human nature, needs to be cleansed from his exposure to the atrocities of war, which, like Coleridge, he personifies in animal form.[34] Although both poets subscribe to a harmonious pantheism that incorporates historic calamity as fully realistic material for the poetic imagination, Dickey postulates nothing like a divine providence—as does Coleridge when he "recentre[s] his immortal mind"—as a subsumptive or unifying principle to which he can appeal for relief.[35] Instead, on a personal level, Dickey dramatizes an inferred magical animism in which life and death are not exclusive opposites but shared moments in a cycle of perpetual motion. In a world in which life and death constantly merge into and emerge out of each other, Dickey's snake—unlike Coleridge's birds, "the famish'd brood of prey"—has a double nature. First, the boa constrictorlike coiling and physical mutilation of the snake constitute a confrontation or death encounter for the speaker, a poetic event that has an emotional analogy with his vast experience of death from war and simultaneously stands for his desire for the symbolic death of his mutilated war-self. With what appears at first to be an appalling movement, the snake then enters its subject from behind and an opposite movement begins: the renewal of the soldier, which is initiated in the poem's final line. Strangely enough, the motion of the snake alters—indeed, re-deems—both serpent and host, for the snake acquires, in Drake's terms, a "mysterious energy" that transforms the soldier, Christlike, into "the new prince of peace":

> I felt myself opened
> Just enough, where the serpent staggered on his last
> Colors   needles gasping for air   jack-hammering
> My right haunch burned by the hundreds
> Of holes, as the snake shone on me complete   escaping
> Forever   surviving   crushing   going home
> To the bowels of the living,
> His master, and the new prince of peace.
>
> (*EB*, 41)

As is the case with Dickey's animals in many of his poems, such as "Approaching Prayer," "Eagles," "Reincarnation I and II," and "The Sheep Child," the snake now functions redemptively by assuming the role of what is a shamanic commonplace in anthropological literature, namely, a power animal. In keeping with the classic mythological character of a power animal, Dickey's snake acquires a mysterious power that is both malign and benign. On the one hand, as a crosscultural symbol of the range of human evil (including war), the snake is a traditional object of terror. Joseph Campbell says: "In its threatening character, as a traveling aesophagus, the serpent is . . . an image of the consuming power of the . . . will [in nature], foreboding death to all that lives." On the other hand, Campbell notes, "The ability of the serpent to shed its skin and thus to renew itself, as the moon is renewed by sloughing its shadow, has recommended it, throughout the world, as an obvious image of the mystery of the [same] will in nature, which is ever self-renewing in its generation of living beings."[36] This ancient mythological connection between snake and moon thus enables the serpent to play its double role by providing it with the "self-renewing" power that is passed on to the soldier. In "Victory," as in "May Day Sermon" and "The Eye-Beaters," Dickey establishes yet another magical setting in which his poetic agent is energized as he tries to overcome overwhelming odds. On the road of this momentous psychic journey, Dickey's soldier struggles forward to rid himself of war by acquiring traits of natural objects that are really rhetorical, self-animating aspects of his own mind.[37] That nature should seem beneficent and helpful, rather than another debilitating oppressor, adds considerably to the momentum of the healing process.

Consequently, in Dickey's ritual scene, the moon is not static but carries with it a renewing, ancient, and magical light. For example, "two birthdays / Ago" in "Victory," when the soldier got drunk—drunkenness being another variation of the hallucinatory state of shamanic transition—he did so at night when "the moon burned with the light it had when it split // From the earth" (EB, 39). Dickey's soldier, like this moon, has been "split" by war from the human and emotional ground that he desperately requires. But this moon retains the light or the energizing possibility to split, then become something different and uniquely powerful. This possibility and process bear direct analogy to the soldier's ritual journey of healing and self-empowerment. While expressing a dynamic relation between life and death, metaphors throughout the poem further bind the motions of snake and moon, suggesting once more that in Dickey's world, there operates something analogous to Frazer's principle of a power-exchanging, contagious magic. When the soldier says, "I reached for the bottle. It was dying and the moon / Writhed closer to be free," the dying energy of whiskey's liberating hallucination gives rise to the snakelike motion of the moon, which sheds its animating light on the soldier's "smile of fore-knowledge" that he will survive the war. Similarly, just before the visionary snake emerges from the bottle, the speaker indicates another, closer, lunar connection between snake and moon that images the archetypal movement of life out of death: "Had the Form in the moon come from the dead soldier / Of your bottle, Mother?" (*EB*, 39). Finally, even during the tattooing process, the passive host gives himself over to the animating, magical motion of the snake. Earlier, he described the snake by saying "the angel / Of peace is limbless" (*EB*, 39–40). Yet as the snake covers his body, the soldier identifies with the shape and motion of this "dreadful . . . superhuman agency" (Drake's words) and so takes on its sustaining and renewing moon-energy as he notes, "limbless I fell and moved like moonlight / On the needles" (*EB*, 40).

Even though Dickey's poem suggests that the "Form in the moon" (which I read to be an incipient image of the snakehead) comes from a masculine source (albeit from his mother. "the dead soldier / Of your bottle") (*EB*, 39), and though the form's shape suggests a phallocentric image, the serpent is by no means a universal sign of masculine power. As an instrument of self-revelation and transformation, the serpent is conceived in many cultures as a feminine totem that symbolizes modes of coming to consciousness that bear directly on central religious components in Dickey's poem. For example, Campbell notes that in "India's Kundalini Yoga . . . the energy of life—all life—is symbolized as . . . a female serpent." In this sect, "The aim of the yoga is to wake this Serpent Maiden, coiled in upon herself, and bring her up the spine to full consciousness, both of herself and of the spiritual nature of all things. She is awakened by the sound of the energy of the light of consciousness (the sound of the syllable 'om'), which is brought to her first on the rhythm of the breath, but fully heard only when she has uncoiled and ascended to the center of the heart."[38] As it does in this Indian ritual initiated through feminine power, the snake in "Victory" covers the soldier's body with a motion that constitutes a hypnotic somatic meditation, a meditation that like Dickey's poem involves the total transformation and awareness of its participant. Examples of the movement of Dickey's snake warrant repeating here to confirm this striking analogy: "the snake . . . was at my throat / Beginning with its tail . . . moving under my armpit . . . He coiled around me . . . I turned with him side / To side . . . he grew . . . I lay and it lay / Now over my heart . . . and I knew that many- / colored snakeskin was living with my heart our hearts / Beat as one" (*EB*, 40–41).

In Campbell's view, the symbolic purpose of the Indian snake is to unify all of man's emotional and psychic centers, whether at the lowest point in the genitals or at the higher reaches of the human heart. This somatic concordance then leads each center along the "one way trail" to full consciousness at "the crown of the head." To carry the whole man—sensory and cognitive, conscious and unconscious—through a comprehensive healing process, Dickey's serpent enters the soldier's bowels with the ritual motion of the mythic *ouraboros*, the serpent eating its tail in the eternally circular process of separation and return to an energizing source. When Dickey's serpent passes the navel (that part of the body which Campbell interprets as a mythological symbol of the will to power and aggression) and enters the soldier, this event may be read as the poem's climactic moment, a culmination of the fully conscious, circular transformation by the aggressive, war-torn, and exhausted phallus into an instrument of peace and renewal.[39] Thinking through the physical imagery of the male body, Dickey transcends the merely physical by concluding in the mystical tradition of T. S. Eliot's poem "East Coker." Although in Eliot's words there may be a pun equal to Kenneth Burke's word-play in his essay on the bodily tropes, there is also a standard religious oxymoron that locates Dickey's poetic attitude in a well-documented series of theological traditions, namely, that "in my end is my beginning" (129).[40]

If this kind of closural magic (or, indeed, the formal snakelike movement of Dickey's poem down the page) seems trivial or reducible to static, sensory experience, one need only examine similar forms of religious meditation in other cultures, ranging from that of the Hopi Indians to certain oriental religions.[41] Consistent with the worldviews in many of these beliefs, Dickey's magical method in "Victory" is not a form of escapism but rather a nondualistic way of clearing the ego of earthly pain in order to stand outside dominating sensation and emotion, and thus to free oneself from their tyranny.[42] In many ways, the animating emotional form of "Victory" is analogous to the utterance of the mythic syllable *aum*, which carries its practitioner through levels of consciousness, beyond myriad mental opposites, to the infernal and celestial vision deep within one's soul. Dickey's magical, religious method of closure is thus both ancient and crosscultural; it is directed to an external narrative of traumatic historical events yet is also inner-directed to the most sensitive reaction to these events by the human body. That this method should involve a sexual component becomes even more intelligible when it is related to certain religious principles shared by Buddhist and Hindu sects. As Campbell notes of the Sahajiya cult in the Pala Dynasty of Bengal, between A.D. 700 and 1200,

> It was held that the only true experience of the pure rapture of the void was the rapture of sexual union, wherein "each is both." This was the natural path . . . to

the innate nature (*sahaja*) of oneself, and therewith of the universe: the path along which nature itself leads the way.

So we read . . . "This sahaja is to be intuited from within." "It is free from all sounds, colors, and qualities; can be neither spoken of nor known." "Where the mind dies out and the vital breath is gone, there is the Great Delight supreme: it neither stands steady nor fluctuates; nor is it expressible in words." "In that state the individual mind joins sahaja as water water." "There is no duality in sahaja. It is perfect, like the sky."

. . . One knows then: "I am the universe: I am the Buddha: I am perfect purity: I am non-cognition: I the annihilator of the cycle of existence."[43]

"Victory" originally appeared in the *Atlantic Monthly* in 1968. Twenty-five years later, in the fall of 1993, Dickey dramatized yet again his paramount interest in mystical momentum by using word-magic to conclude *To the White Sea*. Here, his hero-predator, the American tailgunner Muldrow, shot down over Japan, is killed by Japanese soldiers. As their bullets go through him, he does not die exactly, but rather enters a desireless, objectless, bodiless world, like the Sahajiyaian realm of supreme rapture in which "the mind dies and the vital breath is gone," which "neither stands steady nor fluctuates," and in which there is "no duality," for "the individual mind joins [nature] as water water." This absolute, circular flow—the union of life and death, waking and dreaming, pain and the absence of sensation—then hypnotically transports him to a kind of waking trance beyond even these harmonious opposites. In the novel's final lines, Muldrow's predatory quest ends when he closes his eyes and the individuality of his speaking voice dissolves into a darkened silence. Campbell calls this the "fourth element" of *aum*, "the sphere of bliss," described in the *Mandukya Upanishad* as "neither inward- nor outward-turned consciousness, nor the two together . . . neither knowing nor unknowing . . . the coming to peaceful rest of all differentiated, relative existence: utterly quiet: peaceful-blissful."[44] In the purity of his motionless motion, this soldier, like the soldier in "Victory," is propelled by the momentum of Dickey's extraordinary word-magic into the ecstatic silence that is his and its final form:

When I tell you this, just say that it came from a voice in the wind: a voice without a voice, which doesn't make a sound. You can pick it up any time it snows, where you are, or even just when the wind is from the north, from anywhere north of east or west. I was in the place I tried to get to. I had made it in exactly the shape I wanted to be in, though maybe just a little beat up. But the main thing was that I had got to the landscape and the weather, and you can remember me standing there with the bullets going through, and me not feeling a thing. There it was. A red wall blazed. For a second there was a terrific heat, like somebody had opened a furnace door, the most terrible heat, something that could have burned up the world, and I was sure I was gone. But the cold and the snow came back. The wind mixed the flakes, and I knew I had it. I was in it, and part of it. I matched it all. And I will be everywhere in it from now on. You will be able to hear me, just like you're hearing me now. Everywhere in it, for the first time and the last, as soon as I close my eyes.[45]

Conclusion

A. R. Ammons

> A substitute for all the gods:
> This self, not that gold self aloft,
>
> Alone, one's shadow magnified,
> Lord of the body, looking down,
>
> As now and called most high,
> The shadow of Chocorua
>
> In an immenser heaven, aloft,
> Alone, lord of the land and lord
>
> Of the men that live in the land, high lord.
> One's self and the mountains of one's land,
>
> Without shadows, without magnificence,
> The flesh, the bone, the dirt, the stone.
>
> —Wallace Stevens,
>   "The Man with the Blue Guitar"

The first chapters of this book examined how, through his invention of myth and ritual, A. R. Ammons approaches prayer. Though dwelling in a universe no longer inhabited by a transcendental deity directly involved in the affairs of man, Ammons' speaker nonetheless reveals an emotional need for religious belief that is exceptionally strong. Ammons shares this need to approach prayer with a considerable number of modern and postmodern poets, believers and nonbelievers, ranging from T. S. Eliot to D. H. Lawrence to Dylan Thomas. One

of the most prominent in this group is Wallace Stevens. To be sure, the topics
of religious belief and its relation to poetry inform much of Stevens' work,
whether in "A High-Toned Old Christian Woman," whose divinities are "dis-
affected flagellants," or in "Notes Toward a Supreme Fiction," where he claims
that "the death of one god is the death of all."[1] In *Opus Posthumous,* Stevens
underscores the seriousness of these concerns for his poetics: "To speak of the
origin and end of gods is not a light matter. It is to speak of the origin and ends
of eras of human belief. . . . In an age of disbelief . . . it is for the poet to supply
the satisfactions of belief." Although Stevens does not want the poet to replace
the gods, he nonetheless claims that the poet has a spiritual role to fill in this
existential crisis:

> To see the gods dispelled in mid-air and dissolve like clouds is one of the great hu-
> man experiences. It is not as if they had gone over the horizon to disappear for a
> time, nor as if they had been overcome by other gods of greater power and pro-
> founder knowledge. It is simply that they came to nothing. Since we have always
> shared all things with them and have always had a part of their strength and, cer-
> tainly, all of their knowledge, we shared likewise this experience of annihilation.
> It was their annihilation, not ours, and yet it left us feeling that in a measure, we,
> too, had been annihilated. It left us feeling dispossessed and alone in a solitude,
> like children without parents, in a home that seemed deserted, in which the ami-
> cable rooms and halls had taken on a look of hardness and emptiness.[2]

Twenty years after Ammons began his Sumerian quests, this condition of
spiritual dispossession and solitude—and its poetic consequences—continues
to dominate his speaker's consciousness in the book-length poem *Sphere,* winner of the 1973 National Book Award:

> the gods have come and gone
> (or we have made them come and go) so long among us that
> they communicated something of the sky to us making us
>
> feel that at the division of the roads our true way, too,
> is to the sky where with unborn gods we may know no
> further death and need no further visitations
>
> (*S,* 49)

If, as has been noted throughout, a central concern of Ammons is "the creation
of false gods to serve real human needs" (*OM,* 4), then this study may conclude
with an examination of his Near Eastern materials from yet another mytholog-

ical perspective, that is, as elements in the construction of his own supreme fiction. In *Sphere*, Ammons employs Stevens' famous phrase, asserting that "if truth is colorless, fictions / need be supreme, real supreme" (*S*, 36). If truth is colorless and needs concrete embodiment to make its universals intelligible, then Ammons' Sumerian vistas provide framing stories (or fictions) that reposition and redefine him within a secular world whose theological solitude requires the poet to reperform his cosmos in primal foundational elements that stabilize its random nature. In "The Man with the Blue Guitar," the realm of this return to basics is described by Stevens as a land "Without shadows, without magnificence, / The flesh, the bone, the dirt, the stone."[3]

Flesh, bone, dirt, and stone are certainly prominent in Ammons' Sumerian universe, but they are by no means all of the fictional strategies by which he approaches prayer. In addition to his invocation of elementary powers, this poet can also reinvent the gods, whose absolute "annihilation" is, for Ammons, premature: "If the gods have gone away, only the foolish think them gone / for good" (*S*, 48). Consequently, another major aspect of Ammons' mythological impulse appears in a constructive mode and is exemplified by *Sphere*. This later approach is a much less concrete and more supreme—or at least physically "higher"—fiction than that of his desert laments. The nature of Ammons' higher fictional view is indicated in the lines above, when the poet notes that even though they have "come and gone," "the gods . . . communicated something of the sky to us" and that "our true way, too, / is to the sky." With regard to this skyward approach, Ammons may well be taking his inspiration from Emerson, who claims that "prayer is the contemplation of the facts of life from the highest point of view."[4] One may also interpret this higher view as an extension of the Eastern impulse in Ammons. If at Sumer he begins to disengage himself from the sensations and pain of a profane ego, this process achieves its final disengagement (or least earthly status) in *Sphere*, whose circular design may be read as the ritual reorganization of the realm of sky gods and thus of the poet's relation to these gods. However new Ammons' direction was in 1973, his purpose is still similar to that of *Ommateum* in 1955. In Stevens' words, this goal is to provide "the satisfactions of belief" so that, as Ammons says with regard to the gods, "we may know no / further death and need no further visitations" (*S*, 49).

One key to Ammons' skyward method of prayer—and thus to his ritual mode of thinking—lies in the title to the first section of Stevens' "Notes Toward a Supreme Fiction"—"It Must Be Abstract." Stevens' argument for poetic abstraction is that one must become "an ignorant man" to truly see the sun. In other words, one must divest oneself of layers and years of interpretation to see clearly the idea of heaven while one is reinventing it: "How clean the sun when seen in its idea, / Washed in the remotest cleanliness of a heaven / That has expelled us and our images."[5] Ammons' abstractions, on the other hand, are designed to produce a vision that is less Stevens' phenomenological reduction than Ammons' own grand inclusion. In *Sphere* he says that the abstract poem should encompass "the whole measure" in order to free "the rational mind" from "starved definition," that is, to "force mind from boxes to radiality" (*S*, 50). Ammons' gods are invisible movements of mind giving shape to perception and cognition. These gods are not only ideas but also the shapes and combinations of forms that ideas acquire. Ammons' mental deities are disembodied and characterless, more like the Sumerian wind-ghosts than Stevens' robust "ring of men" chanting "in orgy on a summer morn / Their boisterous devotion to the sun, not as god, but as a god might be":[6]

> the gods near
> their elemental or invisible selves turn or sweep or
> stand still and fill us with the terror of apprehending . . .
>
> shape, definition, ease: thank the gods for those
>
> though only the least gods will take them on or those
> gods are least who do: but the real gods, why talk
> about them, unavailable: they appear in our sight when they
>
> choose and when we think we see them whole, they stall
> and vanish or widen out of scope: the highest god
> we never meet . . .
>
> (*S*, 16–17)

The truly false god that Ammons must battle is, like Stevens', a complex of outmoded fiction or, more specifically, "the god that rolls up circles of our linear / sight in crippling disciplines / tighter than any climb" (*CP*, 35). This god of "crippling disciplines" is Ammons' Sumerian version of Blake's Urizen; and Ammons' seer is, in this regard, Blake's Los. As the "Prophet of Eternity" who reveals truths to man and beats on the "iron links" of the limiting "dark Demon" Urizen, Los brings light to "the dark regions of sorrow, / Giving to airy nothing a name and a habitation."[7] So Ammons' seer grapples with the deities of mental darkness and loss of light by climbing higher and higher in circles of comprehension rather than confining himself to the limiting motion of straight lines. To remove layers of fictions, religious and otherwise, the poet's view also goes outward. Ammons says that it should "ramble around without constriction or distortion / (debilitating exclusion) until the big sky opens the freedom // between design and designed airiness" (*S*, 71). In the long poem "Essay on Poetics" he answers Stevens' key question from "Sunday Morning"—"where, then, is paradise?"—by using the Sumerians once again and by sounding like Stevens, even though he develops a special abstract idiom centering on one of his favorite pair of terms, *the One* and *the Many:*

> . . . [many] expresses itself into the
> manageable rafters of salience, lofts to comprehension, break
>
> out in hard, highly informed suasions, the "gathering
> in the sky" so to speak, the trove of the mind, tested
> experience, the only place to stay, where the saints
>
> are known to share accord and wine, and magical humor floats
> upon the ambient sorrow: much is nearly stable there,
> residence perpetual, more than less, where gold is utterly
>
> superfluous and paves the superfluous streets, where phenomena
> lose their drift to the honey of eternity: the holy bundle of
> the elements of civilization the Sumerians said: the place
>
> where change is mere disguise, where whatever turns turns
> in itself
>
> (*CP*, 300)

A second key to Ammons' skyward approach to prayer may be found in Stevens' observation from his prose piece "Two or Three Ideas," which is that "the style of a poem and the gods themselves are one."[8] To this equation may be added the fact that the style of Ammons' poetic Sumer—where is found "the holy bundle of the elements of civilization"—is also one with the poem and the gods. Ammons' paradise is not a spatial entity but a lyric synthesis of thought and ritual; it employs an abstract diction but is dramatized structurally by a mode of motion that alternates between shape (generated primarily by uniform three-line stanzas and discrete units of consecutive argument) and shapelessness (an overall pattern of episodic argument). In this mode the power of the poet, like that of the ancient gods, is manifested by segments of order alternating with semantic chaos and thus continuously embodies a process of creation by which Ammons makes his cosmos habitable and intelligible. In this ritual flow effected by abstract (or invisible) gods, Ammons employs an analogy to the Sumerian wind god, Enlil, who exemplifies the synthetic power of the abstract poem in which structure, style, and gods become one:

> . . . the abstract poem goes out and never
> comes back, weaves the highest plume of mind beyond us . . .
>
> the abstract poem, yearning
> into the lean-away, acquires a skeleton to keep it here, and
>
> its jangling dance shocks us to attend the moods of lips
> the liquid changes of the spiritual eye: the abstract poem
> cleaves through the glassy heights like the hump of a great
>
> beast, the rising reification, integration's grandest, most
> roving whale: in this way Enlil became a god and ruled
> the sky: in this way earth became our mother: in this way
>
> [section break]
> angels shaped light
>
> (S, 71)

By referring to Enlil, Ammons once again reminds us of the degree to which his world is mythopoeically formulated. The world-ordering motion of his poetic form not only assumes the archetypal shape of the sphere, it does so within a cosmos that takes the life-enhancing possibility of orderly motion from a meteorological myth of the Sumerian skies. Because of this assumption, the poem's magical "way" is the way of Ammons' Sumerian wind god, which is also the heavenly way that "angels shaped light." All of these ways share central properties with the wind, which was an essential force in Sumerian cosmology. In *History Begins at Sumer*, Samuel Kramer notes that the Sumerians "recognized a substance which they called *lil*, a word whose approximate meaning is 'wind' (air, breath, spirit); its most significant characteristics seem to be movement and expansion, and it therefore corresponds roughly to our 'atmosphere.'"[9] Ammons' Sumerian firmament is analogous to the "mist" of creation from Genesis 2:6, which "watered the whole face of the ground" and thus enabled the plants and herbs of the fields to grow. An even closer analogue to the creation narrative in Genesis is Ammons' use of "lil," which is like the breath of the Lord God, who took "the dust of the ground" and "breathed . . . the breath of life" into Adam's nostrils so that "man became a living soul" (Genesis 2:7). The movement and expansion of Ammons' poem, which destroys and reinvents the supreme fictions of its own divinities, moves like Enlil in his double nature as benign and malign wind:

> The mighty one, Enlil,
>   whose mighty utterance cannot be changed,
>   he is the storm, is destroying the cattle pen,
>   uprooting the sheepfold.
>   My roots are torn up! My forests denuded![10]

In the mythopoeic sky (or mythic space) that responds to Ammons' "mighty utterance"—an utterance that he both believes and disbelieves, like Dickey in "Approaching Prayer," when at one point he calls it "magnum hokum" (*S*, 77)—the divinely comic atmosphere of the mind is a magically charged monism. In such a world of transformation and possibility, when a poetic image becomes a synecdochic representative of its own class of things—say, for instance, like a god standing for a class of human powers—it explodes the boundaries of that classification, producing in the mind a liberating mystical radiance. This radiance destroys the boundaries and limits of that class, dissolving its content into the originary image of "a mere seed / afloat in radiance." This liberating event, which frees the mind from the restrictions of division, is "the source of spirit" and generates Ammons' version of eternity; for, he says, "the mind will forever work in this way," and thus "the spiritual, the divine" will "always be with us" (*S*, 39). In a radically assimilative ontology of circular internalized motion, the elements of setting, style, gods, and poem fuse into a whole, marked by an upward motion of mind reminiscent of Plotinus' magical monism. In such a world, Ammons' sphere becomes the ultimate ground of luminous undifferentiation—beyond the traditional dualisms of subject and object, knower and known, ego and desire—where quester, quest, poem, and prayer become one: "The quester holds knowledge still of the ground he rests on, but, suddenly, swept beyond it all by the very crest of the wave of Intellect surging beneath, he is lifted and sees, never knowing how; the vision floods the eyes with light, but it is not a light showing some other object, the light is itself the vision. No longer is there thing seen and light to show it, no longer Intellect and object of Intellection; this is the very radiance that brought both Intellect and Intellectual object into being . . . and allowed them to occupy the quester's mind. With This he himself becomes identical with that radiance."[11]

JAMES DICKEY

Woman of the child

I was, I am shone-through now
In circles, as though the moon in my hand were falling

Concentrically, on the spirit of a tree
With no tree thought of, but with

High-concentrate quiet, and the curving essence of God-ruined
                                                    God-willed
God-moved slow stone   I am shining for the first time   at last
All-told. . . .

—JAMES DICKEY,
"Deborah, Moon, Mirror, Right Hand Rising"

If A. R. Ammons approaches prayer through an archetypal method of ascension that propels him by forces analogous to the breath of a Sumerian wind god, James Dickey also finds the power of prayer in somatic modes of mythological motion. In the above excerpt from *Puella*, Dickey effects a liminal rite— one by which he enters "into / / New Being angled with thresholds"—through the rejuvenating power of his wife, Deborah, an Energized Woman whose mythopoeic body is similar in its strengths to that of the stewardess-goddess in "Falling." Deborah is yet another of Dickey's life-giving and life-transforming women who traverse the realms of life and death, whom Dickey began to dramatize in the middle and late sixties in such major poems as "May Day Sermon," "The Fiend," and "Mercy." Like the cumulative power that Ammons effects by gathering stones, Deborah's primal strengths manifest themselves through an ancient combination of circles, stones, and trees. This combination demarcates a sacred space—which constitutes not only Deborah's body but the world's body and the poet's body as well—in a magical atmosphere of meteorological forces equivalent to Ammons' Sumerian *lil*. Thus, Dickey's mythopoeic Deborah can claim that the "moon . . . moves in strong rings / Through me, leaving something in the air between / the moon and sun" (*PU*, 15). In Dickey's concentric world of moons, suns, and rings, the power of God is also circular (or curving), and it is invisible, an essence rendered sensible through the elemental substance of "slow stone," which is "God-ruined / God-willed," and "God-moved." Insofar as Dickey uses circles to transform linear, historic time into what Eliade calls the "eternal mythical present," the stone is "slow" because the time of the poem is "indefinitely recoverable," "reversible," and "repeatable." In a world of time and space that is "periodically reintegrated by means of rites," Dickey is eternally reborn through the goddesslike power of the "Woman of the child / I was."[12] The result is a ritualized mode of renewal that defines all of creation in terms of feminine space:

> A woman's live playing of the universe
> As inner light, stands clear,
> And is, where I last was.
>
> (*PU*, 16)

By making sacred space accessible to sensory experience through the body of a woman—a feminized version of Ammons' "way" that the "angels shaped light" (*S*, 71)—Dickey reveals a major mode of prayer that runs throughout his poetry. Much of his work, to use Eliade's apposite phrase from *Myth, Dreams, and Mysteries,* constitutes a "quest for sanctity," that features what Eliade calls "a religious use of 'sensibility,'" thus making many of Dickey's narrative forms sacramental. While discussing shamans as "*specialists in ecstasy,*" Eliade poses a question that focuses on this sacred aspect of Dickey's ritualized technique when he asks "to what degree . . . the attainment of a condition regarded as superhuman may be reflected in the senses." This question serves as an especially fitting conclusion to this book's discussion of Dickey, insofar as the concern has been with how, romantically and mythologically, he renders his conception of nature supernatural, or to put it another way, how he spiritualizes natural objects, which in his world become "God-ruined / God-willed / God-moved." If any doubt remains that Dickey's work has a strong sacramental aspect, one should turn again to Eliade, who indicates that ecstatic spiritual transport to God, effected through the senses, is not limited to shamans and so-called primitive cultures: "These privileged beings are [not] the only ones in whom sensory activity is capable of taking on religious values or significance. . . . When the collective religious life is centered in a 'sensory experience'—such as . . . the communion of the first-fruits, which lifts the tabus on food-stuffs and makes it possible to eat the new harvest—the act in question is at once a sacrament and a physiological action. . . . In short, throughout religious history, sensory activity has been used as a means of participating in the sacred and attaining to the divine."[13]

As in "Deborah, Moon, Mirror, Right Hand Rising," this ancient method of approaching prayer is especially relevant to *Puella*, in which Deborah's body—and by extension, women's bodies—renders space and time both sensuous and sacred through Dickey's accumulated complex of hyphenated compounds. In "Ray-Flowers," for instance, Deborah "as Winged Seed" descends in an originating motion—again, analogous to that of the stewardess–sky goddess in "Falling"—which transforms the poet's cosmos into a fertile realm of light and flowers; for she is "Sight-softening   space-massing / Time-thickening   time-floating   more // Light // Unparalleled" in "harmonic distances" filled with "Sunflowers   dandelions   thistles" (*PU*, 27). In so descending, Deborah energizes and sanctifies the space around her by means of a specific mythological method which Cassirer, in *The Philosophy of Symbolic Forms*, describes in a way that echoes Eliade's pairing of the sacred and the sensual: "At primitive levels of mythical consciousness, 'power' and 'sacredness' . . . appear as kinds of things: sensuous, physical somethings which adhere to specific persons or things as their vehicle." In this kind of somatic consciousness, the god's power and its space are one, for "the relation between what a thing 'is' and the place in which it is situated is never purely external and accidental; the place is itself a part of the thing's being." In such a realm, space thus becomes sacred: "The rigid limit between 'inside' and 'outside,' the 'subjective' and the 'objective,' does not subsist as such but begins . . . to grow fluid. The inward and outward do not stand side by side, each as a separate province; each, rather, is reflected in the other, and only in this reciprocal reflection does each disclose its own meaning. . . . Hallowing begins when a specific zone is detached from space as a whole, when it is distinguished from other zones and one might say religiously hedged around."[14]

In Dickey's mythological mode of poetic prayer, Deborah's body flows into and out of conventional coordinates of space and time, thus turning the two into an "eternal mythical present" (Eliade's phrase), or what Dickey calls "millennial air-space." Within this reconstituted cosmos, this reflexive reciprocity coverts—or disembodies—her into a pure spirit of motion, an inward and outward force that so detaches her own sacred zone from "space as a whole" that she is "empowered with blurr." Deborah is

> Super-nerved with weightlessness:
>
> All girls of cloud and ego in your time,
> Smoked-out of millennial air-space,
> Empowered with blurr, lie down
> With bindweed force   with angelic clutter and stillness
>
> As I hold out and for you unfold
> This feather-frond of a bird
> Elsewhere . . .
>
> (*PU*, 28)

The "feather-frond of a bird" is especially relevant here, for in addition to Dickey's deification of women, another major aspect of how he renders the spiritual sensory—and thus attains to the divine—may be found in the ritual magic of the flight of birds. In his nine-page poem "Reincarnation II," an unidentified office worker finds himself transformed fantastically into a migrating sea bird, flying by instinct over the South Pole. Like many of Dickey's lucidly hypnotic forms, this lyric begins with a chant, a circle, and a spirit:

> One can do   one begins to   one can only
>
> Circle   eyes wide with fearing the spirit
> Of weight   as though to be born   to awaken to what one is
> Were to be carried   passed out
> With enormous cushions of air under the arms
> Straight up   the head growing stronger
> And released between wings near an iceberg
>
> It is too much to ask   to ask
> For   under the white mild sun
> On the huge frozen point to move
>
> As one is so easily doing
>
> Boring into it with one's new
> Born excessive eye   after a long
> Half-sleeping self-doubting voyage . . .
>
> (*P,* 243)

Even in these opening fourteen lines, key terms and word-groups suggest that this poem involves more than the mere material description of a bird in flight. "Circle," "fearing the spirit / / Of weight," "born   to awaken to what one is"— all point to a direction of ascension that is not merely upward but also from a limiting condition, a "weight," into a new birth or fuller consciousness of what one can become. Renewal is signaled by the prominence of the word "born" in line 3 and by the same word being featured in lines 12 and 13, where the subject possesses a "new / born excessive eye."

This eye is excessive because it is not human. It is the monstrous vision of an agent in transformation, whose "head" is "growing stranger" while finding itself mysteriously "released between wings near an iceberg" in its strange new animal form. As was noted in "Approaching Prayer" (additionally, in "The Sheep Child," "Madness," and "Reincarnation I"), animals that traverse species in Dickey's world of radical exchange effect ancient rites of renewal through multiple perspectives that render them totemic. They not only possess dynamic kinds of strengths from their animal natures—for example, the ability to fly, soar, hunt, see great distances, and their ferocity and courage—they enable Dickey's narrators to make human passage by means of the same empowering traits and thus become the human agents' emblems of power and protection. Among their ancient primitive functions, totem animals enabled primitive man to return to a paradise to which humans once could ascend and talk with the gods but from which they have fallen, either because of original sin or a rupture that catastrophically interrupted the celestial communication between heaven and earth. Thus, through the language of animals or the imitation of their behavior, a weakened or fallen mortal can attain a spiritual life far greater than that of his present condition. So it is in "Reincarnation II" that the human aspect of the subject is lame when compared with its powers of animal flight, which propel him in "a new start" in which the "air in the upper world" splits his human "lips," turning them into an appropriate instrument for the language of animals:

> With a cold new heart
> With celestial feathered crutches
> A "new start" like a Freudian dream
> Of a new start   he hurtles as if motionless
> All the air in the upper world
> Splitting apart on his lips.
>
> (*P*, 244)

The paradise—or state of mind—to which man returns is not, according to Eliade, mere nostalgia for a mythical solution to economic problems for which religion is an opiate; it is the source of real options and possibilities, a source of actual transcendence, personal freedom, and change: "Upon the different but interconnected planes of . . . active imagination, of mythological creation and folk-lore, of ritual and of metaphysical speculation, and, finally, upon the plane of ecstatic experience, the symbolism of ascension always refers to a breaking-out from a situation that has become 'blocked' or 'petrified,' a rupture of the plane which makes it possible to pass from one mode of being into another—in short, liberty 'of movement,' freedom to change the situation, to abolish a conditioning system."[15] Dickey echoes exactly these liminal dynamics when he notes toward the end of his poem that "to be dead / In one life is to enter / Another   to break out   to rise above   the clouds" (*P*, 249). Dickey's terminology of ascension leads me to believe that "Reincarnation II" is a primordial paradisiac myth, not of escape but of freedom and possibility effected through the friendship and language of animals; this transformation is by no means mere regression to a lower biological level. Rather, it is an ecstatic unification of those aspects of the psyche that operate in dream space or in a "waking-dream," where *"weight is abolished,"* such that "an ontological mutation has occurred in the human being himself."[16]

This flight may very well be a naturalistic allegory for the magical movement of the mind, which is analogized in the *Rig Veda* to the flight of birds. Like Ammons' rituals of circling and chanting, Dickey's animal rite takes us through a comprehensive, somatic, and religious experience that evokes and unifies conscious and unconscious elements through its vast word blocks of celestial imagery, analogous in their powers of transport to the cumulative effect of Whitman's great catalogs. Dickey's restorative experience specifically assumes—to modify two of Eliade's poignant observations about the efficacy of myths in archaic societies—that a *"return to* [instinctive or intuitional] *origins gives a hope of rebirth"* and that "life cannot be *repaired,* it can only be *recreated* by a return to [instinctual, animal] sources."[17] Thus, the essential emotion of "Reincarnation II" is that of a wonderful purifying hope effected by the poem's mythological narrative of rebirth, return, and recreation, all dramatized on the wings of the poet's animal totem:

> Dawn   Panic   one moment of thinking
> Himself in the hell of thumbs   once more   a man
> Disguised in these wings   alone   No   again
> He thinks   I am here   I have been born
> This way   raised up from   raised up in
> Myself   my soul
> Undivided at last . . .
>
> (*P,* 248)

What Dickey returns to is not mere animal or sensory instinct but rather a poetic action that models itself on the continuous repetition of a paradigmatic act of creation, whereby a sacred space of human possibility is demarcated and defined by the motion of its empowering agent. In the poem's concluding lines, Dickey's subject ends up, like the mythic Deborah and like so many of Dickey's totemic animals, with a double vision: half human, half instinctive, in a motion that neoplatonically aligns itself with larger modes of cosmic rhythm, uniting heaven, earth, man, and the objects of nature; Dickey's bird-man is, finally,

Oriented by instinct   by stars
By the sun in one eye the moon
In the other   bird-death

Hovers for years on its wings
With a time sense that cannot fail
Waits to change
Him again   circles   abides   no feather
Falling   conceived by stars and the void
Is born perpetually
In midair   where it shall be
Where it is.

(*P,* 251)

For A. R. Ammons, the God of his early poetry is some kind of supreme fiction or personified ritual whereby deities are destroyed and then invented through the reconstituted self in ceremonial symbols constructed within sacred zones. Similarly, for James Dickey, God is a romanticized, energized construct of personal realignment of the human soul through larger forces of nature to a variety of empowering emotional ends. In *The Symbols of Transformation,* Jung provides an apt summary of this reader's experience of what is "God-ruined / God-willed" and "God-moved" in Dickey's work:

Psychologically . . . God is the name for a complex of ideas grouped round a powerful feeling; the feeling-tone is what really gives the complex its characteristic efficacy, for it represents an emotional tension which can be formulated in terms of energy. . . . If one worships God, sun, or fire, one is worshipping intensity and power, in other words the phenomenon of psychic energy as such, the libido.
    . . . psychic energy or libido creates the God-image by making use of archetypal patterns, and that man in consequence worships the psychic force active within him as something divine. . . . From the psychological point of view, the God-image is a real but subjective phenomenon. As Seneca says, "God is near you, he is with you, he is within you," or, as in the First Epistle of John, "He who does not love does not know God; for God is love," and "If we love one another, God abides in us."[18]

Yet as Laurence Lieberman has pointed out, Dickey is not only an inward but also a worldly mystic, so that his divinity entails both directions simultaneously, as does Whitman's in "Song of Myself":

And I know that the hand of God is the promise of my own,
And I know that the spirit of God is the brother of my own,
And that all the men ever born are also my brothers, and the
    women my sisters and lovers.[19]

In their mythological modes, Ammons and Dickey give the reader access to a God-moved, primitive world of archetypal forces so emotionally refreshing that one may very well agree with Eliade's claim "that modern man's only real contact with cosmic sacrality is effected by the unconscious, whether in his dreams and his imaginative life or in the creations that arise out of the unconscious (poetry, games, spectacles, etc.)."[20]

If one should wonder to whom Ammons and Dickey pray, I will offer these sentiments of Frederic W. H. Myers, cited by William James in *The Varieties of Religious Experience.* Myers gives as good a general definition of prayer as one is likely to find for the informing, lyric stances of Ammons and Dickey: "*Prayer* is the general name for that attitude of open and earnest expectancy. If we then ask to *whom* to pray, the answer (strangely enough) must be that *that* does not much matter. The prayer is not indeed a purely subjective thing;—it means a real increase in intensity of absorption of spiritual power or grace;—but we do not know enough of what takes place in the spiritual world to know how the prayer operates;—*who* is cognizant of it, or through what channel the grace is given."[21]

In their willingness to experiment with a wide range of mythological and ritual motifs, Ammons and Dickey share this poetic attitude of "open and earnest expectancy"—one of their most appealing features—though neither claims, by any means, to know how prayer operates or how grace is given. Indeed, they may both say with Whitman that "I hear and behold God in every object, yet understand God not in the least."[22] Furthermore, both reveal a wonderful "intensity of absorption of spiritual power," whether they build cairns in mid-desert or put the head of a ceremonial boar over their own. This absorption is most strongly reflected in their faith in the linguistic miracle of prayer, a miracle that their poetry constantly approaches, whereby the barren human condition is continually transformed from chaos into cosmos or, as Eliade notes, from chaos into culture, where "*the World reveals itself as language.*"[23] Just such a place is found in Dickey's moving conclusion to "Approaching Prayer," a poetic place where past and present are recoverable in a sacred stillness that unites blood and memory, angels and planets, a living son and a dead father—in short, an ancient yet fully contemporary place, which all can approach and where all can pray:

> Where I can say only, and truly,
> That my stillness was violent enough,
> That my brain had blood enough,
> That my right hand was steady enough,
> That the warmth of my father's wool grave
> Imparted love enough

And the keen heels of feathery slaughter
Provided lift enough
For something important to be:

That, if not heard,
It may have been somehow said.

(*P*, 168)

NOTES

PREFACE

1. René Girard, *Violence and the Sacred* (Baltimore, 1977), 124.

2. Robert Kirschten, *James Dickey and the Gentle Ecstasy of Earth: A Reading of the Poems* (Baton Rouge, 1988), 125.

3. Throughout this study, I cite Frazer, Joseph Campbell, and Mircea Eliade, to name but three, as serious commentators on myth and ritual. All three writers have been vigorously attacked by a considerable number of scholars and critics, ranging from anthropologists of various conceptual persuasions to recent proponents of rhetorical deconstruction. Indeed, although the first edition of Frazer's *The Golden Bough* was published in 1890, anthropologist Edmund Leach argued in 1966 that as early as 1910, "Frazer had ceased to matter" in British anthropological circles ("On the 'Founding Fathers,'" *Current Anthropology*, VII [1966], 561). Social anthropologist Marilyn Strathern goes even further in noting that "Frazer has not for many years—some would say never—held a respectable place in the history of the discipline. On the contrary, modern British anthropology knows itself not just non-Frazerian but quite positively anti-Frazerian" ("Out of Context: The Persuasive Fictions of Anthropology," in *Modernist Anthropology: From Fieldwork to Text*, ed. Marc Manganaro [Princeton, 1990], 85). Of course, such debates are vastly beyond the scope of a book of practical criticism on Ammons and Dickey. My own use of Frazer, Campbell, and Eliade is pragmatic, psychological, and poetic. All of their statements are used herein primarily as hermeneutic analogies designed to explore how myth and ritual are employed by the two poets under consideration, not as unassailable authoritarian descriptions of a wide diversity of cultural practices. My employment of Campbell (and others), for instance, coincides with William Doty's estimation of Campbell's value in *Mythography: The Study of Myths and Rituals* (Tuscaloosa, Ala., 1986): "His works have had importance more as resources for comprehending a wide range of mythological perspectives than as contributions to a methodological posture" (176). Whatever the strengths or limits of these anthropological perspectives, they are designed to show how Ammons and Dickey think through their

"primitive" materials; and if the reader believes that, say, Frazer's conception of sympathetic magic is irrelevant to contemporary human experience and culture—literary or otherwise—I urge him or her to examine such counterstatements as Daniel Lawrence O'Keefe's six-hundred-page *Stolen Lightning: The Social Theory of Magic* (New York, 1982), which traces magic as a form of social action through a vast range of contexts extending from religion to depth psychology to legal institutions and practices. See also the chapters "Rhetoric and Primitive Magic" and "Realistic Function of Rhetoric" in Kenneth Burke's *A Rhetoric of Motives* (Berkeley, 1969), 40–46. One may also add that my line of inquiry is not, to put it mildly, the only one that has employed Frazer for literary purposes, as John Vickery attests in his magisterial study *The Literary Impact of "The Golden Bough"* (Princeton, 1973) and in his collection *Myth and Literature: Contemporary Theory and Practice* (Lincoln, Nebr., 1966).

On the other hand, the reader—including the practical critic—should be aware of the criticisms leveled against the anthropological commentators cited in this volume. See, for example, Marc Manganaro's insightful yet extremely aggressive deconstruction of Frazer and Campbell in *Myth, Rhetoric, and the Voice of Authority: A Critique of Frazer, Eliot, Frye, and Campbell* (New Haven, 1992), plus articles by Vickery and Roth in Manganaro's edited volume *Modernist Anthropology*. See also Jonathan Z. Smith's critique of Frazer in "When the Bough Breaks" (*Map Is Not Territory: Studies in the History of Religions* [Chicago, 1978], 208–39), and critiques of Eliade in *Religion on Trial: Mircea Eliade and His Critics*, by Guilford Dudley III (Philadelphia, 1977). For an excellent comprehensive overview of the conflicting literary uses of "ritual," see Richard F. Hardin's "'Ritual' in Recent Criticism: The Elusive Sense of Community," *PMLA*, XCVIII (1983), 846–62.

4. E. B. Tylor, *Primitive Culture* (London, 1929), 453.

5. William Harmon, "Herself as the Environment," *Carolina Quarterly*, XXXV (Fall, 1982), 91.

6. Sir James George Frazer, *The Golden Bough* (New York, 1963), 13.

7. T. S. Eliot, *The Complete Poems and Plays* (New York, 1950), 39.

8. See Joseph Campbell, *The Flight of the Wild Gander: Explorations in the Mythological Dimensions of Fairy Tales, Legends, and Symbols* (New York, 1990), 154.

9. *Ibid.*, 151, 155.

10. David I. Grossvogel, "Interview: A. R. Ammons," *Diacritics*, III (Winter, 1973), 52.

11. A. R. Ammons, "Poetry Is a Matter of Survival" (interview by Nancy Kober), *Cornell Daily Sun*, April 27, 1973, p. 12.

12. Except for an essay by Robert Morgan ("The Compound Vision of A. R. Ammons' Early Poems," *Epoch*, XXII [1973], 343–63), little has been done critically on Ammons' early work. If, however, one believes that the poems of *Ommateum* (1955) and *Expressions of Sea Level* (1964) are in any way inferior to Ammons' later lyrics—a claim that I have heard several critics vigorously make—one may turn with equal vigor to a counterstatement by the poet, with which I completely concur. In an interview in the *Michi-*

gan Quarterly Review (XXVIII [Winter, 1989], 105–17) with William Walsh, Ammons describes the initial commercial failure of *Ommateum,* then discusses the personal value of his early work:

WALSH: Your first book of poetry, *Ommateum,* failed miserably.
AMMONS: I believe the publisher knew it wouldn't sell and so they only bound one hundred copies of the three hundred sheets pressed. It sold sixteen copies the first five years. Five libraries bought it—Princeton, Harvard, Yale, Berkeley, and Chapel Hill, only because they bought everything. My father-in-law sent forty copies to people he knew in South America. I bought back thirty copies for thirty cents each. So I guess you could say it failed miserably. . . . But now *Ommateum* goes for about thirteen hundred dollars a copy.
    . . . *Ommateum* remains a very powerful influence with me. . . . It may be my best book. *Expressions of Sea Level,* though more widely welcomed, more obviously ingrati- ates itself to an easier kind of excellence. The *Ommateum* poems are sometimes very rigid and ritualistic, formal and off-putting, but very strong. The review I got said, these poems don't care whether they are listened to or not. Which is exactly true. I had no idea there was such a thing as an audience; didn't care if there was. . . . Someone else said that I was a poet who had not yet renounced his early poems. I never intend to re nounce those poems.

1.   THIS BLACK RICH COUNTRY

1. David I. Grossvogel, "Interview: A. R. Ammons," *Diacritics,* III (Winter, 1973), 47.
2. *Ibid.,* 50, 47.
3. For an argument the opposite of mine, namely, that Ammons' "early work can be quite overtly Christian," see Frank Lepkowski's "'How Are We to Find Holiness?': The Religious Vision of A. R. Ammons," *Twentieth-Century Literature,* XL (Winter, 1994), 447–98.
4. Jane Ellen Harrison, *Themis: A Study of the Social Origins of Greek Religion* (Cleve- land, 1957), 378.
5. Rollo May, *The Cry for Myth* (New York, 1991), 50–51. As one may easily gather from surveying the forty-page list of references in William G. Doty's formidable *My- thography: The Study of Myths and Rituals* (Tuscaloosa, Ala., 1986), there is an over- whelming number of definitions of myth and ritual. For my own practical purposes in this book, I have chosen those that seem to best fit the elements in Ammons and Dickey under discussion. My central sense of ritual as poetic action may be found in note 42 of Chapter 3, on Dickey's "Approaching Prayer." The meaning of both these terms should be evident in my analysis. If, however, the reader requires a more complex conception of myth than that of Harrison or May, I offer Doty's definition of a "mythological cor- pus," each segment of which he defines carefully in his first chapter and sections of which I use throughout this book. Each segment in his definition has been numbered by Doty:

(1) a usually complex network of myths that are (2) culturally important (3) imaginal (4) stories, conveying by means of (5) metaphoric and symbolic diction, (6) graphic imagery, and (7) emotional conviction and participation, (8) the primal, foundational accounts (9) of aspects of the real, experienced world and (10) humankind's roles and relative statuses within it.

Mythologies may (11) convey the political and moral values of a culture and (12) provide systems of interpreting (13) individual experience within a universal perspective, which may include (14) the intervention of suprahuman entities as well as (15) aspects of the natural and cultural orders. Myths may be enacted or reflected in (16) rituals, ceremonies, and dramas, and (17) they may provide materials for secondary elaboration, the constituent mythemes having become merely images or reference points for a subsequent story, such as a folktale, historical legend, novella, or prophecy. (Doty, *Mythography*, 11)

6. Ammons, interview in *Diacritics*, 47.

7. That performance is important for Ammons may be found in this commentary on his poetry: "It is true that I use the discursive in my work a great deal, but always as a character in a play: I don't particularly care what I say; I care only that the dramatic placing of the thought is accurate in the piece as if it were a stage play. So and so enters from the left and says his thing, and it either fits in and promotes the dramatic action, or it doesn't. Whether or not it is literally true is of little interest to me because I don't think that the truth can be arrived at in that mode; but I do believe a character can represent that truth" (interview in *Diacritics*, 47).

8. In an interview in the *Manhattan Review*, I (Fall, 1980), Ammons says, "Circles and radial points coming from circles are very prominent in my work, including the painting. . . . [In an article on archeo-astronomy in *Midwest Quarterly*] they talk about something called the sacred center, and once you have a ring of stones, as you approach the center of this, you approach the highest kind of integration you can imagine between the material and the spiritual, between the stone that lasts forever and the starlight which is ephemeral, between man and his time and the larger, apparently eternal" (8).

9. Ovid, *Metamorphoses*, X, 512–13 (cited by Joseph Campbell in *The Masks of God: Oriental Mythology* [New York: 1976], 395).

10. Arnold Van Gennep, *The Rites of Passage* (Chicago, 1975), 18.

11. Samuel Noah Kramer, *The Sumerians* (Chicago, 1963), 20.

12. See Joseph Campbell, *The Masks of God: Primitive Mythology* (New York, 1959), 145ff.

13. For a similar set of critical questions on how to read a contemporary poem, see Paul Breslin's perceptive chapter, "Deep Images, Shallow Psychologies," in which he cites James Atlas on W. S. Merwin's idiomatic poem "The Night of the Shirts," in *The Psycho-Political Muse: American Poetry Since the Fifties* (Chicago, 1987), 120–27.

14. Kenneth Burke, *Permanence and Change: An Anatomy of Purpose* (New York, 1965), 69.

15. Mircea Eliade, *Myths, Dreams, and Mysteries: The Encounter Between Contemporary Faiths and Archaic Realities,* trans. Philip Mairet (New York, 1957), 79–81.

16. *Ibid.,* 83.

17. Burke, *Permanence and Change,* 69.

18. Patricia A. Parker, "Configurations of Shape and Flow," *Diacritics,* III (Winter, 1973), 29, 30.

19. Victor Turner, *The Anthropology of Performance* (New York, 1986), 54–55.

20. Émile Durkheim, cited by Catherine Bell in *Ritual Theory, Ritual Practice* (New York, 1992), 218.

21. Turner, *Anthropology of Performance,* 24–25.

22. *Ibid.,* 55.

23. *Ibid.,* 81.

24. Theodore W. Jennings, "On Ritual Knowledge," *History of Religions,* LXII (1982), 115.

25. Sir James George Frazer, *The Golden Bough* (New York, 1963), 792.

26. Joseph Campbell, *The Hero with a Thousand Faces* (Princeton, 1968), 335

27. Campbell, *Primitive Mythology,* 121.

28. See Joseph Campbell, *The Masks of God: Occidental Mythology* (New York, 1964), 489.

29. At the beginning of his career, isolated from major centers of poetry and with a background in science and business, Ammons undertook a search for poetic wisdom that was heroic indeed. As noted in my preface, after its initial appearance *Ommateum,* published privately, sold sixteen copies in five years. Consequently, Ammons' struggle to have his work attended to must have easily given him the feeling that he was tied to a great oak and that supernal knowledge, similar to Odin's, was necessary to succeed. Any enabling rite of assistance would have been welcome, even if that rite had to be constructed by the beginning writer. In the search for a mythopoeic motto for sustainment, perseverance, and the invention of a poetic self through the telling of tales, the advice given by Odin to an aspirant for his poetic wisdom is applicable. Like any beginner, the ephebe requires considerable guidance, for among other things, he is bewildered by the forms and names given by legend to the poet-god (who refers to himself as "him"): "It is truly a vast sum of knowledge to rake into rows. . . . [T]here being so many branches of tongues in the world, all people believed that it was needful for them to turn his name into their own tongue, by which they might the better invoke him and entreat him on their own behalf. But some occasions for those names arose, also, in his wanderings; and that matter is recorded in tales. Nor canst thou ever be called a wise man if thou canst not tell of those great events" (Campbell, *Occidental Mythology,* 489).

30. Campbell, *Primitive Mythology,* 121.

31. Mircea Eliade, *The Sacred and the Profane: The Nature of Religion* (New York, 1957), 190.

32. Mircea Eliade, *Shamanism: Archaic Techniques of Ecstasy* (New York, 1964), 246; Frazer, *The Golden Bough,* 131.

33. Ammons, interview in *Diacritics,* 51.

34. Laotse, *Tao Te Ching,* trans. Arthur Waley, cited by Joseph Campbell in *Oriental Mythology,* 426–27.

35. Kramer, *Sumerians,* 15ff.

36. Joseph Campbell, *The Power of Myth* (New York, 1988), 222.

37. Campbell, *Oriental Mythology,* 428.

38. Laotse, *Tao Te Ching,* trans. Waley, cited by Campbell in *Oriental Mythology,* 428.

39. Campbell, *Oriental Mythology,* 428.

40. In his chapter "Modes of Ritual Sensibility" from *Beginnings in Ritual Studies* (Columbia, S. C., 1982), Ronald L. Grimes offers a rich conception of liturgy, one that involves the idea of Tao and effectively describes much of the ritual action in Ammons' poetry, especially regarding the complex combination of receptivity and power (even in walking) in his work:

> [L]iturgy . . . refers to any ritual action with an ultimate frame of reference and the doing of which is understood to be of cosmic necessity. Liturgy begins with the ritual cultivation of being and is typified by a deep receptivity. Power is more comprehensively understood in liturgy than in ceremony or magic. Liturgical power is not the force of labor, a way of achieving results, but is a mode of tapping the way (*tao*) things flow or connecting with the order and reason (*logos*) that things manifest. Liturgy is a way of coming to rest in the heart of the cosmos.
>
> . . . In liturgical rites people try to walk on the ground of their being, to walk, as Lakotas say, "in a sacred manner." In such an effort it is easy to overstep oneself, and as a result there is always something inherently clumsy about the liturgical stride. For this reason, ritualists humble themselves and apologize by confessions of sin, cleansings, sweats, baptisms, and incensations.
>
> What is unique to liturgy is . . . that it asks. Liturgically, one approaches the sacred in a reverent, "interrogative" mood, waits "in passive voice" and finally is "declarative" of the way things ultimately are. In liturgy, ritualists "actively act" in order to be acted upon. . . . Liturgy occurs in moments when power does not need to be seized and held, as is the case in ceremony, or put to immediate use, as in magic. . . .
>
> [L]iturgy is a structured waiting upon an influx of whole-making (holy) power, it is . . . not only preparatory, it is also the thing itself. The exercise *is* the hierophany.
>
> (51–52)

41. René Girard, *Violence and the Sacred* (Baltimore, 1977), 124.

42. Campbell, *Oriental Mythology,* 424–25.

2. AMMONS' SUMERIAN SONGS

1. David I. Grossvogel, "Interview: A. R. Ammons," *Diacritics,* III (Winter, 1973), 51.

2. Harold Bloom, "The Internalization of the Quest-Romance," in *Romanticism and Consciousness: Essays in Criticism,* ed. Harold Bloom (New York, 1970), 8, 16, 13, 11, 15, 12, 17.

3. Joseph Campbell, *The Mythic Image* (Princeton, 1974), 478.

4. Ananda K. Coomaraswamy, *Hinduism and Buddhism* (New York, n.d.), 9.

5. Philip Fried, "'A Place You Can Live': An Interview with A. R. Ammons," *Manhattan Review,* I (Fall, 1980), 11.

6. Bloom, "Quest-Romance," in *Romanticism and Consciousness,* ed. Bloom, 13.

7. The relevance of such a process for this poet is extremely important, for Ammons has suffered dry spells, extended periods in which he has not been able to write, throughout his career. This may sound unlikely for so prolific and well known a poet, but he was unhappily in one of these spells when I arrived to teach at Cornell in the late seventies. During this period he turned from writing poetry to painting watercolors.

8. Mircea Eliade, *Myths, Dreams, and Mysteries: The Encounter Between Contemporary Faiths and Archaic Realities,* trans. Philip Mairet (New York, 1957), 79–81.

9. Ralph Waldo Emerson, "Plato; or, The Philosopher," from *Representative Men,* in *Ralph Waldo Emerson: Essays & Lectures* (New York, 1983), 645.

10. In his interview in the *Manhattan Review,* Ammons is explicit about this disengagement from his religious upbringing: "The religious thing is very strong in my background, where we had all kinds of preaching and dancing and holy rolling. . . . Going to college, I began to inquire into this religious background which was so strong and severe, and I got it more and more on a rational and historic level, which moved me intellectually from those positions that my family and aunts and uncles would have taken to be natural. . . . I was already in exile in that country. . . . Was no longer able to accept the doctrine familiar throughout my youth" (14–15). I share this thesis with Frederick Buell ("To Be Quiet in the Hands of the Marvelous," *Iowa Review,* VIII [Winter, 1977], rpr. in *Modern Critical Views: A. R. Ammons,* ed. Harold Bloom [New York, 1986], 196) and Janet DeRosa ("Occurrences of Promises and Terror: The Poetry of A. R. Ammons" [Ph.D. dissertation, Brown University, 1978], 64–65); my inquiry into ritual differs considerably from theirs, however.

11. Joseph Campbell, *The Masks of God: Primitive Mythology* (New York, 1959), 50–51.

12. Geoffrey Hartman, "Romanticism and Anti-Self-Consciousness," in *Romanticism and Consciousness,* ed. Bloom, 47, 50, 49.

13. Heinrich Zimmer, *Philosophies of India* (Princeton, 1951), 334.

14. A. R. Ammons, "Poetry Is a Matter of Survival" (interview by Nancy Kober), *Cornell Daily Sun,* April 27, 1973, p. 12.

15. C. Leonard Woolley, *The Sumerians* (Oxford, 1929), 13–14.

16. Samuel Noah Kramer, *History Begins at Sumer* (Philadelphia, 1981), 181, 113–14.

17. John Gardner, *Gilgamesh,* trans. John Gardner and John Maier (New York, 1984), 18.

18. Cited by Thorkild Jacobsen in *The Treasures of Darkness: A History of Mesopotamian Religion* (New Haven, 1976), 207.

19. *Ibid.,* 204.

20. Buell, "To Be Quiet," rpr. in *Modern Critical Views: A. R. Ammons,* ed. Bloom, 196.

21. Samuel Noah Kramer, *Sumerian Mythology* (Philadelphia, 1944), 76.

22. Gardner, *Gilgamesh*, 178.

23. Eliade, *Myths, Dreams, and Mysteries,* 95–96.

24. *Ibid.,* 96, 243.

25. Mircea Eliade, *Myth and Reality,* trans. Willard R. Trask (New York, 1963), 129.

26. *Ibid.,* 136.

27. *Ibid.,* 133.

28. Denis Donoghue, "Ammons and the Lesser Celandine," *Parnassus,* III (Spring/ Summer 1975), rpr. in *Modern Critical Views: A. R. Ammons,* ed. Bloom, 173–74.

29. Eliade, *Myth and Reality,* 133–34.

30. William Wordsworth, cited by Hartman, "Anti-Self-Consciousness," in *Romanticism and Consciousness,* ed. Bloom, 47–48.

31. Campbell, *Primitive Mythology,* 186.

32. Joseph Campbell, *The Masks of God: Occidental Mythology* (New York, 1964), 163–64.

33. *Ibid.,* 57–58.

34. *Ibid.,* 54, 57.

35. *Ibid.,* 78.

36. Mircea Eliade, *The Sacred and the Profane: The Nature of Religion* (New York, 1957), 29.

37. *Ibid.,* 32.

38. *Ibid.,* 87, 24.

39. Joseph Campbell, *The Masks of God: Creative Mythology* (New York, 1968), 216.

40. Chuang Tzu, trans. Arthur Waley, cited by Joseph Campbell in *The Masks of God: Oriental Mythology* (New York, 1962), 427.

41. *Ibid.*

42. Edward Conze, *Buddhism: Its Essence and Development* (New York, 1965), 106, 110–11.

43. Harold Bloom, Introduction to *Modern Critical Views: A. R. Ammons,* ed. Bloom, 7.

44. Laotse, *Tao Te Ching,* trans. Stephen Mitchell (New York, 1988), 27.

45. Emerson, *Essays & Lectures,* 645.

46. Conze, *Buddhism,* 101; DeRosa calls this "mirror-consciousness" in Ammons' poetry, 128.

47. *Ibid.*

48. Joseph Campbell, *The Flight of the Wild Gander: Explorations in the Mythological Dimensions of Fairy Tales, Legends, and Symbols* (New York, 1990), 195, 198.

49. A. R. Ammons, "Guide," *Hudson Review,* XIII (Autumn, 1960), 354.

50. Geoffrey H. Hartman, *"The Fate of Reading" and Other Essays* (Chicago, 1975), 118.

51. Conze, *Buddhism,* 101.

52. Arthur Waley, cited by Campbell in *Oriental Mythology,* 26.

53. Emerson, *Essays & Lectures*, 645.

54. *The Bhagavad Gita*, trans. Franklin Edgerton (New York, 1944), 34.

55. Arthur Waley's note, cited by Campbell in *Oriental Mythology*, 26.

3.   DICKEY'S "APPROACHING PRAYER"

1. Harold Bloom, Introduction to *Modern Critical Views: James Dickey*, ed. Bloom (New York, 1987), 11.

2. In addition to Bloom's two-paragraph discussion, the fullest treatment of "Approaching Prayer" is found in Ernest Suarez' *Assessing the Savage Ideal: James Dickey and the Politics of Canon* (Columbia, Mo., 1993), where he argues that "Approaching Prayer" "does not result in discovery of a god who holds out the promise of an immortal soul, but in a vision which holds many dimensions of experience" (66). In *James Dickey* (Boston, 1983), Richard J. Calhoun and Robert Hill claim that in "Approaching Prayer," Dickey turns "to overt ritual" and "ritual dress" to achieve "mystical simultaneity: the son is both animal and man, father and child, the hunter and the hunted" (60–61). Ronald Baughman notes in *Understanding James Dickey* (Columbia, S.C., 1985) that this poem enables Dickey to discover "the right relationship with nature—as a hunter with the hunted" and that through "the boar's viewpoint" the poet has "a premonition of his own mortality, and an understanding of the difference between life and death" (50–51).

3. T. S. Eliot, *The Complete Poems and Plays, 1909–1950* (New York, 1930), 139, 144.

4. Mircea Eliade, *The Sacred and the Profane: The Nature of Religion* (New York, 1957), 128, 129.

5. Joseph Campbell, *The Hero with a Thousand Faces* (Princeton, 1968), 98–99.

6. Eliade, *Sacred and Profane*, 32.

7. See Victor Turner, *The Ritual Process: Structure and Anti-Structure* (Ithaca, 1969), 23.

8. With regard to the power of things to create sacred space, Lévi-Strauss argues in *The Savage Mind* (Chicago, 1962) that "a native thinker makes the penetrating comment . . . 'All sacred things must have their place.' It could even be said that being in their place is what makes them sacred for if they were taken out of their place, even in thought, the entire order of the universe would be destroyed. Sacred objects therefore contribute to the maintenance of order in the universe by occupying the places allocated to them. Examined superficially and from the outside, the refinements of ritual can appear pointless. They are explicable by a concern for what one might call 'micro-adjustment'—the concern to assign every single creature, object or feature to a place within a class" (10).

9. Campbell, *Hero with a Thousand Faces*, 98. Ronald Grimes's discussion of "flight"—as dramatized in marginal theatrical movements he calls "parashamanism," beginning in the mid-1970s—is suggestive here. In *Beginnings in Ritual Studies* (Columbia, S.C., 1982), Grimes compares the contemporary *parashaman* ("the composite figure, shaman-trickster-fool") with ancient figures of shamanism: "Whereas flight in

shamanism refers to an ecstatic trance, or journey out of the body, it refers in para-shamanism to one's own discovered bodily attunement—to a rhythm or some very simple dance, for example, a circle dance. Flight is not viewed as a magical trance so much as unintellectalized, unformalized, spontaneous, or minimally structured move-ment. The flight to 'other' worlds is a rhythmic visit to what is other than the merely academic, commercial, medical, theatrical, or decorous. To fly is to be in one's body with soul. It is not to leave the body but to fill it. This is why drums and flutes are . . . important. . . . [T]hey do not transport so much as embody." For Grimes, parashamanic gesturing also has a reflexive or visionary dimension relevant to Dickey's relationship with his father: "Flight . . . for the parashaman . . . is an ascent above social structures in order to attain a perspective on the various collectives such as families" (262).

10. Sir James George Frazer, *The Golden Bough* (New York, 1963), 12–13.

11. For the psychology of both believing and disbelieving narrative elements in the "ritual management of distress" in ritual drama, see psychotherapist and sociologist T. J. Scheff's discussion (in *Catharsis in Healing, Ritual, and Drama* [Berkeley, 1979]) of effecting emotional catharsis by means of "aesthetic distance" that may be defined as "the simultaneous and equal experience of being both participant and observer" (115): "Any device which allows people to be both participants in, and observers of, their own distress accomplishes . . . distancing. . . . The ritual of prayer exactly distances the com-municant so that he or she is as much participant as observer, so long as the communi-cant both believes and disbelieves that he or she is in communication with a supernatu-ral being. This double vision, of both believing and not believing simultaneously . . . [enables] the communicant who is both participant and observer [to] experience re-pressed emotion and discharge it" (119). For a comprehensive treatment of psychologi-cal rituals and families, see *Rituals in Families and Family Therapy* (New York, 1988), ed. Evan Imber-Black, Janine Roberts, and Richard Whiting.

12. Eliade, *Sacred and Profane*, 70.

13. *Ibid.*, 179–80.

14. Campbell, *Hero with a Thousand Faces*, 42.

15. Eliade, *Sacred and Profane*, 177, 180.

16. See Grimes on the ritual function of masking, especially "Masking as Concre-tion" and "Masking as Embodiment," in *Ritual Studies*, 79–87.

17. E. B. Tylor, *Primitive Culture* (London, 1929), 453.

18. Mircea Eliade, *Shamanism: Archaic Techniques of Ecstasy* (New York, 1964), 92, 179, 263, 460.

19. In *Shamanism*, Eliade claims: "The presence of a helping spirit in animal form . . . or incarnation of such an animal spirit by the shaman . . . is another way of showing that the shaman can forsake his human condition, is able, in a word, to 'die.' From the most distant times almost all animals have been conceived either as psychopomps that ac-company the soul into the beyond or as the dead person's new form" (93).

20. Bloom, Introduction to *Modern Critical Views: James Dickey*, ed. Bloom, 12; Bloom notes that although Dickey's poem "shares a magic vitalism with Yeats," "Ap-proaching Prayer" has "nothing Yeatsian . . . in its vision" (11).

21. Eliade, *Sacred and Profane*, 189.

22. Eliade, *Shamanism*, 33.

23. Eliade, *Sacred and Profane*, 190.

24. Eliade, *Shamanism*, 246.

25. Dickey uses blood in a similar way in another of his initiatory poems, namely, "The Shark's Parlor," when the two young boys bait their hook with "a bucket of entrails and blood" (*P*, 205). When they land the shark, it enters their poled cottage on the waters of Cumberland Island and throws "pints / Of blood over everything we owned" (*P*, 207). At the end of the poem, "Blood hard as iron on the wall" is "black with time" but "Can be touched" by the memory and thus retains its ritual power (from the ordeal of overcoming great obstacles) as "one black mark . . . against death" (*P*, 207–208).

26. In Chapter 8 of *Ritual Studies*, Grimes discusses the theories of psychiatrist Gotthard Booth, which he finds to be a convincing psychosomatic ground for gestural symbolization in ritual. In Grimes's words, Booth aims at discovering "a hermeneutics of the body" and "the grammar of bodily language, especially the language of illness." Especially relevant for my inquiry into Dickey's use of blood and his ritualizing body language is Booth's claim, as Grimes puts it, that "the blood stream . . . is the symbolic internalization of the environment. The blood stream is to human beings what the sea was to primitive organisms" (127). See also Jack Goody's observation about the widespread purgative and separational powers of water in *Death, Property, and the Ancestors: A Study of the Mortuary Customs of the Lodagaa of West Africa* (Stanford, 1962), where he discusses the "river of Death" in the African tribal mythology of the Lodagaa of northwest Ghana. Although focusing on this particular culture, Goody also speculates generally "why in so many societies we should find the Land of the Living separated from the Land of the Dead by a river or similar stretch of water" (374).

27. Campbell, *Hero with a Thousand Faces*, 155.

28. In *Stone Men of Malekula*, using sacrifical boars as examples, John Layard reinforces Eliade's point made earlier about an enabling "*new identity*" for ritual performers who take on the powers of an "animal spirit." Arguing that it is through the violence of sacrifical rites, whereby practitioners gain power over their own victimage and death, Layard notes that on the festival of Maki, a hundred or more boars may be offered at a single time on massive stone altars. He claims that "the efficacy of this sacrifice results from the fact that the sacrificial animals have themselves been consecrated through sacrifice of yet other boars, and have by this means become identified with the Guardian Ghost, and in the highest grades have been invested with a title similar to its own. At the moment of sacrifice the ghost of the boar passes into the sacrificer, who by this means himself becomes identified with this Being, and in this way builds up a power within him that he hopes will ensure him from being devoured when he dies" (cited by Campbell in *The Mythic Image* [Princeton, 1974], 456).

29. Eliade, *Sacred and Profane*, 188.

30. In his discussion of ritual masking, Grimes is relevant on this point: "An embodied moment is like a mystical experience, because it can only appear to an interpreter as a meaningful exterior. An interpreter of ritual has no direct access to interiority; one

has only imaginative, indirect access. What appears to a wearer as either the naked power of another or the bare power of selfhood can only appear to an observer as a stylization" (86).

31. Victor Turner, cited by Mary Schmidt, "Crazy Wisdom: The Shaman as Mediator of Realities," in *Shamanism: An Expanded View of Reality*, ed. Shirley Nicholson (Wheaton, Ill., 1987), 64.

32. Schmidt, *ibid.*, 68.

33. Arthur Deikman, cited *ibid.*, 70.

34. Schmidt, *ibid.*, 68.

35. Eliade, *Shamanism*, 246.

36. Eliade, *Sacred and Profane*, 191; Claude Lévi-Strauss, *Structural Anthropology*, trans. Claire Jacobson and Brooke Grundfest Schoepf (New York, 1963), 200.

37. Lévi-Strauss, *The Savage Mind*, 18–21.

38. I am grateful to Kimberly Breitenbecher and John Skowronski in the Department of Psychology at Ohio State University for emphasizing that this claim and others like it should be presented as psychoanalytic speculation, not as empirically grounded fact. Now much out of favor in contemporary psychology, both theoretically and practically, psychoanalysis needs to be supplemented with more empirical inquiry. Consequently, for current perspectives on the emotional bases of Dickey's ritual, the reader is urged to consult the following studies on the process of grieving: Nancy O'Connor, *Letting Go with Love: The Grieving Process* (Tucson, 1984), 53–73; Therese A. Rando, *How to Go on Living When Someone You Love Dies* (New York, 1991), 36ff., 227–32, and on how to design your own grieving ritual, 265–78; Elizabeth Kübler-Ross, *On Death and Dying* (New York, 1969) and *Death: The Final Stage of Growth* (Englewood Cliffs, N.J., 1975); Rabbi Marc D. Angel, *The Orphaned Adult* (New York, 1987); Ernest Morgan, *Dealing Creatively with Death: A Manual of Death Education and Simple Burial* (Burnsville, N.C., 1984); and Edward Myers, *When Parents Die: A Guide for Adults* (New York, 1986).

39. Lévi-Strauss, *Structural Anthropology*, 181, 198.

40. *Ibid.*, 200, 202.

41. Sigmund Freud, cited by Rollo May in *The Cry for Myth* (New York, 1991), 72; *ibid.*, 7. Grimes is perceptive on the openness of rituals and, by extension, on the critical challenge of reading Dickey's poem too precisely: "Rites are events; they have lifespans. Only secondarily do they reside in texts, scenarios, scripts, or rubrics. . . . They are not artifacts. They are not structures in the sense that a building is a structure. They are structurings. They surge and subside, ebb and flow. One can infer the structure of a rite, but the inference is not the event. A ritual structure, like a ritual text, is a residue. And texts, as Walter Ong . . . reminds us, are like funerary monuments. Rites deteriorate. Entropy is the rule; therefore, they must be raised up constantly from the grave of book, body, memory, and culture" (62).

42. May, *Cry for Myth*, 50–51. Of the myriad conceptions of ritual that I have encountered while researching this subject, three others are also central to my reading and should be mentioned to anticipate critical concerns about the meaning of this ex-

tremely ambiguous term. First, there is Janine Roberts' psychotherapeutic definition taken from *Ritual in Families and Family Therapy* (New York, 1988): "*Rituals are co-evolved symbolic acts that include not only the ceremonial aspects of the actual presentation of the ritual, but the process of preparing for it as well. It may or may not include words, but does have both open and closed parts which are 'held' together by a guiding metaphor. Repetition can be a part of rituals through either the content, the form, or the occasion. There should be enough space in therapeutic rituals for the incorporation of multiple meanings by various family members and clinicians, as well as a variety of levels of participation*" (8). Second, there is this poignant, enabling definition of ritual from *Imagining Religion: From Babylon to Jonestown* (Chicago, 1982) by Jonathan Z. Smith: "*Ritual represents the creation of a controlled environment* where the variables (*i.e.*, the accidents) of ordinary life may be displaced *precisely* because they are felt to be so overwhelmingly present and powerful. *Ritual is a means of performing the way things ought to be in conscious tension to the way things are in such a way that this ritualized perfection is recollected in the ordinary, uncontrolled, course of things*" (63). Finally and most important are these considerations from Kenneth Burke in *The Philosophy of Literary Form: Studies in Symbolic Action* (New York, 1941): "The general perspective that is interwoven with our methodology of analysis might be summarily characterized as a *theory of drama*. We propose to take *ritual drama* as the Ur-form, the 'hub,' with all other aspects of *human* action treated as spokes radiating from this hub" (87). "The general approach to the poem might be called 'pragmatic' in [that] [i]t assumes that a poem's structure is to be described most accurately by thinking always of the poem's function. It assumes that the poem is designed to 'do something' for the poet and his readers, and that we can make the most relevant observations about its design by considering the poem as the embodiment of this act" (75). "[P]oetry *is* produced for purposes of comfort, as part of the *consolatio philosophiae*. It is undertaken as *equipment for living*, as a ritualistic way of arming us to confront perplexities and risks. It would *protect* us" (51).

43. Eliade, *Sacred and Profane*, 209.

44. May, *Cry for Myth*, 163.

45. Eliade, *Sacred and Profane*, 211.

46. For a similar pragmatic and performative analysis of prayer from Native American culture, see Sam D. Gill's "Prayer as Person: The Performative Force in Navajo Prayer Act," *History of Religions*, XVII (1977), 143–57.

47. Lévi-Strauss, *Structural Anthropology*, 199.

48. Theodore Roethke, *The Collected Poems of Theodore Roethke* (New York, 1961), 172.

4.   FORM AND GENRE IN DICKEY'S "FALLING"

1. Joyce Carol Oates, "Out of Stone, into Flesh," in *Modern Critical Views: James Dickey*, ed. Harold Bloom (New York, 1987), 101.

2. Monroe Spears, *Dionysus and the City: Modernism in Twentieth-Century Poetry* (London, 1970), 257.

3. Joyce Pair, quoted in Michael Hirsley, "On Wings of Words," *Chicago Tribune,* May 10, 1987, Sec. 10, pp. 8–10, 29.

4. There is considerable evidence that Dickey has read extensively in anthropology and is strongly influenced by non-European poetry and song: "I've tried to come into conjunction in one way or another with Eskimo dance rituals and Bantu hunting songs and that sort of thing. And the revelations of those so-called folk as far as poetic imagery is considered are marvelously rich and evocative. They have nothing to do with Alexander Pope's use of the heroic couplet or Wordsworth's use of Milton's blank verse or any of that sort of thing. . . . Those people are saying something out of a condition with which they are in a precarious and dangerous and sometimes desperate harmony, but always a harmony of some kind which, even when the environment destroys them, is some kind of harmony. I'm looking for some way to *relate* to things again and this is the reason I dislike so much these poets of alienation who feel humiliated by everything and who are endlessly examining their own motives" (*NH,* 251). See also Gordon Van Ness, "Living Beyond Recall," and Ron McFarland, "An Interview with James Dickey," in *The Voiced Connections of James Dickey: Interviews and Conversations,* ed. Ronald Baughman (Columbia, S.C., 1989), 253, 184–85.

5. In addition to Oates, Spears, Pair, and Dickey, others have mentioned briefly that the stewardess in "Falling" is some kind of goddess. Richard J. Calhoun and Robert Hill perceptively say that her function is "to serve the American agricultural heartland as a new-found fertility goddess" (*James Dickey* [Boston, 1983], 84). Neal Bowers claims that "Falling" is "the myth of the stewardess turned goddess in free-fall over Kansas" (*James Dickey: The Poet as Pitchman* [Columbia, Mo., 1985], 49). Ronald Baughman uses Dickey's own term to call her a "goddess" as well "as a sexual and religious symbol of renewal" (*Understanding James Dickey* [Columbia, S.C., 1985], 93). Marion Hodge rightly notes that she is "the earth-goddess, mother earth" who "transforms those who come near her body" ("James Dickey's Natural Heaven," *South Atlantic Review,* LVI [November, 1991], 66). Laurence Lieberman accurately sees the positive power of the stewardess when he asks, "Who would have guessed that a woman's falling to her death from a plane could be converted by Dickey's imagination into a symbol of fantastic affirmation of life?" ("James Dickey: The Deepening of Being," in *Modern Critical Views: James Dickey,* ed. Bloom, 9).

6. Robert Kirschten, *James Dickey and the Gentle Ecstasy of Earth: A Reading of the Poems* (Baton Rouge, 1988), 119.

7. The gaps in the run-in text follow Dickey's spacing in the poem.

8. Erich Neumann, *The Great Mother,* trans. Ralph Manheim (Princeton, 1963), 145–46.

9. Erich Neumann, *The Origins and History of Consciousness,* trans. R. F. C. Hull (Princeton, 1954), 76.

10. Heinrich Zimmer, "The Indian World Mother," in *The Mystic Vision,* ed. Joseph Campbell (Princeton, 1968), 84.

11. Carol Christ, *The Laughter of Aphrodite* (San Francisco, 1987), 168, 166.

12. Joseph Campbell, *Historical Atlas of World Mythology,* Vol. II, *The Way of the Seeded Earth* (New York, 1989), Pt. 2, pp. 143–46.

13. Charles H. Long, *Alpha: The Myths of Creation* (New York, 1963), 125–26.

14. Neumann, *Great Mother,* 222, 212.

15. D. H. Lawrence, *Etruscan Places* (New York, 1963), 49.

16. Christ, *Laughter of Aphrodite,* 169.

17. James Dickey, "The Energized Man," in *The Imagination as Glory: The Poetry of James Dickey,* ed. Bruce Weigl and T. R. Hummer (Urbana, Ill., 1984), 164.

18. Jane Harrison, *"Epilegomena to the Study of Greek Religion" and "Themis: A Study of the Social Origins of Greek Religion"* (Hyde Park, N.Y., 1962), 68.

19. Campbell, *World Mythology,* Vol. II, Pt. 2, pp. 153–54.

20. Marija Gimbutas, *The Goddesses and Gods of Old Europe* (Los Angeles, 1982), 152.

21. Campbell, *World Mythology,* Vol. II, Pt. 2, p. 156.

22. Zimmer, *Mystic Vision,* 89, 87, 71, 93, 96.

23. Friedrich Nietzsche, *The Birth of Tragedy,* trans. A. Haussmann (Edinburgh, 1909), 21.

24. Spears, *Dionysus and the City,* 259.

25. Nietzsche, *Birth of Tragedy,* 22–24.

26. Spears, *Dionysus and the City,* 258–59.

27. Nietzsche, *Birth of Tragedy,* 67–69, 27.

28. Friedrich Nietzsche, *Twilight of the Idols,* in *The Portable Nietzsche,* trans. Walter Kaufmann (New York, 1954), 518.

29. Nietzsche, *Birth of Tragedy,* 128.

30. Herbert Marcuse, *Eros and Civilization* (Boston, 1955), 166, 201, 235.

31. Theodore Roethke, cited in Neal Bowers, *Theodore Roethke: The Journey from I to Otherwise* (Columbia, Mo., 1982), 8–10.

32. Campbell, *World Mythology,* Vol. II, Pt. 1, p. 36.

33. Neumann, *Great Mother,* 162.

34. Joseph Campbell, *The Masks of God: Primitive Mythology* (New York, 1959), 186.

35. Joseph Campbell, *The Power of Myth* (New York, 1988), 109.

36. Campbell, *Primitive Mythology,* 177.

37. Kenneth Burke, "The Vegetal Radicalism of Theodore Roethke," in *Language as Symbolic Action: Essays on Life, Literature, and Method* (Berkeley, 1966), 244.

38. Theodore Roethke, "Root Cellar," in *The Collected Poems of Theodore Roethke* (New York, 1961), 38.

39. Campbell, *Primitive Mythology,* 181; Zimmer, *Mystic Vision,* 96.

40. Mary Ellmann, *Thinking About Women* (New York, 1968), 29.

41. Equally wrongheaded are two sets of claims against "Falling" by Paul Ramsey and Ralph Mills. Ramsey charges that the stewardess is a "stripteaser aiming at seducing all the farm boys and men in Kansas, on her way to death" ("James Dickey: Meter and Structure," in *James Dickey: The Expansive Imagination,* ed. Richard J. Calhoun [De-

land, Fla., 1973], 192). To be sure, the stewardess' sexual power increases dramatically when she removes her clothes; her energy is not, however, the provocation of a striptease but the Dionysian amplification and purification of natural sexual instinct that passes not only to "the farm boys and men in Kansas" but to the women as well and to the entire earth. Mills criticizes "Falling" for being "drawn out, repetitive, overwritten, blurred, and diffuse." The idea behind the poem, he charges, is "contrived" and "cannot be sustained even by Coleridge's 'willing suspension of disbelief'" ("The Poetry of James Dickey," in *Imagination as Glory,* ed. Weigl and Hummer, 41). Many of these issues center on the very conception of "form" I discuss. "Falling" is not "drawn out" if it is in the shape of a ritual conversion that requires considerable dramatic length to effect emotionally the transformation at the heart of the poem. Neither is the poem "repetitive" or "overwritten," for the stages of its story are clearly demonstrable in terms of the changes the stewardess experiences, several of which shade off into each other but do not merely replicate the same aspect of development. If my reading of the form and genre of the poem are accurate, then the piece is not "blurred" but is quite focused as to what happens and the kind of action that happens. Perhaps Mills confuses one aspect of the stewardess' hallucinatory sight as she falls with the heart of the poem. What is "diffuse" is not the poem but rather her energy, which is diffused throughout the setting and animates everything it touches. Finally, the premise of "Falling" is contrived only if it is assumed that the transformation of a stewardess into a goddess is somehow trivial or even, as Mills says, "boring."

42. Christ, *Laughter of Aphrodite,* 111.

43. Campbell, *Primitive Mythology,* 315.

44. Campbell, *World Mythology,* Vol. II, Pt. 2, p. 156.

45. Christine Froula, "When Eve Reads Milton," in *Canons,* ed. Robert von Hallberg (Chicago, 1983), 160.

46. Christ, *Laughter of Aphrodite,* 154–55.

47. Alicia Ostriker, "Dancing at the Devil's Party: Some Notes on Politics and Poetry," in *Politics & Poetic Value,* ed. Robert von Hallberg (Chicago, 1987), 221.

48. Dickey, "Energized Man," in *Imagination as Glory,* ed. Weigl and Hummer, 164–65.

5.   THE MOMENTUM OF WORD-MAGIC IN DICKEY'S *THE EYE-BEATERS*

1. Louis Untermeyer, "A Way of Seeing and Saying," *Saturday Review,* May 6, 1967, p. 55.

2. Peter Davison, "The Difficulties of Being Major: The Poetry of Robert Lowell and James Dickey," *Atlantic Monthly* (October, 1967), 223–30; James Tulip, "Robert Lowell and James Dickey," *Poetry Australia,* XXIV (October, 1968), 39–47; John Simon, *Commonweal,* December 1, 1967, p. 315.

3. Herbert Leibowitz, "The Moiling of Secret Forces: *The Eye-Beaters, Blood, Victory, Madness, Buckhead and Mercy,*" in *The Imagination as Glory: The Poetry of James Dickey,* ed. Bruce Weigl and T. R. Hummer (Urbana, Ill., 1984), 130.

4. Benjamin DeMott, "The 'More' Life School and James Dickey," *Saturday Review,* March 28, 1970, p. 38.

5. Richard Howard, "Resurrection for a Little While," *Nation,* March 23, 1970, pp. 341–42. In all fairness to Howard, his review of *The Eye-Beaters* cannot be described as entirely negative, although he certainly seems dismayed at much of the material in that book.

6. Poems that I should like to nominate as major in this collection are "Under Buzzards" (Pt. 2 of "Diabetes"), "Mercy," "Victory," "Pine," "Madness," "The Eye-Beaters," and "Turning Away."

7. For example, "the stagy, unpleasant hysteria" with which Leibowitz faults Dickey may in fact be an emotional sign that Dickey has formally achieved exactly the kind of poem he intended to produce, with "hysterical" effects totally appropriate to its genre. See my discussion of "Madness," "Mercy," and "Victory." Also, Ernest Suarez deals perceptively with the considerable critical misperception of Dickey in *James Dickey and the Politics of Canon: Assessing the Savage Ideal* (Columbia, Mo., 1993), especially chap. 4. See also Romy Heylen's valuable distinction between "reflection poetry" and "a participation poem or performance poem that quite simply must be experienced," with Dickey falling under the latter heading ("James Dickey's *The Zodiac:* A Self-Translation?" *James Dickey Newsletter,* VI [1990], 2–17, rpr. in *Critical Essays on James Dickey* [New York, 1994], 187–200).

8. For a comprehensive treatment of magic as social and legal action, psychological therapy, and religious symbolism, to name but four aspects of its multifaceted character, see Daniel Lawrence O'Keefe's *Stolen Lightning: The Social Theory of Magic* (New York, 1982).

9. Dickey's presentation, entitled "The G.I. Can of Beets, the Fox in the Wave, and the Hammers over Open Ground," was published in *NH,* 124–40.

10. Hart Crane, *The Complete Poems and Selected Letters and Prose of Hart Crane,* ed. Brom Weber (Garden City, N.Y., 1966), 36, 221.

11. Whether one agrees that "Spindrift" cannot be part of this seal's vision—recall Crane's vigorous defense of his language in a famous letter to Harriet Monroe (*Poems,* 234–40)—Dickey's comments on Crane's word selection lead to further considerations about magical word-play in poetry that is relevant for my argument in this chapter.

12. "James Dickey on Yeats" (interview by W. C. Barnwell), *Southern Review,* XIII (Spring, 1977), 311–16, rpr. in *The Voiced Connections of James Dickey: Interviews and Conversations,* ed. Ronald Baughman (Columbia, S.C., 1989), 155.

13. Sir James George Frazer, *The Golden Bough* (New York, 1963), 13.

14. Joseph Campbell, *Historical Atlas of World Mythology,* Vol. II, *The Way of the Seeded Earth* (New York, 1988), Pt. 1, p. 9.

15. Ernst Cassirer, *Mythical Thought* (New Haven, 1955), 36, 64, Vol. II of *The Philosophy of Symbolic Forms,* trans. Ralph Manheim.

16. *Ibid.,* 38, 55.

17. Cassirer, *Language and Myth,* trans. Susanne K. Langer (New York, 1946), 57–58.

18. Dickey calls this mode of lyric "country surrealism" (*S,* 100).

19. My own reading of "Pine" differs from yet is indebted to Suarez' analysis (*Politics of Canon*, 134–36).

20. Denis Donoghue, "Walt Whitman," in *Leaves of Grass*, ed. Sculley Bradley and Harold W. Blodgett (New York, 1973), 964.

21. Cassirer, *Mythical Thought*, 64, 55.

22. *Ibid.*, 77.

23. Gerard Manley Hopkins, *Poems and Prose of Gerard Manley Hopkins*, ed. W. H. Gardner (Baltimore, 1953), 13.

24. Cassirer, *Mythical Thought*, 65.

25. *Ibid.*, 83.

26. Longinus, "On the Sublime," in *Criticism: The Foundations of Modern Literary Judgment*, ed. Mark Schorer, Josephine Miles, and Gordon McKenzie (New York, 1948), 16.

27. Edmund Burke, in *Critics and Criticism: Ancient and Modern*, ed. Ronald Crane (Chicago, 1952), 446, 447.

28. Nathan Drake, *ibid.*, 447.

29. Samuel Taylor Coleridge, "Dejection: An Ode" and "Ode to the Departing Year," in *English Romantic Poetry and Prose*, ed. Russell Noyes (New York, 1956), 419, 388.

30. If one were to apply Drake's criteria as well as conventional standards of the ode to "Victory" and "Ode to the Departing Year," one would find that both poems qualify as singular representatives in the genre of terror. First, the poems are long—Dickey's at 131 lines, Coleridge's at 161—which enables each to develop a considerable vastness of conception regarding war and the toll it takes on human emotion. Further, both possess an occasional reference of considerable if not ceremonial importance—Dickey's to V-J Day, Coleridge's to the year 1796 and a preceding tragic history; each occasional reference produces the feeling of an elevated status of public utterance, even though each poem is represented in a profoundly personal mode of address. Both poems entail elaborate stanzaic organization, exquisite detail and coloring, and a somewhat similar style of indention, although Dickey's is more pronounced as much less regular than Coleridge's. Although Dickey uses no rhyme and his tone is less heightened, both lyrics convey a considerable seriousness that slowly alters and transports the reader into a state of empassioned dread. Rhetorically, this dread aids these poets' political position by giving each a vulnerable sincerity that makes them sympathetic and morally convincing.

31. Coleridge, "Ode to the Departing Year," in *English Romantic Poetry and Prose*, ed. Noyes, 389.

32. Arguing for the value of poetic rather than merely semantic meaning, Kenneth Burke puts the issue in a poignant statement that could well represent Dickey's poetic stand against certain self-indulgent aspects of confessional poetry:

I wonder how long it has been since a poet has asked himself . . . Suppose I did not simply wish to load upon the broad shoulders of the public medium my own ungainly appetites and ambitions? Suppose that, gnarled as I am, I did not consider it enough simply to seek payment for my gnarledness, the establishment of communion through evils held in common? Suppose I would also erect a structure of encouragement, for all of us? How should I go about it, in the sequence of imagery, not merely to bring us most poignantly *into* hell, but also *out* again? . . . Must there not, for every flight, be also a return, before my work can be called complete as a moral act?

(*Philosophy of Literary Form* [New York, 1957], 138–39)

33. Coleridge, "Ode to the Departing Year," in *English Romantic Poetry and Prose*, ed. Noyes, 389–90.

34. As critic Ronald Baughman poignantly points out in "James Dickey's War Poetry: A 'Saved, Shaken Life,'" it is not just the snake that terrorizes Dickey but also a veteran's residual terror of surviving the war (*South Carolina Review*, X [April, 1983], 38–48, rpr. in *"Struggling for Wings": The Art of James Dickey*, ed. Robert Kirschten [Columbia, S.C., 1997], 118–28). It is a well-known biographical fact that Dickey spent the formative years of his young adulthood (1942–46) serving in the army air force in the South Pacific. Dickey flew scores of missions with the 418th Night Fighters, saw his compatriots killed and mutilated by the enemy, and was an integral part of the killing mechanism of war. It is little wonder, then, that so much of his poetry is driven by a need to deal emotionally with the shock of combat.

35. Coleridge, "Ode to the Departing Year," in *English Romantic Poetry and Prose*, ed. Noyes, 390.

36. Joseph Campbell, *Historical Atlas of World Mythology*, Vol. II, *The Way of the Seeded Earth* (New York, 1989), Pt. 3, p. 378.

37. This self-enabling rhetoric is extremely important, especially on a personal and emotional level. The reader has only to ask how many times he or she has had to fight back from psychological or physical attack, whether in a major social arena such as world war or in the wars conducted on the battlegrounds of one's profession, family, or love life, where the threat of failure is the constant enemy. For a similar rhetoric, though presented in a more explicit mode of direct address, see Whitman's "A Noiseless Patient Spider" (*Leaves of Grass*, ed. Bradley and Blodgett, 450). See also "Rhetoric and Primitive Magic" and the "Realistic Function of Rhetoric" in Kenneth Burke, *A Rhetoric of Motives* (Berkeley, 1966), 40–46.

38. Campbell, *World Mythology*, Vol. II, Pt. 3, p. 291.

39. *Ibid.*

40. Kenneth Burke, "The Thinking of the Body" and "Somnia ad Urinandnum," in *Language as Symbolic Action: Essays on Life, Literature, and Method* (Berkeley, 1966), 308–58. See also William James's famous essay on mysticism in *The Varieties of Religious Experience* (1903; rpr. London, 1969), 299–336.

41. See Joseph Campbell's description of the Hopi Indian snake dance, which occurs in late August in the lunar month called "the Big Feast Moon," in *World Mythology*, Vol. II, Pt. 3, p. 290.

42. Dickey's revitalizing war myth/ritual and its narrative persona recalls Susanne K.

Langer's definition of myth in *Philosophy in a New Key: A Study in the Symbolism of Reason, Rite, and Art* (Cambridge, Mass., 1942). Her definition has considerable relevance for many of Dickey's mythological strategies, both in his poetry and prose:

> Myth . . . is a recognition of natural conflicts, of human desire frustrated by nonhuman powers, hostile oppression, or contrary desires; it is a story of the birth, passion, and defeat by death which is man's common fate. Its ultimate end is not wishful distortion of the world, but serious envisagement of its fundamental truths; moral orientation, not escape. That is why it does not exhaust its whole function in the telling. . . . Because the mythical hero is not the subject of an egocentric day-dream, but a subject greater than any individual, he is always felt to be superhuman, even if not quite divine. He is at least a descendent of the gods, something more than a man. His sphere of activity is the real world, because what he symbolizes belongs to the real world, no matter how fantastic its expression may be. (176–77)

43. Joseph Campbell, *The Masks of God: Oriental Mythology* (New York, 1962), 351.

44. Cited by Joseph Campbell in *The Masks of God: Creative Mythology* (New York, 1968), 666.

45. James Dickey, *To the White Sea* (New York, 1993), 274–75.

CONCLUSION

1. Wallace Stevens, *The Collected Poems of Wallace Stevens* (New York, 1965), 59, 381.

2. Wallace Stevens, *Opus Posthumous* (New York, 1957), 205–207.

3. Stevens, *Collected Poems*, 176.

4. Ralph Waldo Emerson, "Self-Reliance," in *Selections from Ralph Waldo Emerson*, ed. Stephen E. Whicher (Boston, 1957), 162.

5. Stevens, *Collected Poems*, 381.

6. *Ibid.*, 35.

7. William Blake, *The Complete Writings of William Blake*, ed. Geoffrey Keynes (Oxford, 1972), 259.

8. Stevens, "Two or Three Ideas," in *Opus Posthumous*, 209.

9. Samuel Noah Kramer, *History Begins at Sumer* (Philadelphia, 1981), 76.

10. Cited by Thorkild Jacobsen in *The Treasures of Darkness* (New Haven, 1976), 101.

11. Plotinus, "Ennead VI," in *Plotinus*, trans. A. H. Armstrong (Cambridge, Mass., 1984), 590.

12. Mircea Eliade, *The Sacred and the Profane: The Nature of Religion* (New York, 1957), 69–70.

13. Mircea Eliade, *Myths, Dreams, and Mysteries: The Encounter Between Contemporary Faiths and Archaic Realities*, trans. Philip Mairet (New York, 1957), 73–74.

14. Ernst Cassirer, *Mythical Thought* (New Haven, 1955), 81, 92, 99, Vol. II of *The Philosophy of Symbolic Forms*, trans. Ralph Manheim.

15. Eliade, *Myths, Dreams, and Mysteries*, 118.

16. *Ibid.,* 63, 104.

17. *Ibid.,* 105, cited by Eliade: "'Intelligence (*manas*) is the swiftest of birds'" (*Rig Veda,* Pt. 6, pp. 9, 5), 30.

18. C. G. Jung, *The Symbols of Transformation: An Analysis of the Prelude to a Case of Schizophrenia,* trans. R. F. C. Hull (Princeton, 1956), 85–86.

19. Walt Whitman, *Leaves of Grass,* ed. Sculley Bradley and Harold W. Blodgett (New York, 1973), 33.

20. Eliade, *Myths, Dreams, and Mysteries,* 77.

21. Frederic W. H. Myers, cited by William James in *The Varieties of Religious Experience* (1903; rpr. London, 1969), 363.

22. Whitman, *Leaves of Grass,* ed. Bradley and Blodgett, 86.

23. Mircea Eliade, *Myth and Reality* (New York, 1963), 141.

Index

Abreaction, 81–82

Absolute, 56

Adam, 46, 102, 136–37

Adonis, xviii, 9, 76

Aesthetic distance, 156n11

Africa, 157n26

Algonquin Indians, xviii, 72

Ammons, A. R.: darkness in, xix–xx, 3–4, 22–28, 33–34, 36, 40, 42, 44–51, 53; religious implications in, generally, xx–xxiii, 131–32, 144–45; Sumerian landscapes in, xx–xxiii, 2–43, 133–37; and Eastern mystical philosophies, xxi–xxii, 32, 33, 43, 56–60; ritualizing strategies in poetry by, xxi, 8–13; and identity with things around him, xxii–xxiii; youth of, xxii–xxiii; myth and narrative in, 1–2, 5–6; on somatic narrative, 1–2, 5; as southerner, 4; ritualized narrative of, 5–6, 18–19; natural objects in, 6–12; stones, spaces, and reality in, 6–14; dismemberment images in, 8–9, 32, 41, 44; circular imagery in, 10–11, 52, 150n8; water dreams in, 10; "bliss" in, 11, 26; Emerson's influence on, 11, 22, 30, 45–46, 56; many-sided view in poetry of, 12–13; merging and tearing in poetry of, 14–15; self in, 14–19, 53–55; and flow, 16, 18–19, 57; and reflexivity, 18–19; ritual violence and transformation in, 19–22, 32; literary fathers of, 22–23; monstrosity and the Quietist Way in, 22–28; "interweaving of purgatory and paradise" in, 32–33; on the One and the Many, 32, 51–55, 59, 135; sacrificial action in, 32; Christian upbringing of, 33, 35–36, 153n10; Sumerian laments by, 34–43; dust imagery in, 40; and anamnesis, 41–42; criticisms of, 43, 148–49n12; division, renewal, and undifferentiated darkness in, 43–51; death in, 44–45, 48–55; nature in, 44–45; on wisdom beyond death, 51–55; higher way or mysterious assimilative principle in, 55–63; and skyward method of prayer, 133–38; nature of God in, 144–45; performance as important for, 150n7; beginning of poetry career of, 151n29; and dry spells in writing, 153n7. See also specific titles of works

Anamnesis, 41, 43

Anima, 90

Animal totems. See Totem animals; specific animals

Animism, 90, 110, 111, 125

Aphrodite, 9

Apollo, 93–94

"Apologia Pro Vita Sua" (Ammons), 6–8, 20, 22

"Approaching Prayer" (Dickey): basic narrative of, xviii, 64–66; as ritual narrative of shamanic dismemberment, xviii, 21, 64–65, 75; Dickey's own assessment of, 64–65, 137; originality of, 64–65; biblical images in, 65, 79–81; critical responses to, 65, 74, 155n2, 156n20; exposition in opening section of, 66–67; separation in opening section of, 66–71; stages of initiation in, 66–83; preparation in opening section of, 67–71; sacred space and sacred time in, 67–69; ceremonial garb in, 68; body-house sym-